WOMEN EDUCATION AND DEVELOPMENT
Perspectives, Issues and Concerns

WOMEN EDUCATON AND DEVELOPMENT

Perspectives, Issues and Concerns

Edited by

Rajarshi Roy

SHIPRA

First Published 2009

Rs. 1250; US$ 62.50

ISBN: 978-81-7541-459-4

2014 Impression

Women Eduation and Development
Perspectives, Issues and Concerns

Published by:
SHIPRA PUBLICATIONS
LG 18-19, Pankaj Central Market,
I.P. Ext., Patparganj, Delhi 110092, India
Ph.: +91 11 22235152/6152
Email: info@shiprapublication.com
Website: www.shiprapublication.com

PREFACE

Sixty-two years of policy-intervention since independence for a developing nation appears as 'too narrow span' to change the social bent of mind at large towards gender-equilibrium in India, which would have been best implemented through formal system of education. It is a trajectory that even at the present juncture of time, women in Indian subcontinent, and possibly in various other parts across the globe, starts facing a hostile environment since in the womb. Even in the progressive nation-states across globe and province-states in India, a girl child is lucky enough to see the light of the earth. She often experiences discrimination since her infancy and consequently grow-up with formal education, which helps just to be accustomed with the gender-role-stereotyping and thereby become 'women' in society.

Present day studies on social science reveal that women's education and fertility are strongly interconnected. Studies have shown that increased literacy and school attendance in general delay marriage and increase the opportunity-cost of having children. Moreover, as female education and female wages rise, the differential between female and child wages widens. This in itself tends to reduce fertility since it means that the family's loss of the mother's income when children are young is not easily and quickly made up by children's work. Researchers have also demonstrated that educated girls become more effective mothers who have higher survival rates among children because they have better nutrition and health practices. There is also an intergenerational impact where the children of educated women are likely to be educated and thus carry the benefits to successive generations.

These are the social impacts of education irrespective of culture. Due to these sequels of reasons, the rate of women's education can be regarded as an effective index of development for a nation. While higher education is important in building up a quality human resource base of a nation, the basic elementary education system holds much more significance. In fact, since the inputs of the Higher Education system are nothing but the outputs of the elementary education system, the latter serves as the base over which the superstructure of the whole education system is built up.

Historically and physiologically men hold more power than women. Rules and major philosophy texts are mostly men-made and maintained male dominance. Gender discrimination manifests itself not only in the patterns of patriarchal male domination, but also in behaviors that make the experience of males central in every area of life. Men have constructed the prevailing theories, written history, and set values that become guiding principles for women. Compulsory educational establishments originally were founded by men for the education of men. Later teachers absorbed and repeated the teachings of Rousseau that women are less intellectual that means that they are made to please men and to obey. Belenky, et al. (1997) observed that women often feel alienated in academic settings and experience formal education as either peripheral or irrelevant to their central interests or development, often feel unheard. Stereotypical assumptions that women's thinking is emotional, intuitive has contributed to the devaluation of women's minds and contributions.

Social constructivism underlines that humans are socially constructed. Male domination has always been an important part of that construction. This all has resulted in imposing educational laws and social norms designed by men on women. These rules become constitutive not only of what women are allowed to do but also what they are allowed to be: how they are able to conceive themselves that their preferences are. It is a proven fact that construction of reality takes root in our language. Woman usually is not the subject of her language. In most cases women's language is defined by men, therefore, a woman represents herself through the language of the others. Male defined categories of meaning become barriers to women's self-definition, epistemology itself is restraint because 'dominant ways of knowing and categories of knowledge encode and derive from patriarchal constructions of women'.

Besides, some groups of people structurally have more power to do construction than others. This means that women are less free within the terms of masculinistic discourse itself. Of course, excluded groups participate in social construction in varying degrees. As Young (1990) argues, this is not true to say that all men are free and all women are unfree. No one is fully free. Some women are better placed to support patriarchy than men by virtue of class or other privileging factors.

However, the issue of gender equality is far from solved. Despite of a worldwide evidence of the low level of female participation in political and educational spheres, there is still tendency not to see it as a 'serious' issue. Centuries of status-injury and intellectual misrecognition mean that women themselves more often do not know their worth. It appears difficult for some women to state boundaries or negotiate for better material remuneration as this contradicts gendered identities. The ingrained reflexes of gender domination will remain alive for generations. Yet, the economic need to incorporate women into labor force, the pressures of feminist movement creates new ground for gender equality in all spheres of the society.

The challenge of the day is to situate gender equality economically, culturally and politically and overall, educationally. Popular stereotypes about gender-roles need to be challenges by the system of Education and mass media. In all levels the focus must be shifted on the needs and priorities of women by the way of promoting the education of girls and the career for young women.

The present volume is a humble attempt in the direction to fetch up the issues and concerns of education and development for women.

Rajarshi Roy

CONTENTS

LIST OF TABLES AND FIGURES

TABLES

FIGURES

1.

UNIVERSAL WOMEN'S EDUCATION IN INDIA
Government Policies and the Challenges Ahead

KARUBAKI DATTA

Introduction

Education is the basic and fundamental requirement of the citizens of a nation. The impacts of high level of literacy on both economy and society of a country are many. Attainment of basic education is important both due to its impact on the living standards of the people as also in augmenting their capabilities. Possession of reading and writing skills empowers an individual to participate in modern economic processes and transforms this embodied capital into higher earning and better living.

For the development of the country as a whole, it has been seen that bouts of long term economic growth are usually preceded by increases in the population's literacy level. The examples of Japan and Korea are the classic cases in which an educated population base has provided the necessary infrastructure for industrial advances to take place at a later date.

It is said that education also encourages migration. It makes the worker aware of employment opportunities elsewhere or simply makes him or her employable in other contexts and thereby instigates a more efficient allocation of labour to the most productive wages.

Health status is a very important part of human well-being. Several studies have shown that literacy and other measures of education are more closely correlated with life expectancy than per capita income is. This because education helps determine both the levels of knowledge about how to combat disease and the ease with which it can be transmitted and utilized.

Another often mentioned impact of education is that of having a more informed body of consumers and a literate electorate, leading to democratic government.

While these are some of the general impacts of education, education of women in particular is important for the development of a society. This is not only because women constitute half of the population and therefore they naturally have a right to education but also because women's education has far reaching impact on the society as a whole. Education empowers a woman to participate in political and economic decision-making in the community as well as in the household and thereby enables her to participate in development efforts in both the family and the community.

Here also the impacts are both economic and social. Educated women are more likely to enter the formal labour market. This contributes to overall efficiency in the economy to the extent that her market wage is higher than her implicit, shadow wage of being engaged in household activities.

There is also a relationship between women's education and fertility. Studies have shown that increased literacy and school attendance in general delay marriage and increase the opportunity cost of having children. Moreover, as female education and female wages rise, the differential between female and child wages widens. This in itself tends to reduce fertility since it means that the family's loss of the mother's income when children are young is not easily and quickly made up by children's work.

Researches have demonstrated that educated girls become more effective mothers who have higher survival rates among children because they have better nutrition and health practices. There is also an inter-generational impact in that the children of educated women are likely to be educated and thus carry the benefits into succeeding generations. These are the social impacts of education. Due to all these reasons, the rate of women's education can be regarded as an index of development of a state.

While higher education is important in building up a Quality Human Resource base of a nation, the basic elementary education system holds much more significance. In fact, since the inputs of the Higher Education system are nothing but the outputs of the elementary education system, the latter serves as the base over which the super structure of the whole education system is built up.

India has made remarkable progress in the expansion of higher education. The progress in spreading elementary education is nominal in comparison to that. Even in whatever has been achieved the girls have been largely left out of the capacity building process. The Government has undertaken many schemes for the education of girls and women and it is only in course of the recent decade that the trend has begun to show a positive change.

The chapter describes the status of literacy and basic elementary education among the girls of India. This has been done in the context of international guidelines and the education policy of the government of India.

International Trends and Guidelines

As mentioned above, social phenomenon like Birth rates(CBR), Death rates (CDR), Infant Mortality rates (IMR), and Population Growth rates (PGR) decelerate with improvements in literacy levels. In addition, improvements in literacy levels lead to uplifting of living standards also. It is generally seen that percentage of people below poverty level has a significant negative association with literacy. Significantly, in all these cases the association is found to be stronger with female literacy than male literacy. This can be said to be an international trend in general.

Nearly a quarter of the world's population of 6 to 11-year-old girls, 85 millions, remains out of school, constituting roughly 60 per cent of all out-of-school children in the age group. The total number of out-of-school girls is projected to double by the year 2015 compared with the 1990 rates. (Pandey, p. 5)

Primary participation varies by region. The lowest rate of participation is in Sub Sahara Africa and the largest gender gap is in South Asia. East Asia and Latin America have high rates of participation for both boys and girls and in the latter there is even a small gender gap favouring girls. The largest disadvantage for females is found mainly in Western and Central Africa, North Africa and South Asia. Rates of completion also vary from region to region. South Asia has the lowest rates and the Middle East and North Africa and East Asia have the highest rates of completion. (Pandey, p.5.6) Given this reality, several international conferences have been held and guidelines have been set to expand basic primary education among the children in general and bridge the gender gap in education in particular.

A world conference on the theme of Education for All (WCEFA) was held in Jomtien, Thailand, on March 10, 1990, attended by 1,500 participants from 155 governments, 20 inter-governmental bodies and 140 NGOs from all over the world. The objective was to make fresh start and a new commitment to fulfilling the goal of education for all, especially for girls. Participants made a global commitment to ensure access to and improve the quality of education for girls and women and to remove every obstacle that hampers their active participation. Getting girls into schools and ensuring that they benefited from the experience in a supportive, enabling environment was identified as critical to achieving education for all. The World Declaration on Education for All, Jomtien 1990, was an important milestone in the march towards universal elementary education and girls' and women's access to basic education. '*More than an end in itself, it is the foundation of lifetime learning and human development*' - it declared.

This rights perspective on educational access and equality got a tremendous boost during the International Conference on Population and Development in Cairo, 1994. *'Everyone has a right to education, which shall be directed to the full development of human resources, and human dignity and potential, with particular attention to women and the girl child. Education should be designed to strength for human rights and fundamental freedoms, including those related to population and development' (Page 10, Agenda for Action, ICPD, 1994)*

Women and girls' education was placed center stage in the struggle for human development and social justice in the Copenhagen Declaration on Social Development in 1995. *'We affirm that, in both economic and social terms, the most productive policies and investments are those that empower people to maximize their capacities, resources and opportunities'* *(Paragraph 7 of the Copenhagen Declaration, 1995)

The fourth World Conference on Women, Beijing 1995, reaffirmed the commitments made by governments and called upon the intellectual community to intensify efforts.

The United Nations Organization has repeatedly highlighted the discrimination against women and endeavored for its elimination through different programmes.

The U.N General Assembly adopted Conventions on the Elimination of all Forms of Discriminations Against Women (CEDAW) on 18 December 1970. Discrimination means "*any distinction, exclusion or restriction made on the basis of sex in the political, economic, social, cultural, civil or any other field*". The spirit of the Convention reaffirms UN goals and faith in fundamental Human Rights, in the dignity and worth of the human person, in the equal rights of men and women. It enjoins all state parties to take "*appropriate measures including legislation to ensure the full development of women, for the purpose of guaranteeing them the exercise and enjoyment of human rights and fundamental freedom on a basis of equality with men*" (Nayar, P. 22).

Finally, education received priority in the United Nations Millennium Development Goals. The second Goal is to ensure that all boys and girls complete a full course of primary schooling while the third Goal is to eliminate gender disparity in primary and secondary education preferably by 2005 and at all levels of education no later than 2015.

The declaration was signed by world's leaders of 189 countries in 2000. It established 2015 as the deadline for achieving most of the Goals.

Education Policy of the Government of India

India, the home of 16 per cent of World's total population, has a long way to go before reaching a level of universal primary education. According to World Education Report 1998, about one third of the world's non-literate aged 15 years and above live in India (Mukherjee, p.2) . In the age group of 0-9 years, the literacy rate is no higher than 68 per cent. The situation has only slightly improved since then and this is in spite of the repeated policy recommendations for the improvement of the same.

The Constitution of India itself has recognized the importance of education. It made a commitment that *"the state shall endeavor to provide, within a period of ten years from the commencement of the Constitution, free and compulsory education for all children until they complete the age of fourteen years"*. (Article 45, The Constitution of India) The National Commitment to provide free and compulsory education to all children in the 6- 14 years age group is now a Fundamental Right of every child in India after the passing of the Constitution (86th Amendment) Act in December 2002. Throughout this period Commissions have been constituted and policies undertaken for the welfare and empowerment of women, which naturally implied their access to education.

One important document on the education policy of the government was the Report of the Durgabai Deshmukh Committee on Education of Women (1959). It highlighted the necessity to treat girls' education as a special problem. The report, in fact became a policy document for the subsequent Five Year Plan formulation. This Committee was followed by Hansa Mehta Committee on Differentiation of Curricula (1964) and Education Commission of 1964-66. The Report of the Committee on the Status of Women (CSWI)-Towards Equality, 1974 revealed the discriminatory condition of women in the society. This included declining proportion of women in the population, low female literacy and education, higher female mortality, low economic participation and poor representation in political process.

The U.N. Development Decade of 1975-'85 saw the growth of various women oriented policies and setting up of different departments for the welfare of women. These include Department of Women and Child Development, Women's Development Corporations, Development of Women and Children in Rural Areas, ICDS, etc. There was also the movement from 'welfare' to 'development' and finally to 'empowerment' in the Eighth and Ninth Five Year Plans. The National Perspective Plan for Women (1988-2000) chalked out the national gender agenda till the turn of the 20th century with a strong focus on the rural and disadvantaged women. These policies naturally implied an emphasis on the spread of education among them.

Coming specifically to the policy regarding women's education, one very important document is the National Policy of Education. It was hailed as a major breakthrough in addressing gender issues in government policy.

The chapter on Education for Women's Equality states that

> "Education will be used as an agent of basic change in the status of women. In order to neutralise the accumulated distortions of the past, there will be a well-conceived edge in favour of women. The National Education System will play a positive, interventionist role in the empowerment of women. It will foster the development of new values through redesigned curricula, textbooks, the training and orientation of teachers, decision makers and administrators, and the active involvement of educational institutions. This will be act of faith and social engineering..."
>
> "The removal of women's illiteracy and obstacles inhibiting their access to, and retention in elementary education will receive overriding priority, through provision of special support services, setting of time targets, and effective monitoring. Major emphasis will be laid on women's participation in vocational, technical and professional education at different levels. The policy of non-discrimination will be pursued vigorously to eliminate sex stereotyping in vocational and professional courses and promote women's participation in non-traditional occupations as well as in existing and emerging technologies".

The New policy was widely debated over and discussed by representatives from all walks of life. The process was initiated in 1985 and continued for a year. This was accepted by the Parliament in 1986. The policy was debated again in 1992 and accepted with minor modifications.

In the meantime the Government of India launched the National Literary Mission in 1988-89. It was a multi pronged programme aimed at the acquisition of literary skills, social awareness and functional development by the participants. As it consciously tried to move away from being identified with the Government programme, it provided for greater participation of voluntary agencies.

The period 1986-91 witnessed three other national initiatives to promote basic education with a focus on greater participation of girls and women. Operation Blackboard was launched in 1987 with focus on construction of school buildings and appointment of second teacher in single teacher schools. Non-Formal Education (NFE) initiative was also launched with government's own resources. The scheme provided grant-in-aid to State Governments and NGOs to start NFE centres for out of school children. 100 per cent central funds were promised for NFE centres for girls. The District Primary Education Project (DPEP) was proposed in 1992 and formally launched in 1994. This was envisaged as an intensive area specific and decentralized effort to revitalize the primary education system. The document *Three years of DPEP- Assessment and Challenges* brought out in 1998 notes that successful community awareness and mobilization campaign under DPEP have contributed to significant increase in enrolment especially of girls.

In addition, the Government of India also launched six new initiatives during the same period. British ODA supported the Andhra Pradesh Primary Education Project and the Swedish aided the Rajasthan Shiksha Karmi Project in 1987, Netherlands supported Mahila Samakhya-Education for Women's Equality in Karnataka, Uttar Pradesh and Gujarat in 1988, UNICEF funded the Bihar Education Project, World Bank supported the Uttar Pradesh Basic Education Project in 1990 and the Swedish aided Rajasthan Lok Jumbish in 1992. All this opened up the basic education to external assistance.

Finally the Sarba Shiskha Abhiyan (SSA) or education for all programme once again put girls' education at the top level of priority. It recognizes that ensuring girls' education requires changes not only in the education system but also in societal norms and attitudes. A two pronged gender strategy was therefore adopted to make the education system responsive to the needs of the girls through targeted intervention which serve as a pull factor to enhance access and retention of girls in schools and on the other hand to create a push factor through generation of a community demand for girl's education through training and mobilization. It also promises motivation and mobilization of parents and the community at large, enhancing the role of women and mothers in school related activities and participation in school committees and strengthening the linkages between the school, teachers and communities.

One part of this SSA is the National Programme of Education of Girls for Elementary Level (NPEGEL), which was launched in 2003. It aims to provide additional provisions for enhancing the education for underprivileged or disadvantaged girls at elementary level through more intense community mobilization, development of model schools, gender sensitization of teachers, development of gender sensitive learning materials, early child care, provision of need based incentives like escorts, stationery, books, uniforms, etc. for girls.

Literacy Trends and Patterns

As a result of the policies undertaken by the Government of India, literacy and level of education have definitely increased in India but it is still a long way to go. Universalization of girl's and women's education is a great challenge indeed.

In the beginning of the century in 1901 literacy in India was a mere 5.3 per cent. It has increased to 65.4 per cent in 2001. However, the improvement has been much more pronounced for the males compared to the females especially till 1981. As a result, the gender gap (GG) in literacy soared from 9.2 points in 1901 to 26.8 points in 1981, but declined thereafter to 21.7 points in 2001.

Rural urban and inter group disparities were sharp in 1991, the sharpest being among the females themselves. Urban females were twice as well off in literacy compared to their rural counterparts. SC and ST females also lagged far behind, the rate of literacy being 81 per cent for urban males, 64 per cent for urban females, 58 per cent for rural males, 31 per cent for rural females, 50 per cent for SC males, 24 per cent for SC females, 41 per cent for ST males, and 18 per cent for ST females (Nayar, p.35). The decade of 1991-2001 has been significant for increase in the literacy rate of the population aged seven and more: the rate being 65.38 per cent of which 75.85 per cent are males and 54.16 per cent are females. This is a jump of 13.17 points from 52.21 in 1991.What is significant is that the female literacy rate is higher - being 14.87 points compared to 11.72 points for males.

ZThis attainment however is not uniform all over the country. Mizoram recorded the literacy rate of 88.49 per cent with the minimum gap in male female literacy rates of 4.56 points while Kerala has achieved 91 per cent literacy level in 2001 with the GG of only 5.73 points. In Meghalaya where the combined literacy rate is below the national average, the gender gap is a small 5.73 points.

Male female differentials are also high in the states of Gujarat (32.50), Rajasthan (32.12), Dadra and Nagar Haveli (30.33), Jharkhand (29.56), Uttar Pradesh (27.30), Madhya Pradesh (26.55), Orissa (25.02), Jammu and Kashmir (23.83), Uttaranchal (23.75) and Haryana (23.24). Bihar has recorded the lowest literacy rate (51 per cent) both in case of males (60.32 per cent) and females (33.57 per cent) the GG being 26.80 (Nayar, 36-37).

Formal Education: Enrolment in Schools

The step beyond literacy leads to schools. Here also the progress has been substantial. Numbers of schools have increased and simultaneously with it has gone up the number of enrolments even though in this respect also the rate is not uniform for the males and the females and the regional variations are also vast.

Table 1.1: Literacy and gender gap in some states of India during 1991-2001

Year	1991				1995				2001			
States	Male	Female	Total	Gender Gap	Male	Female	Total	Gender Gap	Male	Female	Total	Gender Gap
Andhra Pradesh	55	33	44	22	60	37	49	23	71	51	61	20
Bihar	52	23	38	29	59	28	44	31	64	37	51	27
Delhi	82	67	75	25	86	74	80	12	87	75	82	12
Gujarat	73	49	61	24	77	50	64	27	81	59	70	22
Haryana	69	40	56	29	72	52	63	20	79	56	69	23
Himachal Pradesh	75	52	64	23	81	61	71	20	86	68	77	18
Karnataka	67	44	56	23	67	51	59	16	76	57	67	19
Kerala	94	86	90	08	95	89	91	06	94	88	91	6
Madhya Pradesh	58	29	44	29	61	34	48	27	77	51	64	26
Maharastra	77	52	65	25	83	62	73	21	86	68	77	18
Orissa	63	35	49	28	66	42	54	24	76	51	64	25
Punjab	66	50	59	16	68	54	62	14	76	64	70	12
Rajasthan	55	20	39	35	59	26	43	33	76	44	61	32
Tamil Nadu	74	51	63	23	76	54	65	22	82	65	73	17
Uttar Pradesh	56	25	42	31	63	34	49	29	75	50	60	25
West Bengal	68	47	58	21	76	55	66	21	78	60	69	18

Source: Dipa Mukherjee, Women's Education in India: Trends, Interlinkages and Policy Issues, 2005,MPRA, paper No: 4871, http://mpra, ub.uni-muenchen.de/4871

During the period 1950-51 and 2000-2001 the number of primary schools went up from 20, 9,671 to 63, and 8,738. The numbers of middle schools have increased from 13,596 to 20, 6,269. The numbers of high and higher secondary schools have also gone up from 7,416 to 12, 6,047. However, for every 100 primary schools there are only 32 middle schools, 14 high schools and 6 higher secondary schools. (Nayar, p.41)

Enrolment in primary schools has increased from 19.2 million in 1950-51 to 113.6 million in 2001. During the same period enrolment in the middle and high schools has increased from 3.1 million and 1.5 million to 42 million and 28.2 million respectively. Here too can be observed a gender disparity as only 86 per cent and 49 per cent of girls of the relevant age groups enroll for primary and middle schools respectively.

As in the case of literacy, the decade of 1990-91 to 2000 -01 has shown considerable progress in this respect also. In course of this period, enrolment at the primary stage increased by more than seventeen million. Girls accounted for close to ten million while boys' share was a little over seven million. At the middle stage enrolments increased by eight million - girls accounting for 4.4 million of the enhanced enrolments and boys' share being 3.6 million (Nayar, p.42) .

Completion of Schools

Only a percentage of the children who get enrolled complete their schooling. It is observed that even in 2000 only 63 per cent, 46 per cent and 33 per cent of the relevant age group children complete primary, middle and secondary level education respectively. The completion rate (CR) has increased for the middle and secondary levels but declined for primary level during 1995-2000. The CRs are lower for the girls with only 37 per cent, 26 per cent of which completing middle and secondary schools. Kerala is the only exception where 100 per cent CR has been achieved for primary and middle stages. Even in the secondary level CR for girls is higher than for boys (Mukherjee, p. 6) .

At the secondary level Delhi has achieved a CR of 100 per cent, but it is only 10 per cent and 22 per cent for Bihar and West Bengal respectively. Just 5 per cent and 9 per cent of girls in Bihar and Rajasthan complete their schooling. This type of regional disparity has increased at all levels of education during 1995-2000. This disparity is noticeably high at the secondary level for girls (Mukherjee, p. 6).

On the whole it can be said that in an overall sense, enrolment of children in all stages of education in India have improved over the years though universalization of basic education has remained elusive till today.

Table 1.2: Completion Rates of Primary, Middle and Secondary Levels– 2000

States	*Completed Primary*			*Completed Middle*			*Completed Secondary*		
Gender →	*Boys*	*Girls*	*Total*	*Boys*	*Girls*	*Total*	*Boys*	*Girls*	*Total*
Andhra Pradesh	69	58	63	47	33	40	29	21	25
Bihar	29	15	22	28	11	20	16	5	10
Delhi	81	82	82	44	42	43	100	100	100
Gujarat	100	95	99	70	45	58	26	22	24
Haryana	84	76	80	76	62	69	69	45	57
Himachal Pradesh	88	85	86	96	77	86	82	68	75
Karnataka	93	94	94	60	54	57	45	37	41
Kerala	100	100	100	100	100	100	76	84	80
Madhya Pradesh	98	79	90	45	27	37	45	21	33
Maharashtra	104	93	98	79	68	74	63	49	56
Orissa	68	45	56	55	30	41	30	22	26
Punjab	70	70	71	56	56	56	66	61	63
Rajasthan	65	23	43	57	19	38	27	9	18
Tamil Nadu	70	96	83	100	88	100	47	53	56
Uttar Pradesh	48	28	39	36	15	26	46	18	33
West Bengal	67	53	60	42	31	37	29	16	22

Source: Women's Education in India: Trends, Interlinkages and Policy Issues, 2005.

As the data points out, the participation of girls in elementary schooling is greater now but male female gap in enrolment ratios and share of girls in total enrolments is still not uniform all over the country. In fact, the regional variations are very vast – ranging from 61.46 in Bihar, to 138.48 in Sikkim for girls and from 66.30 in Chandigarh to 153.43 in the Union territory of Dadra and Nagar Haveli at the primary stage; from 22.04 for Bihar to 93.36 in Kerala for girls and from 41.38 for Bihar to 105.89 in Rajasthan for boys at the upper primary /middle stage (Nayar p.42) .

What is of significance is that though the trend in general is that of lower educational participation by girls, in some states they are doing better than the boys.

This is what is happening at the primary stage in Haryana, Punjab, Andaman and Nicobar Islands and in Meghalaya. The same trend is seen for the middle stage at the states of Nagaland, Sikkim, Chandigarh, Delhi and the Andaman and Nicobar Islands. Similar trends were noted in earlier studies for Bombay, Kolkata and Delhi (Nayar, 43).

These variations are largely due to cultural variations. This has been explained by Nayar at length. Meghalaya is a matrilineal society and girls are favoured more, Sikkim is gender egalitarian, and Nagaland though patrilineal and patriarchal, does not discriminate between girls and boys on matters of education. The union territories of Andaman and Nicobar Islands and Lakshadives are also gender egalitarian though for different historical reasons. Mumbai, Delhi and Kolkata are metropolitan cities where boys are freer to get different odd jobs for livelihood while girls continue to study more and more. Chandigarh, Punjab and Haryana are affluent and unfavourably biased against women with high rates of female foeticide on the one hand and predominance of girls in both primary and higher education.

It is a fact to be noted that the substantial regional disparity and considerable GG, that is the trend in general, is more acute in the primary level compared to the higher stage and this is in spite of the declared approach, policy and strategy of the Government of India.

The basic cause of this, as all the policy documents recognize, is poverty. Women from poor communities, especially in rural areas in general, are in need of special attention. This is also the cause of the high rate of dropouts from among the girls. Traditionally drop out rates (DOR) have been quite high in India though it has been showing a downward trend over the years. The drop out rate for the primary classes I-V has gone down from 62 per cent to 39 per cent for boys and from 71 per cent to 42 per cent for girls during the period 1960-61 to 1999-2000. At the middle stage the drop out rate has come down from 75 per cent to 52 per cent for boys and from 85 per cent to 58 per cent during the same period (Nayar, 45). That the male female gaps in drop out rates is narrowing down is a positive sign for the educational participation for the girls.

At the regional level, zero DOR have been achieved in Kerala for primary and middle levels and in Delhi in the secondary level. In contrast, Bihar has a DOR of more than 70 per cent at primary and middle levels and both Bihar and West Bengal have more than 80 per cent DOR at the secondary level. These have resulted in high regional disparity. The data also implies that DOR has increased for the primary and middle levels between 1995 and 2000. The increase has been more pronounced for the girls than boys (Mukherjee, p. 6).

The second stumbling block is social status especially when considering children from disadvantaged communities like Scheduled Castes, Scheduled Tribes, some minority groups and nomadic tribes. While affirmative actions in the form of reservation of jobs and places in institutions of higher learning have been provided, there is stumbling block at the elementary level. Scheduled Castes and Scheduled Tribes are far behind compared to the rest of the population in respect of literacy rate. The 2001 census (provisional) does not have separate accounts for

Scheduled Castes and Scheduled Tribes and therefore no comparison is possible with the general population. The following table gives an idea about their educational status till 1991. As to the girls of these communities-data shows that the percentage share of SC and ST girls to the total Scheduled Caste and Scheduled Tribe children is not very remarkably different from the overall percentage share of girls in general population at the primary stage. It is at the middle stage that the Scheduled Castes and Scheduled Tribes girls are far behind. (Nayar, p.42-43)

***Table 1.3*: Difference in Literacy Rates between Scheduled Castes and Scheduled Tribes and Rest of the Population**

Year	*Scheduled Castes*	*Scheduled Tribes*	*Rest of the population*
1961	10.27	8.53	27.86
1971	14.67	11.30	33.80
1981	21.38	16.35	41.22
1991	37.41	29.60	52.21

Source: 'Development and Empowerment of Disadvantaged People of India', in Development of Scheduled Caste, (Ed.), New Delhi.

***Table 1.4*: Literacy Rate of Scheduled Castes and Scheduled Tribes**

Year	*Scheduled Castes*	*Scheduled Tribes*
1961	17.59	19.33
1971	19.13	22.50
1981	19.84	24.87
1991	17.20	25.01

Source: 'Development and Empowerment of Disadvantaged People of India', in Development of Scheduled Caste, (Ed.), New Delhi.

The Kasturba Gandhi Balika Vidyalaya (KGBV) scheme, initially launched in July 2004 and later on merged with SSA in the XI Plan with effect from 1st April, 2007 targets these communities in particular. Its objective is to set up residential schools at upper primary level for girls belonging predominantly to the SC, ST, OBC and minority communities in educationally backward blocks of the country where the female rural literacy is below the national average and GG is above the same. The scheme provides for a minimum reservation of 75 per cent of seats for girls belonging to SC, ST, OBC, and minority communities. Priority for the remaining 25 per cent is accorded to girls from families below poverty lines.

As per the Government records, the scheme is being implemented in 24 states (Assam, Andhra Pradesh,, Arunachal Pradesh, Bihar,

Jharkhand, Gujarat, Haryana, Himachal Pradesh, Karnataka, Jammu& Kashmir, Madhya Pradesh, Chhattisgarh, Manipur, Maharashtra, Meghalaya, Mizoram, Orissa, Punjab, Rajasthan, Tamil Nadu, Tripura, Uttar Pradesh, Uttaranchal, West Bengal and the Union Territory of Dadra Nagar Haveli.)

It is reported that 2,180 KGBVs were sanctioned by the Government till March 2007. Of these 1,226 were made operational in the states and 80,853 girls enrolled in those. The share of girls from the Scheduled Castes, Scheduled Tribes, Other Backward Classes, minority communities and Bellow Poverty Level (BPL) families is 25 per cent, 29 per cent, 25 per cent, 17 per cent and 5 per cent respectively. It is too early to gauge the actual impacts of these developments.

Conclusion

With the international initiative and government efforts, Net Enrolment Ratios (NER) have risen almost everywhere.. While in developed countries NER were already universal or close to it in 1990, the average level of NER in the developing countries was 85.6 per cent for boys and 77.2 per cent .The levels were projected to be 87.9 per cent for boys and 81.5 per cent for girls in 2000. NER for primary school girls has risen in all regions since 1990 and is projected to increase further up to 2010. However, the absolute number of girls of primary age (world wise) out of school has risen since 1990 and is expected to continue rising up to 2005. In all regions of the developing world girls' enrolment has grown more than boys, particularly in East Asia and the Arab states. However, the girls are still less likely to be in school than boys. (Pandey, p. 15-16) The trend is not very different in India.

Girls and women's education is a developmental priority in India. In keeping pace with the international guidelines and its own Constitutional directives, almost every conceivable strategy and approach has been covered in policy documents of the government of India. As discussed above, schemes after schemes have been undertaken and are still being formulated. Availability of international development assistance for basic education and women's education has also gone up considerably. The efforts have yielded results and significant progress has been made in course of the last decade.

The number of enrolment of girls and women has increased considerably and the GG is also decreasing. But there is still a long way to go. About 35 per cent of Indians are still illiterate and the percentage is much higher for girls and women. Even though DOR for girls has recorded a downward trend when considered from a long-term perspective, it has actually increased in course of the last few years. The results of the implementation of the various educational schemes are not uniform and the regional variations are stark.

The two stumble blocks that stand in the way of universal education and women's education in particular are poverty and social status. Unless and until these are eradicated through the implementation of other economic and social policies, the goal of "education for all" is bound to remain unachievable. India is yet to make long strides in this direction.

Bibliography and References

Bhuimali, Anil, 'Development and Empowerment of Disadvantaged People of India', in *Development of Scheduled Caste*, (ed) Anil Bhuimali, Serials Publications, New Delhi, 1907.

Girls' and Women's Education in India , United Nations Educational, Scientific, and Cultural Organisation, Bangkok (Thailand), http://www.unescobkk.org/education/appeal/girls &women/india.pdf

Girls Education at Elementary Level, http://ssa.nic.in/girlseducation/Girls-EDU-WEBSITE.pdf

Mukherjee, Dipa, *Women's Education in India: Trends, Interlinkages and Policy Issues*, 2005, MPRA, paper No. 4871, http://mpra,ub.uni-muenchen.de/4871

Nayar, Usha, 'Gender Bias in Education' in *Education, Employment and Empowering Women*, (ed) Anil Bhuimali, Serials Publications, New Delhi, 2004.

Velkoff, Victoria A. *Women's Education in India*, Washington D.C., Bureau of the Census, 1998, International Programs Center, Women of the World: WID/98-1, October 1998, http://www.census.gov/ipc/prod/wid-9801.pdf

Misra, R.C., *Women Education*, A. P. H. Publishing Corporation, New Delhi, 2005.

Encyclopedia of Education, volume II, A.P.H. Publishing Corporation, New Delhi, 2005.

Gupta Mukta, *Women and Educational Development,* Institute of Environment Development Studies, Lucknow, Sarup and Sons, New Delhi, 2000.

Pandey, V.C., *Girls' Primary Education,* Isha Books, Delhi, 2004.

2.

WOMEN, HIGHER EDUCATION AND CHANGE

A Critical Pedagogy For Women

DZINTRA ILIŠKO

Transitional time towards new democracy in Latvia (Eastern Europe) outlines new trends that affected educational system as well. Although significant progress has been achieved in reforming and modernizing higher education in Latvia, new issues come up to deal with. The Law on Education (1991) introduced significant reforms in the status of higher education: depolarization of educational content, authorization of private higher education as well as administrative decentralization. This chapter outlines the situation of women in higher education in Latvia as well as points to the major challenges women are facing today. The most common approaches conceive gender equality as the inclusion of women in higher education. This perspective generally does not challenge the form of institutions, their power dynamics or epistemological frameworks. Critical approaches highlight gendered processes within institutions, often obscured by rhetoric and complex means of silencing. Critical approach towards women in higher education advocates connections between aspirations for gender equality within higher education and wider social justice concerns. This approach requires a consideration of questions of gender equality within and beyond the institution pointing to the need for further work on deepening meanings of gender equality in higher education.

Women in Higher Education

The system of higher education in Latvia is undergoing rapid and profound changes. Educational system is undergoing huge transitions since 1991 The major transitions that are taking place are from teacher centered towards a child – centered and humanistic pedagogy. Among significant accomplishments one can mention a compliance of the educational system with the Bologna Declaration through the adoption of a common framework for comparable degrees and the introduction of it in undergraduate and postgraduate levels. New vision for science and technology has been worked out. Some progress has been made in enlarged learning opportunities of diverse groups of students. Despite the significant progress that has been achieved in reforming higher education, new problems have come up that pose new challenges to higher education institutions and society at large. In particular, the growth of a global knowledge-based economy creates great opportunities and poses great challenges, particularly for Latvia that is dealing with difficult transitions from centralized forms to new forms of economic organization. Academicians in cooperation with specialists from other fields are working towards developing a multi-faceted national strategy for building and sustaining a knowledge-based economy. Majority of teachers in the academic sphere in Latvia are taking an active part in the reform making processes in education on both legislative and the grassroots level. Women are taking active role in policy-making processes in the country. In total there were 100 members, 18 from them are women. Members of city councils in Riga, the capital of Latvia, are 60 in total, 11 of them are women; in the second biggest city Daugavpils – only 15. In Latvia women hold the posts of president, the speaker of Parliament, four ministries (foreign affairs, welfare, culture, public health) and the candidate for EU commissioner. Still, the overall picture in Latvia indicates relatively low representation of women in politics compared to the European countries. There is lack of public acceptance of women taking part in politics and the resistance among the representatives of existing power structures towards prevailing common reasons for the uneven distribution of political power among women and men. Gender equality is still the question to be solved and academicians need do a lot to build a more sustainable world in the future. In mass media women are still represented in stereotypical roles of housewives, prostitutes, consumers of cosmetics, but not as equals in profession, business and political life (Cimdina, 2002).

Women undergraduate and graduate students increasingly enter nontraditional fields such as dentistry, engineering, law and business and aspire to combine family and career responsibilities. Still, majority of women choose to work in the field of education. Women's education level is higher than men's, especially in the cities (see the table 2.1). From table 2.1 it is evident that in all higher education institutions, except Riga Technical university, female students are represented more as men. Women choose to study more in the field of humanities rather than in the field of technical sciences. Women are under-represented in science and technology within University setting.

Table 2.1: **The Number of Female Students and Graduates**

Higher education institutions	*Females out of total number of students, %*	*Females out of total number of degree or qualification obtained persons, %*
Total in Latvia	61	63
University of Latvia	64	63
Riga Technical university	39	37
Latvian University of Agriculture	55	64
Riga Stradins university	76	82
Daugavpils University	83	90
Liepaja Pedagogical higher school	86	97
Ventspils College	52	
Vindzeme University college Latvia	65	79
Rezekne Higher school	72	79
Austria	58	46

Source: Council of Higher Education in Latvia, 2008

Unfortunately, females' monthly average gross wages are lower than males. Still, there is higher unemployment rate among women in Latvia than men. It is very hard for women to get a job at the age of 45 – 55. The majority of women choose education as a sphere of their work that is less paid compared to other spheres of work. Women's employment is primarily in low-paid occupations, such as teaching, nursing, and culture management. Although employment level is equal for men and women, men are more likely to be employers. Women are under represented in political and legislative institutions

Table 2.2: **Educational Institutions: Enrolment of staff**

Institutions	*Enrolment*			*Teaching staff*		
	Total	*of which females*		*Total*	*of which females*	
		Total	*In %*		*Total*	*in %*
Preschool establishments	61759	29326	48	8245	8202	99
General full-time schools	344822	173238	50	28277	24696	87
Of which grades:						
1 – 4	125597	60991	49	8370	8105	97
5 – 9	169010	82012	49	14872	12531	84
10 – 12	50215	30235	60	5035	4060	80
Evening schools	14996	7147	48	1106	952	86
Vocational schools	48625	21287	44	5439	3607	66
Institutions of higher education	118000	62700	53	5396	2840	53

Source: Statistical Yearbook of Latvia, 2002

In Latvia women are the ultimate players in the process of educational change. Women are making their efforts towards bringing a sustainable future by implementing UNESCO guidelines in fostering the ideals and principles of education for a sustainable development.

The Pedagogy of Gaining One's Voice/Agency

Alienation becomes one of the distinct features of our contemporary society. This phenomenon is more fully explained in Fromm's (1976) *Escape from Freedom*. Fromm (1976) describes the process of social manipulation that results in women striving exactly the same as they imagine the majority to be. One of the signs of alienated life is one's inability to engage authentically with work. Fomm (1956) defines alienation as 'a mode of experience in which the person experiences himself as alien... estranged from himself [herself]' (p. 120). Alienation distances people from the world of feelings, so that they become lifeless objects. The process of emergence of freedom in the societal discourse after 1991 in Latvia can be well described by Fromm's central thesis expressed in his book '*Escape from Freedom*' as a situation of growing isolation, insecurity, doubt concerning one's role, the meaning of life. In such a situation, as a rule, people turn to submission to a leader or to compulsive conforming. While conforming to authority one feels powerless in the face of bureaucracy and structures and looses capacity to think critically.

In a poststructuralist discourse, the understanding of the agency involves recognition of the power of the discourse, 'immersion in and indebtedness in that discourse, and a fascination of the play of meaning through which new life-forms may be generated: life forms capable of disrupting old meanings and desires' (In Arnot, Ghaill, 2006, p. 82). Each human person is a moral agent with certain degree of autonomy and self-determination empowered to act according to his/her conscience and freedom. Agency is not the abstract and individualistic agency. It involves a notion of self deeply situated in relationships that is a lacking dimension in one's live in a consumerist society. As Bakan (1966) stresses, a person is 'autonomous' in the sense that he/she has power and ability as well as desire and needs. These all are rational, they come from, exist in the context of, and have meaning only in relation to others.

Paulo Freire (1973) believes in the power of the individual to come to a critical consciousness of his or her own being in the world. Central to his pedagogical work is the understanding that the oppressed are agents who are engaged in the process of constructing and reconstructing meaning. Each individual has an ability to appropriate reality through naming, reading, and thus, knowing reality. He suggests creating situations in which students can articulate their understanding of the world. Women need to develop skills of self-reflectivity and to seek understanding of their presuppositions and assumptions. They must seek to understand the forces of hegemony within their own consciousness as well as in the structured, historical circumstances in which they find themselves. Thus, women can become creators of meaning in their lives. Being recognized as subjects who have knowledge, they can act upon the world, even when their subjectivity is denied in male hegemonic ideology and language. According to post-structuralist theory (Davies, 2000) the self is an ongoing project. Reflection offers new possibilities for change. Thus the person creates spaces of freedom by thinking beyond accepted knowledge, or as Nikolas Rose says, '...If we cannot disinvent ourselves, we might at least enhance the contestability of forms of being that have been invented for us, and begin to invent ourselves differently' (Rose, 1998, p.197). Maria Harris (1988) metaphorically describes the process of finding one's voice as a journey from listening to one's voice, towards finding one's inner voice, and finally, integrating one's voice with voices of other women (In Iliško, 2006, 170).

Return towards One's Authentic Self

Cranton and Carusetta (2004) define authenticity as the expression of genuine self, knowing oneself and one's preferences within the social context of one's work, as well as listening to one's voice. Whitehead (1966) point to narrowness and the exclusiveness of the experience of women in some schools of thought and the significance of each voice to the included in the educational realm:

'Nothing must be omitted, experience drunk and experience sober, experience sleeping and experience drowsy and experience wide-awake, experience self- conscious... experience normal and experience abnormal' (p. 226). The category of voice points to the process through which 'identities are ignored, constructed or experienced; meanings are reaffirmed or questioned; and experiences are formed within the interlocking processes of subjugation, affirmation, and enlightment' (Weiler, 1988, p. xiii).

The generation that grew up within the framework of ideology of Soviet Union has learned a lesson of silence, of not being able to tell one's story, and to speak out for justice. Now women need to relearn to speak out, and make meaning of their experience. Then women can become conscious of their reality, they can begin to define their role, and by doing so, they are integrally engaged in political change for a more just world. Morton describes this process as creation of oneself (As cited in Harris, 1988). In the process one experiences the death of stereotyped images and the birth of oneself. Such a new awareness can be characterized as a process of being, of becoming aware of oneself and one's surroundings. This a separation from the 'false consciousness' (Freire, 1970).

More often teachers follow the standards set by some male authorities. The question of authenticity is a question of who one is, what one believes in and then acts on that. Discussion about authenticity is highlighted in works associated with the existentialist philosophy (Sartre, Heidegger). The search for authenticity can enhance the development of personal integrity and fidelity when people want to pursue their ideals. In teaching, taking an interior turn towards self-development and greater authenticity can have positive consequences when teachers are able to connect the personal and interpersonal satisfaction in their work.

The conscious self while encountering external forces different from oneself acts and changes in response to these pressures. Individuals can be alienated from themselves only because there is something in them to alienate. Alienated person looses himself/herself as centre of his/her experience (Fromm, 2002, [1955]). The person looses his/her own subjectivity and freedom and is trapped in the world defined by others. This leads to loosing person's capacity to respond to life positively, with love and awe. As Fox (1990) argued that when our creativity is suppressed, we strive for power over self and others. 'Self' should be perceived as a continuous reflective project (Leinberger & Tucker, 1991). It should be constantly remade and reaffirmed. The continuous construction of self is a source of creativity, empowerment and change. The goals of being human, according to Fromm (1955), are freedom, spontaneity, and genuine expression of self; anything less is defective. He further argues that failure to realize these goals is indicative of a 'sick society' and to the atrophication of conscience. He argues that the purpose of life is individuation - the continuous process of giving birth to oneself.

Constraints of Women's Authenticity in Education: Some Lessons

Historically men have held more power than women. Men made rules, wrote major philosophy texts and maintained male dominance. The teachings of Aristotle support a dualistic pattern of thought that divides reality into opposite spheres and assigns more value to one part. Gender discrimination manifests itself not only in the patterns of patriarchal male domination, but also in behaviours that make the experience of males central in every area of life. Simone de Beauvoir (1974) captures this in the statement 'woman as the 'Other." A woman is the 'other,' the object whose meaning is determined by men. Androcentric bias reveals itself in prevailing cultural attitudes that assign more significance to the dreams, hopes, and values of men than those of women. Men have constructed the prevailing theories, written history, and set values that become guiding principles for women. Compulsory educational establishments originally were founded by men for the education of men. Later teachers absorbed and repeated the teachings of Rousseau that women are less intellectual that means that they are made to please men and to obey. Belenky, et al. (1997) observed that women often feel alienated in academic settings and experience formal education as either peripheral or irrelevant to their central interests or development, often feel unheard. Stereotypical assumptions that women's thinking is emotional, intuitive has contributed to the devaluation of women's minds and contributions.

The socialist system in Latvia till 1991 officially defined equality of sexes. The socialist system provided welfare, maternity leave, free day care and education. Actually, the Soviet period deformed the notion of gender equality in Latvia. What the Soviet system referred to 'equality' was actually the leveling of all differences regarding gender roles; forcing men and women to do the same work outside the home. Still prevailing cultural traditions in Latvia continue to reinforce women's subordinate status. Women's primary role still was that of mothers and homemakers.

Today *The Latvian Constitution* (1991) defines the right of every individual to be protected from discrimination on the basis of his/her sex. Latvia has signed relevant documents that guarantee equal rights of all women and men. In Latvia men and women have legal rights guaranteeing equal treatment concerning access to employment, equal pay for equal work and career advancement. The Constitutional Law, the Labour Code, Civil Law and international Conventions, ratified by Latvia stipulate the equality of sexes. However, much remains to be done for true equality to emerge both in Latvia and in the world (Iliško, 2008).

According to the Fourth United Nations Conference on Women in Beijing, most of the illiterate of the world are still women, most are underpaid and unemployed are still women. Today consumerism, market economy, a mechanistic paradigm and the male defined standards in the society more often lead a person to alienated condition from the self and others. The consequence is that the person becomes marginalized from the meaningful work and the self. In the product world more often women do not have will of their own, they become alienated 'automatons' (Fromm, 1976), whose tastes, opinions and references are manipulated by the system. Models of teaching imposed above and standardized tests create problems of meaning among teachers who are struggling to work more intuitively, more emotionally than those technical controls permit. The products and measures of learning – essays, test scores, exams stand apart from the learner. The exam does not measure students' engagement in creative work as a means of broadening identity. As Ball (1990) argues, the testing, exams, and streaming in education, as well as formation of certain types of intelligence, ability, and scholastic ability in the process of schooling are strong examples of 'dividing and exclusivist' practices. Educational categories and constructs also play a central role in the formation of human subjects, institutional practices and technologies of control that discipline and normalize identities.

Social constructivism (Foucault) theory underlines that humans are socially constructed. Male domination has always been an important part of that construction. This all has resulted in imposing educational laws and social norms designed by men on women. These rules become constitutive not only of what women are allowed to do but also what they are allowed to be: how they are able to conceive themselves, that their preferences are (Hirschmann, 1996, p. 52). French feminist thinkers and deconstructive thinkers believe that construction of reality takes root in our language. Woman usually is not the subject of her language. In most cases women's language is defined by men, therefore, a woman represents herself through the language of the other. Male defined categories of meaning become barriers to women's self-definition, epistemology itself is restraint because 'dominant ways of knowing and categories of knowledge encode and derive from patriarchal constructions of women' (Hirschmann, 1996, 53).

Besides, some groups of people structurally have more power to do construction than others. This means that women are less free within the terms of masculinistic discourse itself. Of course, excluded groups participate in social construction in varying degrees. As Young (1990) argues, this is not true to say that all men are free and all women are unfree. No one is fully free. Some women are better placed to support patriarchy than men by virtue of class or other privileging factors.

Living a Critical Life

For true authenticity to emerge one should achieve separation from conformity to authority. As Fromm (1956) argues, one needs to experience a fundamental estrangement from commonly accepted ways of thinking and feeling. When one lives in association with others, it becomes difficult to establish the necessary distance for autonomous thought. As Marcuse (1989) emphasizes, only privacy, inwardness, and isolation can play a major role in shifting a focus from submission to the authority to more creative and free forms of being (p. 5).

In order to learn to live a critical life one also needs to develop one's power of critical thinking. This means a critique of interlocking systems of oppression imbedded in the contemporary society. This will help teachers to see disciplinary power, one-dimensional thought, and repressive tolerance. Patti Lather (1991) encourages women 'getting smart', that means engaging in a postmodern praxis which is 'non foundational in epistemology, not prescribed in historical telos, self-reflexive, and oriented towards resistance and committed to social change' (p. 39). It challenges dominant discourses, hegemonic forms of academic discourse and recognizes how one's knowledge is mediated by the concepts and categories of one's understanding.

Many women, in Latvia, show receptivity for the feminist values debated in media. Most women do not call themselves feminists, but still a dramatic change in the values of society, and particular values of women, took place in the society with newly emerging processes of democratization. Equal rights become an institutional goal for most women. Overwhelming majority of women does not accept values underlying the social institution of patriarchal family. The structure of legitimation of patriarchalism has been fundamentally shaken. Women do not accept men's authority any more. Rapid political mobilization of women has made substantial roads in the structure of power of the society.

One of the pedagogical challenges is to create the pedagogical situation in which students can articulate their understanding of the world. At the same time teachers need to be self-reflective and seek to understand their own presuppositions and assumptions and ideological prism through which external reality is sorted and understood (Freire, 1973, p. 56).

Both students and teachers need to understand the forces of hegemony within their own consciousness as well as historical circumstances in which they find themselves.

By emphasizing women's agency and locating women as agents in their choices in relationships and contexts can empower woman. Such a conceptualization requires creation of new contexts that will help both men and women to define themselves and help them to become aware of their capacities and abilities.

In seeking to overcome the individual's alienation from learning, work, and others the educator needs to emphasize cooperative ways of knowing. It would regard individual pursuit of truth, beauty and knowledge. Education should be dialogic, attempting to create a continuous conversation among learners about learning when all voices will be heard.

To sum up, the growth of a global knowledge-based economy has created great opportunities for women and at the same time poses great challenges. One of them is gender equality issue. United Nations Developmental Report (1995) defines equality as the cornerstone of every democratic society. The term of gender equality has been defined in multiple ways in scholarly literature. It often means women having the same opportunities in life as men, for instance, equality to access education and employment, equality under law, and the equality of voice.

In Latvia the representation of women in the previously dominated male-field of business has increased over time, along with women's occupational representation in managerial professions. The effort of some women organizations has focused on removing barriers to entry into higher education, and particularly into traditionally male professions, by challenging the discriminatory policies and practices of educational establishments. Changes in national laws and regulations and greater attention for women's concerns characterizes this effort.

However, the issue of gender equality is far from solved. Despite the worldwide evidence of the low level of female participation in political and educational spheres, there is still tendency not to see it as an issue. Centuries of status injury and intellectual misrecognition mean that women themselves more often do not know their worth. It appears difficult for some women to state boundaries or negotiate for better material remuneration as this contradicts gendered identities. The ingrained reflexes of gender domination will remain alive for generations. Yet, the economic need to incorporate women into labor force, the pressures of feminist movement creates new ground for gender equality in all spheres of society.

Overall, most women continue to enter traditional women's fields as teaching, social work, and nursing. The greater potential increase is in the new technologies, e.g., computer science, where women are also gaining access to some degree.

The challenge is to situate gender inequality economically, culturally and politically. It is not enough simply to increase the number of women in universities, but need to look to the structure and processes within academe that is male-based and explore ways to change that.

Popular stereotypes about gender roles should be challenge by the system of Education and mass media. At all levels the focus must be shifted on the needs and priorities of women. This means promoting the education of girls and the career for young women.

The substantial research in various fields on women in education is necessary to tackle some of the fundamental issues regarding gender and education system. The relationships between gender inequality in education and that in the rest of the society is a fundamental question for further theory and research.

Women enjoy access to higher education that their mothers could not access. It is evident that if women are denied opportunities to full participation in advanced education, research and science, they will not be able to contribute to well being of the future society.

REFERENCES

Arnot, M., MaCan Ghaill, M., *Gender and Education.* Routledge: London and New York, 2006.

Bakan, D. *The Duality of Human Existence: Isolation and Communion in Western Man.* Boston: Beacon, 1966.

Ball, S.J., *Politics and Policy-making in Education: Explorations in Policy Sociology.* New York: Routledge, 1966.

Bejing Declaration (1995*) Fourth World Conference on Women.* New York: United Nation.

Beauvoir, S. (1974) *The Second Sex.* Trans, Parshley, H.M. (ed). New York: Random House.

Belenky, M.F., Clinchy, B.M., Goldberger, N.R, Tarule, J.M. (1997).*Women's Ways of Knowing. The Development of Self, Voice, and Mind.* NY: Basic Books.

Cimdiòa, A. (2002) Enlargement, Gender and Governance. In http:// www.qub.ac.uk/ egg/Summaries/Latvia-WP3summ.doc

Cranton, P. & Carusetta, E. (2004) Perspectives on authenticity in teaching. In *Adult Educational Quarterly*, Adult Association for Adult and Continuing Education, 55, 1, 5-22.

Davies, (2000) *A Body of Writing 1990-1999.* Walnut Creek: Alta Mirta Press.

Freire, P. (1970) *Pedagogy of the Oppressed.* Seabury Press: New York.

Freire, P. (1973) *Education for Critical Consciousness.* New York: Seabury Press.

Fromm, E. (1976) *Escape from Freedom.* New York: Holt, Rinehart and Winstoon.

Fromm, E. (2002) [1955] *The Sane Society. London*: Routledge.

Fromm, E. (1956)'The Application of Humanist Psychoanalysis to Marx's Theory' in Fromm, E. (ed.). (1956) *Socialist Humanism: An International Symposium.* Garden City, NY: Doubleday.

Harris, M. (1988) *Women and Teaching.* New York: Paulist Press.

Hirschman, N.J. (1996) Towards a Feminist Theory of Freedom. *Political Theory*, 24, 1, 46-67.

Iliško, Dz. (2006) The challenges of pedagogy: Reclaiming one's voice to construct a just world. In Sinha, S., Gupta, A. (2006). (Ed.). *Sociolinguistic and Educational Issues.* New Delhi: Dominant Publishers and Distributors, 53-64.

Young, I. (1990) *Justice and the Politics of Difference.* Princeton, MJ: Princeton University Press.

Iliško, Dz. (2007) Women in Times of Changes in Post-Soviet Latvia. In Fisher, I. (ed.) *Theologie von Frauen fur Frauen.* Munster: 157-185.

Iliško, Dz. (2008) Re-imagining Ecofeminist Theology for Eastern Europe. In *Feminist Theology*, 16, 2, 230-237.

Law on Education (1991) Riga: Ministry of Education and Science.

Lather, P (1991) *Getting Smart: Feminist Re-search and Pedagogy with/in the postmodern.* New York: Routledge.

Leinberger, P., Tucker, B. (1991) *The New Individualists: The Generation After the Organzation of Man.* New York: Harper Collins.

Law on Higher Education Establishments (2000), article4, retrieved from http://www.izm.lv/en/default.htm

Marcuse, H. (1989) Philosophy and critical theory, In Bronner, S.E. & Keller, D. M. (ed.) *Critical Theory and Society: A Reader*. New York: Routledge.

Marcuse, H. (2002) *Towards a Critical Theory of Society*. New York: Routledge.

Rose, N. (1998) *Inventing our Selves, Psychology, Power and Personhood.* Cambridge, Cambridge University Press.

Statistical Year Book of Latvia (2002) Riga: Central Statistical Bureau of Latvia.

The Latvian Constitution (1991) Latvia.

United Nations Developmental Report (1995) New York: United Nations.

Overview on Latvian Higher Education institutions in 2002. (2002). Riga: Education and Science Ministry, Department of higher Education and Science.

Weiler, K. (1988). *Women Teaching for Change. Gender, Class and Power.* Massachusetts, MA: Bergin & Garvey Publishers.

Whitehead, A.N. (1966). *Adventure of Ideas*. New York: Crossroads.

3.

RELEVANCE OF EXCLUSIVE WOMEN'S COLLEGES: THEIR MANDATE

JAYA INDERSEN

The earliest women's colleges worldwide dates back to 1800 and they had a specific purpose. In many countries women's colleges were historically the sole or primary points of access for women who wanted to pursue tertiary education. While coeducation eventually became the norm, women's colleges continue to be viable alternatives. The survey carried out by Purcell (2004), points out that full fledged women's colleges can be found in the western world in the U.S., Canada and United kingdom; in Asian countries including Bangladesh, Pakistan, Japan, Korea, the Philippines and India; In the Middle East countries of the United Arab Emirates and Iran and in the African country of Sudan. Certain regions and countries such as Latin America, Australia, and most of Europe, do not have a history of women only universities and colleges.

India has one of the largest systems of higher education with over 355 universities and 18064 colleges. The number of exclusive women's colleges and universities has also been growing at a fast pace. In the past two decades, it has more than doubled from 780 colleges in 1986-87 to 1902 colleges in 2005-06. There are over 10 exclusive women's universities. It is interesting to note that there are exclusive engineering colleges for women being set up in various parts of the country. India also has the distinction of having an exclusive medical college for women. There are no more exclusive colleges for men. Thus, women have access to both women only institutions and coeducational colleges. This brings us to the debate of women's colleges' verses coeducational colleges.

Women's Colleges Verses Co-Educational Colleges

The concept of separate institutions of higher education for women has been debated for several decades. In most countries in the west this idea is outdated. However, in some countries, for instance, the US, there still exist several exclusive women's institutions. In fact, these are coming to acquire a new meaning, though a couple of decades ago they were seen as irrelevant. One of the arguments advanced is that the new feminist movement demands that women have their 'own space' in all aspects of life including higher education.

Several studies both in the west and in India have debated the viability and desirability of having exclusive women's colleges. It is particularly salient in the Indian context, as already pointed out, there are a large number exclusive women's colleges and universities. Both socio-cultural and academic arguments have been forwarded in favour of such colleges. The social argument is that women have always needed protection and that without exclusive colleges, they would not have access to higher education. Originally colleges were meant only for men and women were not admitted. Therefore colleges had to be established specifically for women students. The cultural aspects cannot be ignored either. Parents, especially from conservative background in India, have reservations about sending their daughters to co-educational institutions even today. Providing access is the main rationale for these women's colleges.

More than three decades back, Kim (1978), justifying the existence of separate institutions for women in Korea, argues

> "...women's institutions of higher learning have a definite place in our society, because they can be the place where we can be conscious of our womanhood more critically and existentially... our conscious goal must be to focus our attention on women-women's history, culture, values and religion. We cannot ignore the concrete fact that we are born women and that we have to grow up as women. Therefore, we should learn how to understand and attain humanity, first through a personal and social awareness as women. Liberation is not freedom from men, but from institution of patriarchy and economic discrimination."

In a study based on American data, Riordan (1990) puts forward several arguments for and against single sex education versus coeducation. The points cited in favour of coeducation are that they are economically more efficient and provide a social environment in keeping with the modern world. At the same time, both men and women in mixed institutions are likely to experience some sex bias from teachers, counsellors and fellow students, whereas in single sex institutions sex bias would be minimal

The academic argument in favour of exclusive colleges for women, centres on certain perceived special needs of female students. Desai (1977) points out that men and women require separate curricula, extracurricular activities and types of disciplines. These are based on certain stereotypes and myths about women and their competence, interests and values.

Arguing against separate women's colleges, Nair (1981) opines that these women's colleges often try to perpetuate obscurantist and isolated identities, defying all principals of progressive education. Murugkar (1983) argues that specialized courses in women's institutions, such as polytechnics and home science colleges, are helping in perpetuating the inequality of sexes.

Tidball's (1986) study in the US, is a significant one among the several studies reported in the west on the impact of exclusive women's institutions on women's development. She has shown that graduates from women's colleges are more likely to achieve recognizable and commonly accepted intellectual or career accomplishments than are women graduates from coeducational institutions. It has been argued that the large number of successful female faculty role models and mentors in women's institutions have a salutary influence on women's achievements by counteracting sex stereotypic perceptions in career aspirations and self confidence. The studies of Bressler and Wendell (1980), Pascarella (1984) and others have shown that attending a women's college, may have a positive influence on self-esteem, educational aspirations and career status aspirations. Sagaria (1988) reported that academic programs and curricula such as women studies programs designed primarily to serve women in women's institutions were identified as helpful in developing leadership potential.

It should be pointed out here that the pros and cons of single sex versus co-educational institutions are complex. They could be country specific and could also vary within the country, depending on the region and other culture specific factors.

Perceived Rationale for a Separate Women's College

As pointed out earlier, in India there are a large number of exclusive women's colleges. These colleges are still growing, indicating that there is a perceived need for these institutions. At a national level study carried out by the author (Indiresan, 2002), principals, teachers and students were asked, 'Should there be separate colleges for Women?' Several arguments were put forward. These have been broadly classified as (i) socio-cultural aspects of access (ii) academic advantages (iii) strategic arguments and (iv) meeting the special needs of women.

Socio-cultural aspects of access

There is a feeling that women are still underprivileged and require special attention and protection if they are to be sure of access to higher education. Women's education has been neglected in the past, so there is a need for a special drive to enhance their participation in higher education. The backwardness of women (especially from the rural areas) with the small town culture of conservatism needs to be compensated for and this can be done effectively only through separate colleges for women.

Another major reason put forward is that parents are still conservative and do not approve of men and women mixing freely. They are apprehensive about the women's 'safety' and 'security' in a coeducational college. Parents have inhibitions and resistance and would not permit their daughters to join a coeducational college. If there were no separate colleges for women, their enrolment would go down considerably, as their parents would not send them to coeducational colleges. It is also felt that competition for admission to coeducational colleges would be much greater than to a women's college. Thus, providing access to women students seems to be one of the major arguments in favour of separate colleges for women.

Academic Advantages

There is a feeling that certain courses, which are of interest only to women, would not receive the same attention in a coeducational college. In a women's college it would be possible to introduce courses in women's studies or at least focus on women related issues in the curriculum. Hence, separate women's colleges are required so that these areas can be properly developed. One of the principals has expressed the view that the framework of educational opportunities as it exists today hardly caters to women's interests, in terms of their conditions, powers and limitations.

Strategic Arguments

These arguments centre on the type of atmosphere prevailing in the women's colleges and how it is conducive to the development of women. The exclusiveness is perceived to have several advantages, some of which are:

- Women's education can be given a thrust of its own
- A homogeneous group is conducive to learning and identifying talents and skills
- There is greater scope for discussing women related issues
- Protection from male domination is guaranteed
- There are fewer inhibitions in the absence of men
- There are more opportunities for developing organizational skills which are otherwise dominated by men
- There is freedom to organize programs that are of special interest to women

Another important strategic argument put forward is the security in a women's college. This security is perceived to have the following features.

- It protects the modesty of women
- It saves them from sexual harassment and 'eve-teasing'
- It protects them from drug pushing and alcohol

There is a feeling that there is a more congenial atmosphere in a women's college than coeducational college. There is greater freedom and women who are normally shy and reserved can participate confidently. This congenial atmosphere is expected to help women take on more responsibility and develop leadership skills. There are fewer distractions and diversions, more discipline and hence greater peace. Classes are held regularly leading to better performance. In fact, women are performing better academically compared to men. This congenial atmosphere helps women, especially those from rural background, exclusive girls' schools and from very conservative family background in their adjustment process. Women feel more at ease and are able to express themselves freely in the safe and secure atmosphere of a women's college. Women find it easier to confide their personal problems in female teachers. The teachers also provide role models, especially for students from poor background.

Meeting Special Needs of Women Students

Women students have certain special needs because of their gender and the process of socialization of women. There are certain stereotypes and myths about women, their capability, their values, etc. There is gender inequality in this male dominated society. Women do face certain discrimination. It is not enough that women get just academic inputs. In fact, these can be acquired in a coeducation college also. Women need to be facilitated in their overall development encompassing various dimensions. Women need to be given opportunities to develop life skills to cope with the challenges facing them in society. All these require moving beyond academics and these special needs of women can be effectively achieved in a women's college. In a coeducational college, women get sidelined and do not get enough opportunities to develop their full potential. Women's colleges can greatly facilitate the development of a self respecting and self-fulfilling identity.

Moving Beyond Access and Academics

Having argued that exclusive women's colleges are essential for providing access to women students, the critical question that arises is are these exclusive women's colleges doing anything beyond providing access for the overall development of women students?

The enrolment of women in higher education has crossed 40 per cent of total enrolment. However, it should be pointed out that nearly half of them, that is, 51 per cent of women are in the faculty of arts, 20 per cent in science, 16 per cent in commerce and just 4 per cent in engineering and technology and less than 4 per cent in medicine. While women's access to higher education has gone up, more and more women are entering the world of work in all sectors, including the exclusive male domains of business, police, military, etc., the percentage of women in senior and decision making positions is very small. Women are mainly seen in the low end and soft jobs.

The issues that arise are:

- What is holding back women from achieving significant positions in society?
- Are there structural barriers and glass ceilings?
- Is the climate chilly and gender hostile?
- Are the policies and practices gender insensitive?
- Are there cultural constraints and societal resistance?
- Do women themselves lack achievement motivation and desire to excel?
- Are they diffident and lack self confidence?
- Do they have the required skills and competence to over come barriers?

In fact, the low status of women is a complex interactive outcome of various situational, structural, social and personal variables.

This raises some further critical questions.

- Is the large system of education that is in place geared to change this situation?
- Will mere access and academic inputs be enough to bring out the desired changes?
- Is the education system doing anything to move beyond academics and add value to the education to provide the life skills to empower women students to face the challenges of this complex world that is going through tremendous social transformation?

It is interesting to cite here what the National Policy of Education (1986) has to say on women's education. It says, "Education will be used as an agent of basic change in the status of women, to neutralize the accumulated distortions of the past. The national system will play a positive intervention role in the empowerment of women. This will be an act of faith and social engineering". Delineating the implementation strategy, the policy states that educational institutions will be encouraged to take up active programmes to enhance women's status and further women's development in all sectors.

The National Policy of Education further identifies the parameters of empowerment as:

- Enhancing the self-esteem and self-confidence of women
- Building a positive self-image of women by recognizing their contribution to the society, polity and economy
- Developing the ability to think critically
- Fostering decision making and action through collective processes
- Enabling women to make informed choices in areas like education, employment and health, especially reproductive health
- Ensuring equal participation in developmental processes
- Providing the information, knowledge and skill required for economic independence
- Enhancing access to legal literacy and information relating to their rights and entitlements in society, with a view to enhancing their participation on an equal footing in all areas.

Education of women has become a major concern both as a human right and as a development imperative. Not only the enrolment of women at all levels of education has gone up considerably women are doing academically better than men students. Yet, women lag behind in employment, earnings, social status and recognition, face the challenges of discrimination, bias, stereotype, sexual harassment and so on. Further, enrolment of women and their progress, from the deprived sections of the society is still a matter of concern. The question that arises is, are our educational institutions doing anything beyond providing access and academic inputs for the overall development of women, so that the gender inequality that still exists can be at least reduced if not totally eliminated. What are the roles, responsibilities and agenda for educational institutions, especially the exclusive women's colleges in facilitating the total development of women students?

It is not enough just to give access and academic inputs for the total development of women students, the institutions have to Move Beyond Academics (MBA) by implementing Gender Positive Initiatives (GPI) for the empowerment of women students. Gender positive initiative refers to any programme, project or activity which is implicitly or explicitly designed to promote any dimension of women's development. It could be within or outside the academic or curricular arena. It could be within or outside the classroom. It could be part of the content included in the system of examinations or outside the purview of the grading system. Thus, a gender-positive initiative has a broad definition and includes a variety of happenings in the college.

The focus here is to examine the role and functioning of exclusive women's colleges in facilitating the overall development of women students. Some of the critical issues that are relevant in this context are:

- Do women students have special needs because of their gender?
- What are the dimensions of development that need to be addressed?
- What are the strategies that need to be put in place?
- What should teachers do for the personal development of students?
- What are the approaches adopted by teachers in the developmental process?
- Do the teachers have required skills and competence for carrying out the responsibility?
- What is the impact of these gender positive initiatives?
- What are the driving forces in this effort?
- What are the policy and management implications?

Do women students have special needs because of their gender?

This question becomes relevant when decisions have to be taken about providing special training for women and has been debated extensively. There is one school of thought that argues that men or women, their needs are the same and there should be no distinction made on the basis of gender. However, there is another school of thought that vehemently argues that men and women are equal but different. Women are not only biologically different but have been brought up differently due to various socio-cultural factors and thus have special needs because of their gender.

A large majority of students, teachers and principals contacted during the study, say that women do have special needs because of their gender. If so, what are these needs? A large number of needs have been cited and they fit broadly in the Maslow model of hierarchy of needs.

Physical and Security Needs

All said and done, women do realize that they are vulnerable in this man-dominated world and feel the need for physical protection and security from sexual harassment. They also want good, clean physical surroundings and especially good toilet facilities.

Social and Esteem Needs

Women realize the value of interpersonal relations and would like to improve their communication skills. They would like to be participants in the social life and community around them. They would like the society to give them the respect and regard as a woman and at the same time they would like to contribute in uplifting the social status of those women who are less fortunate. Women face several dilemmas and value conflicts because of the social transformations and their changing roles. They need to enhance their self-concept, find an identity and get their values clarified for meeting their self-esteem needs.

Autonomy Needs

Women are seen to be too dependent on others and are unable to take decisions on their own. They also perceive that they are not allowed to take independent decisions of their lives and are controlled by their family and significant others. They would like to have a career so that they are economically independent.

Aesthetic Needs

Next comes another set of needs to satisfy their aesthetic desires. The femininity in them urges them to appreciate beauty, whether it is in the form of *Rangoli, Mehendi, Batik* or flower arrangement. They want to express their interest in culture through various art forms, be it drawing or painting, music or dance. Women are the preservers of the heritage of art and culture and satisfaction of these needs forms an important part of their needs hierarchy.

Self-actualization Needs

On the satisfaction of all these needs emerge the need for self-actualization. Women want to feel empowered, feel liberated from the various societal and patriarchal shackles which have bound them for ages, want to release the enormous potential they have, want to take leadership roles and above all want to establish an identify of their own.

What are the dimensions of development that need to be addressed?

- Keeping the overall objective of total development of women students and in view of the identified special needs of women because of their gender, there are certain dimensions beyond academic inputs that need to be addressed. They are:
- ***Physical Development:*** This would include providing relevant sex education, awareness about reproduction, AIDS, etc. Knowledge about health and nutrition for physical well-being, coupled with training in martial arts for self-protection, has been cited as essential.
- ***Intellectual Development:*** It has been realized that mere academic inputs are not enough and that the students should be made

intellectually alert through exercises in critical thinking. This also includes providing opportunities for decision making for independence and self-reliance.

- ***Emotional Development:*** Women face several stressful situations because of various conflicts confronting them at home, in the work place and in the society. They need skills to cope with them.
- ***Social Development***: Women have to learn to interact with people at home and outside and they need communication skills, assertiveness and training in handling interpersonal relations to uphold their legal and other rights.
- ***Vocational Development***: There is a general feeling that a large percentage of women are not interested in a career but are marking times in the college to improve their marriage prospect. This is not true any longer. Women are entering the world of work in a big way. Many women have serious career plans. They need information and guidance about the wide choice available in the job market and not be constrained by the prevailing gender stereotypes. They need to be helped in their choice, which would make them also economically independent.

Moral and Spiritual Development and Value Clarification:

As far as women are concerned, there are several myths, stereotypes, prejudices and biases related to gender. While the world is changing rapidly through the impact of globalization, liberalization, urbanization, the media and so on, traditional values are being threatened but women are expected to preserve and perpetuate the cultural heritage. Women are being confronted with a conflict between modernity and tradition. They face the dilemma of how to preserve the qualities of nurturing and tolerance and at the same time face competition, fight for equality, and be assertive without being aggressive or abrasive. The women's colleges should provide a strong support system to help settle these conflicting values.

Women are considered to be emotional and yet they are to be made emotionally independent. Upholding strong moral values amidst deteriorating social conditions is a tough mandate expected of women. Women are expected to maintain humane values while atrocities are perpetuated on them. They are also expected to maintain the traditional Indian culture together with their modern and western oriented education and style of life. Coming from diverse cultural heritage women are also expected to contribute towards preservation of cultural heritage. They are expected to become career minded and be professional in their jobs and at the same time be good wives and mothers. One of the important agendas of the women's colleges is to provide value clarification and help women maintain a balance between these varied and opposing forces of pulls and pushes.

Empowerment

Empowerment has several dimensions and education is seen as a tool in this aspect. Education can help women overcome the social taboos and prejudices and liberate themselves. Women should also be helped to liberate themselves from patriarchy and economic discrimination. In addition, they must be freed from the bondage of restrictive tradition and superstitions. This would enhance their self-image, self-confidence and self-reliance and this would eventually raise their status.

Women should also be empowered to take on leadership roles in various sectors like politics, societal development, professional and international affairs. They should be empowered to handle gender conflicts and injustices and face the challenges of this highly male dominated world. Such empowerment would enhance female participation in all spheres of life and help redefine their roles in this fast changing world. Empowered with economic and psychological independence, women can take on leadership roles and contribute effectively to societal development.

Awareness Building

It is argued that women lag behind because of their lack of knowledge and information. This leads to their exploitation. To overcome this problem, there is a need to raise women's awareness of their rights and entitlements They need to be given basic knowledge on reproductive health, awareness about AIDS, family planning, etc. Awareness in the areas of population education, adult education and environmental education would make women better informed. Awareness of legal rights with respect to marriage, property, etc. is essential. Awareness of various schemes and provisions in the government, specifically meant for women is another area where women's colleges need to make an effort. If women are to play a greater role in societal development, reconstruction and nation building, their social awareness needs to be strengthened.

Cultural development: This should not be sacrificed in the modernization process as women have a responsibility to maintain and promote the rich culture and heritage of the nation.

Thus the dimensions of development are many and varied. Though these dimensions are relevant for both men and women, they are particularly salient for women students, as they have been socialized differently in this highly patriarchal society. The educational institutions have a responsibility to provide opportunities for the proper nurturing and development of all these dimensions to make woman a total person.

Strategies that need to be put in place

Gender-positive initiatives can be broadly classified into two dimensions, namely, (i) academic interventions and (ii) extra-curricular or co-curricular interventions.

Academic Interventions

The foremost objective mentioned is the promotion of women's education that would provide equality of opportunity for women. To achieve this, women need to be trained so that they can compete equally with men. However, it has been observed that women's colleges generally offer courses in arts and humanities and other "female oriented" courses such as home science, thus perpetuating gender stereotype and also denying women an opportunity to get into the frontier and emerging areas where high status and high paying jobs are there. Thus, women's colleges should offer courses in the emerging areas like computers, electronics, microbiology and so on. Women students should be encouraged to take up job-oriented courses in all emerging areas and not confine themselves to gender stereotyped courses.

Academic interventions should also include courses or topics relating to women and their contribution to society. Gender sensitization may be provided as a part of the foundation course or can be incorporated in all the subject areas including arts, science and commerce. Further, any gender bias in any of the texts needs to be carefully eliminated. Incorporating gender issues in the curriculum is not easy for individual colleges that are in the affiliating system. Autonomous colleges have an advantage in this matter. However, under the restructuring of courses gender issues can be built into the curriculum. Where possible, self-financing certificate or diploma courses on gender issues may be offered as add on courses.

Co-curricular and Extracurricular Interventions

The colleges have total freedom in this aspect. Gender positive initiatives and gender sensitization can be provided through several co-curricular and extra curricular interventions. These could be done through various activities of the academic associations, clubs and societies. Debates and discussions could centre on women related issues. Cultural activities can be focused on gender issues. Hobbies promoted could be gender neutral like electronics, photography, etc. and thus go beyond the gender stereotypes of flower arrangement, *rangoli, mehendhi,* etc. Similarly, sports activities can also go beyond gender stereotypes to include riding, swimming, gliding, etc. Adventure activities, tours and trips can all provide opportunities for women's overall personality development.

Teachers' Role for the personal development of students?

The teachers have to realize that it is not enough just to provide academic inputs but they have to move beyond academics if the objective of overall development of women students is to be assured. The teachers will have to develop themselves first so that they can help their student's personal development. The teachers should have confidence in themselves and be an integrated person with inner freedom and correct value system. The teachers should have a sense of personal worth, sensitive to student's needs, have a sense of fairness and be a role model to the students. In brief, some of the desirable characteristics of a good teacher would be

- Accepting one's self
- Being flexible and open minded
- Set an example by their own behaviour
- Understand the student's background and needs
- Create a sympathetic, supportive and friendly atmosphere
- Avoid being condescending and judgemental
- Appreciate, encourage and recognize the student's talents and promote self-esteem, self-actualization, self-image and self-confidence

In addition, some student-centred initiatives would be:

- Help students discover their potential
- Give personal counselling and guidance
- Encourage student's to ask questions without hesitation or inhibition
- Develop critical thinking ability and provide guidance in independent decision making
- Make students aware of their rights and responsibilities
- Provide legal education
- Make them aware of current affairs

Some specific gender related aspects that the teachers can address are:

- Make them proud of their gender and womanhood
- Make them aware of their dignity as women
- Critically evaluate the media and how it depicts women
- Make students aware of the problems faced by women outside the campus

- Raise questions like absence of women in decision making positions
- Sensitize students against gender discrimination at home, in society and workplace
- Take up burning issues concerning women and how to solve them
- Make students present positive aspects of women through pictures, posters and cartoons
- Prepare them to take a public stand to protest against any injustice
- Make them realize that they are no less than men and can work on par with men
- Teach them not to take things for granted.

Approaches to be adopted by teachers in developmental process

The next question that arises is, if all these dimensions of development are to be facilitated, who is responsible for these? Considering that a large section of women are first generation learners and come from socially and educationally deprived backgrounds, it becomes a mandate for the teachers to become MBAs, that is Move Beyond Academics and facilitate Gender Positive Initiatives for the total development of women students. Teachers can take varied approaches in this endeavour.

Academic approach: Firstly, teachers can take initiatives to improve the academic performance of students, especially of those who have been lagging behind, by motivating and encouraging them to perform better. In addition, these students could be given remedial teaching, taught better methods of learning and so on.

Personal approach: The focus of this approach is to take the students into confidence. Talk to them frankly and freely to understand any personal problem they may have and try to help them by giving them guidance and counselling. Giving positive strokes by appreciating the students' performance and efforts goes a long way in enhancing their self-concept and self-image.

Strategic approach: This approach can be taken especially for gender sensitization. Raising issues in class based on newspaper and media reports, organizing "facing the class" session, providing opportunities for debates and discussions in the class on controversial issues and several other methods can be used by teachers to move beyond academics. Basically, teachers have to adopt the humanistic education process for the overall development of the students (Read and Simon, 1975).

Teachers' skills and competence

Not all teachers are conscious that it is their responsibility to facilitate the total development of the students. Some teachers are naturally sensitive to their role as mentors and do a fine job along with their academic responsibilities. Some teachers argue that it is not their responsibility and their mandate is just to teach the subject and conduct the examinations and nothing more. Many teachers are conscious of their responsibility, concerned and committed but do not have the competence or skill to carry out this initiative. It would be helpful if these teachers were themselves given counselling and guidance regarding how they can go ahead with these initiatives. Workshops may be organized highlighting the gender positive initiatives of pace setting women's colleges and how these may be implemented in all institutions.

Impacts of the Gender Positive Initiatives

Students were asked in what way they have benefited by being in a gender sensitive institution. The students did identify several benefits they have derived. It is interesting to see a close match between teacher's identification of the dimensions to be developed and the student's perception of the dimensions on which they feel there has been a significant impact.

First and foremost, the often-mentioned benefit they have derived is gaining in self-confidence. Students have reported that they have shed their shyness, overcome their diffidence, opened up, become independent and more self-reliant which are all indicators of a confident person.

Women students have reported that they have improved their communication skills, learnt to interact with people with greater ease, made several friends, learnt to tolerate people from diverse backgrounds, etc. All these have contributed significantly for their overall social development.

The freedom with which they participate in several sports and physical training activities, participation in martial arts, adventure activities and even horse riding and gliding without having to compete with men or the inhibition posed by the presence of men have benefited the students in their physical development.

A free and secure atmosphere permits women to think critically, be analytical, and participate in discussions and debates and all these help in their intellectual development.

Having to undertake the responsibility for organizing all the activities without being sidelined or marginalised by domineering men around them, the women students feel that they are gaining a lot in developing organization skills. This also helps them to take on leadership roles and learn to work in teams.

Gender sensitive institutions lay a lot of emphasis on morality and ethics through various value education programmes. The students feel this has helped them in their moral development.

Competitions in *Rangoli, Mehendi*, and Flower Arrangement, etc., which are of feminine interest, find a prominent place in the activities of a women friendly institution. Several opportunities are there for cultural programmes of dance and music, painting and drawing. All these contribute to the aesthetic and cultural development of women students.

Another significant impact the students have identified is the Gender Sensitization that they have acquired being in a women oriented institution. The programmes and discussions have made the students understand and realize the status of women, the existence of gender inequality and discrimination that has motivated them to fight for gender justice and work towards achieving equality.

In general, women students feel that the type of exposure they get in a women focused institution, the opportunities provided to them and the safe, secure and supportive climate enhances their sense of overall competence, gives them confidence and makes them feel empowered to face the challenges of life.

Policy and management implications

The study of pace setting women's colleges brought out certain distinguishing features that facilitated these colleges in achieving the objective of total development of women students. It would be useful to highlight some of these features so that other colleges may benefit from these experiences.

- Dynamic leadership of the principal
- Supportive management
- Availability of good infrastructure
- Committed teachers
- Team spirit
- Sensitivity to student background
- Awareness of gender inequality
- Concern for the community around
- Linkages and networking

Conclusion

It has been consistently argued that exclusive women's colleges are still required for providing access to women students for various socio-cultural reasons and to meet the special needs of women students. It has also been argued that it is not enough just to provide access but the exclusive women's colleges have to move beyond academics. Mere academic inputs are available in the co-educational colleges also but the empowerment of women through the provision of life skills required to face the challenges confronting women in this highly patriarchal society, should be a main agenda of the exclusive women's colleges. These can be achieved through both academic and non-academic interventions. The management and super structure has to play a very supportive role in facilitating this process. This requires greater gender sensitivity on the part of educational policy makers and administrators.

The laudable objective cited in the National Policy of Education of utilizing education as an instrument of social change to undo the accumulated distortions of the past will remain a mere rhetoric unless specific gender positive initiatives are put in place. It should be pointed out here that women students are not a homogeneous group. Till a few decades ago, only women from liberated, emancipated, upper caste well to do urban families were enrolling in higher education. Now with the tremendous social transformation-taking place, women from very conservative and traditional families from socially deprived backgrounds are enrolling in higher education, for education is being seen as a means of social and economic mobility. These women are to a large extent, first generation learners and probably the first women in the family to enter the portals of a college.

Women who belong to the first category can perhaps look after themselves. For women who come from the second category, mere academic inputs will not take them far. They need to be provided with additional support to develop required life skills to cope in this highly male dominated society. It should be acknowledged that there still exist several gender stereotypes, discrimination, inequality and injustice. These cannot be wishes away easily. Women need to be empowered to face these challenges effectively. Educational institutions, especially exclusive women's colleges, have a responsibility in capacity building of women so that they have an equal opportunity not only for personal growth but to contribute to societal development. After all, women constitute nearly half of the human resources and their potential should be harnessed for the benefit of the society.

Empowerment is a life cycle process. Due to various socio-cultural and historical reasons women's status has remained rather low. There is now not only *Consciousness* of this status but also a *Concern* to rectify the situation. *Consciousness* and *Concern* while important will not bring about the desired changes, unless there is a commitment coupled with competence on the part of the change agents to initiate the required gender positive initiatives. If all the agenda discussed above are carried through, it would ultimately result in empowering women and liberate them from oppression and discrimination and help them lead a meaningful life of dignity and grace with their heads held high.

REFERENCES

Bressler, M. and Wendall, P. (1980), 'The sex composition of selective colleges and gender differences in career aspirations', *Journal of Higher Education*, 51, 650-63.

Desai, N. (1977), 'The pattern of higher education and role of a women's university' *Journal of Higher Education,* 3(1) Mansoon, 5-20.

Indiresan, J. (2002), *Education for Women's Empowerment: Gender Positive Initiatives in Pace Setting Women's Colleges,* Konark Publishers, New Delhi.

Kim, O. (1978), ' The place of women's colleges- The Korean experience' EWHA University, *New Frontiers in Education*, 8 (1), 42-53.

Murugkar, I., (1983), 'Development goals and women's higher education', *Journal of Higher Education,* 8(3), 78-92.

Nair Ramachandran, K.R. (1981), 'Women's education and women's colleges' *University news*, 19(b), 159-60.

National Policy of Education (1986), Department of Education, Ministry of Human Resources Development, Government of India, New Delhi.

Pascarella, E. (1984), 'College environmental influences on student educational aspirations', *Journal of Higher Education*, 55, 751-71.

Purcell, F.B. (2004), Women's Universities and Colleges: An International Handbook, Center for International Higher Education, Lynch School of Education, Boston College, USA.

Read,D.A. and Simon, S.B. (Ed.) Humanistic Education Sourcebook. Prentice-Hall, New Jersey, 1975

Riordan, C. (1990), *Girls and Boys in School: Together or Separate?* Teacher's College Press, New York.

Sagaria, M.A.D. (1988), 'The case of empowering women as leaders in higher education' in M.A.D. Sagaria (ed.) *Empowering Women in Leadership Development Strategies on Campus,* New Directions for Student Services, No.44, Jossey Boss, San Francisco.

Tidball, M.E., (1986), *Issues for Women in Higher Education*, United Methodist Institute of Higher Education, Vanderbilt University, Nashville, Tennessee.

University Grants Commission Report, 2005-06, New Delhi.

4.

WOMEN AND HIGHER EDUCATION IN INDIA

KAUSAR WIZARAT and VIJAY VRAT ARYA

You can tell the condition of a nation by looking at the status of its women.
—Jawaharlal Nehru

The Dark Shadow of Received Ideas

Many of the prevailing attitudes to the question of educating the Girl Child and Women in India can be traced back to the roles assigned to women in the patriarchal discourse that has informed our social norms for millennia. Manu who has been lionised as the first law giver had this to say about the position of women in 200 B.C.: "by a young girl, by a young woman, or even by an aged one, nothing must be done independently, even in her own house". "In childhood a female must be subject to her father, in youth to her husband, when her lord is dead to her sons; a woman must never be independent". Further the anxiety of man to monopolize his skill in plough culture is reflected in the taboo that is observed almost all over India, against the women's handling the plough. In many societies, she is not even allowed to touch it.

The plough represented a major technological breakthrough in technology of the time and its monopolisation by males is probably an early example of denying women access to technology and to labour saving devises. The denial of excess to the plough also signals the reduction of women to menial labour intensive operations in the productive process and the cornering of all "Highly Skilled" activities in the hands of the males. In the days when the knowledge of the written word, in the languages of the elite, also meant access to spiritual texts, it was prohibited to women, including women born among the dwijas and to the shudras.

Over the centuries it is these attitudes that have been the basis of limiting women's access to education. One must remember that this is nothing unique to India and that all over the world including the developed world the biases that operate against women both in education and employment are a continuation of patently undemocratic attitudes that have been perfected by the patriarchal order over centuries.

Women in India are a little better off than many developed nations because every citizen was granted equal rights before the law from the time our Constitution came into force in 1950, and Indian women did not have to fight a lone battle for the right to vote as women were forced to do in many "Developed Nations". Full Electoral Rights were granted to women in the US only in 1920 and in Canada as late as 1960.

The denial of education to large number of women is akin to denying them equal rights as citizens of a free country, it keeps them out of the employment market and thus denies them an equal chance at earning a livelihood it is no different from denying women the right to equal participation in the affairs of the state.

Our present is shaped by our distant and recent past

Given this tradition of bias is it any wonder that the places where women could go for higher learning were few and far between. The history of higher education for women is not even 200 year old. In fact two USA based colleges for women, Wesleyan College in Macon, GA, and Mount Holyoke College in South Hadley, MA, that started in 1836 and 1837 respectively, claim to be the first women's colleges in that country and perhaps in the world too. Cambridge admitted the first batch of women students in 1882 while Lady Margaret Hall, a college affiliated with Oxford, that admitted only women students was set up in 1878. Both these colleges did not award degrees to their female students though they were allowed to attend courses and sit for exams.

Bethune College, Calcutta, founded as a school in 1849 by John Elliot Drinkwater Bethune, grew into the first women's college in the country in 1871. And in this aspect as well we were a little ahead of our colonial masters.

But having said this let us not forget that many of our leaders were not favourably disposed to women's education. Lokmanya Tilak, Lala Lajpat Rai and Sir Syed Ahmad Khan were not keen to spend the scarce funds for education that had been mobilized with great difficulties, on something as unnecessary as women's education. The opposition and hostilities that Lala Devraj, (the founder, in 1886, of the Kanya Vidyalaya at Jullundhar), Pandita Ramabai (the founder of a school and home for widows in 1889 in Bombay) and Sheikh Mohammad Abdullah of Aligarh (the founder of a school for girls in 1906), had to face is testimony to the mindset that informed even the tallest of our reformers at the end of the 19th and early 20th century. Mind you, these were among the pioneers of women's school education. What the founders of the earliest women's colleges must have had to go through can easily be imagined.

Women's Education: Contemporary Scenario

The Spread of general education and that of girls' and women's education, especially in the colonies of the various imperialist nations, became more marked close to the mid 50s of the 20th century and was directly correlated to the rising tide of the struggles from colonial rule and the general growth of democratic aspirations of the people. According to a study by Louise (2004) impressionistic research reveals that women's colleges and universities have been founded in countries where previously they have been extremely rare—in Africa, much of the Middle East, and China—and their numbers have surged forward in India.

Despite the impressive growth in the number of co-educational institutes of higher learning and the number of separate colleges for women having (from 950 in 1991-92 to 1905 in 2005-06), the fact remains that the prevailing social mores and the dominant mind set continues to hold back women from reaching their potential and taking their due place in this field as well.

The large number of levels that education has been broken into serves as major stumbling blocks for the underprivileged, and women being the most underprivileged suffer the consequences at each level. Each of these levels, *viz.*, Primary, Middle, Secondary, Senior Secondary, Graduation and Post Graduation, work as filters that prevent more and more girls from going across to the next stage.

The commonly accepted desired level for girls education is that they should be kept at functional literacy levels because they have to stay at home to look after siblings when small, tend to their husbands and in laws when young and to care for their children and grand children in later years. (Echoes of Manu dare we say).

This framework has no place for addressing or recognising a girl's interests, capacity and potential for growth, much less having a vision of the future and the place of women in our society. The results are obvious and are evident from the high drop out rates of girls and women as we go up the educational ladder. The courses on offer for women and the familial choices that are made for them only go to exacerbating the situation further.

The other factor that has a telling negative effect on education for females is the popularly held view, without any evidence in its support, that women are incapable of understanding complex and technologically advanced ideas (the plough again). All this continues in the face of strong evidence to the contrary. Year after year girls continue to outperform boys in all subjects across the board. The average pass out percentage for girls appearing for any exam is better than that of the boys. Even among top performers, the proportions are skewed in favour of girls when compared to their counterpart.

Despite this the enrolment of young women at all levels of higher education, *viz.,* Diploma, Certificate, Graduation, Post Graduation and Research, the percentage of women to total enrolment ranges between 32 to 42 per cent, clearly way below their due share. A much higher rate of dropout for girls, as compared to the drop out rates for boys, between the different stages of higher education is the only plausible explanation.

The more jobs oriented and potentially more lucrative or prestigious streams of education are by and large almost exclusively cornered by male students. Women students serve merely as hewers of wood and drawers of water, compelled to be the last and expected to be content with the leftovers of education. They have after all been trained to be the last to eat the left overs, once the males have had their fill.

The courses that thus become available for women, irrespective of their creativity, potential and all round capacities, are courses those that are the least entertained on account of lower post educational pay packages & opportunity. A large number of families, including many with highly educated males, consider educating their girl child to a level that is considered adequate for marriage, in many cases some elementary certificate or diploma is deemed enough. In fact higher educational attainments by young women are in most cases a disqualification in the marriage market.

The courses that young women are encouraged to opt for after school are in most cases totally lacking in a vision for the future professional prospects of the said course and rarely have anything to do with the interests of the student in question. The consequences of such a scenario are obvious; a majority of young women end up with a degree that is totally unrelated to their own interests. This is probably the reason for most young women being unable to give any reasonable justification for their selection of a particular stream of learning. The Choices were limited to begin with and even among the limited choices, the stream eventually chosen was not of their own volition, the choice had been made by a family elder.

Fortunately, due to greater awareness, there is a perceptible shift, though small, yet a shift nonetheless. The shift is a result of growing awareness, greater awareness among young women about career options, there is also, at least in major urban settlements, a little more assertiveness among young women about their individual choices and rights and finally there is a little more sensitivity among parents, again only among more urbanised parents, about the sensitivities and interests of their daughters.

More young women are shifting to courses that were hitherto considered exclusive male bastions.

The results of this change have begun to become visible. Our Indian Institute of Technology (IITs) now have more women students than there were two decades ago, their numbers, though, continue to be abysmally low, still there is a shift and signs of attitudinal change—not among all sections of population but certainly in the larger urban areas, among the more educated, among the more well to do, among the more enlightened and perhaps also among the more market savvy.

We have to, however, keep in mind that we cannot wait indefinitely for this extremely slow process of enlightenment to overcome the traditional resistance to the idea of higher education for women. Educational planners have to play a more proactive role to ensure delivery of the opportunities of acquiring higher education to young women because women constitute the largest underprivileged group cutting across all identities of class, caste, community and region and, therefore, need special mechanisms to be put in place for helping them overcome the built in biases in society.

An idea of the biases that exist and the mechanisms that need to be evolved can be had from one of the relationships that exist between societal anti-social attitudes to women in India and Indian women's need for higher education. The parental fear of their daughters becoming victims of eve-teasing, molestation and other heinous crimes against women, work as one of the deterrents to higher education for women. If the incidence of gender-biased street crimes like eve-teasing, molestation, rape, and sexual harassment in places of study and work are dealt with firmly and the perpetrators brought to book quickly, it will certainly lead to an increasing participation of women in the streams of higher science and in technical and professional education.

In other words women's participation in courses that require students to both spend longer hours of study in the class room or laboratory and to travel longer distances to get to their institutes is directly proportional to how safe the world, outside the confines of the home, is for women. Availability alone is not enough, it has to be converted into 'effective access'.

Another step that will ensure greater enrolment is to establish more colleges of science, medicine and technology exclusively for girls. Such innovative and imaginative practices will bring in their wake a whole host of issues dealing with job creation and the need to stem brain drain. Tackling these will have far reaching consequences both for the female work force in our country and for our economy. These changes will also usher in a greater role for women in the expanding spheres of the new economy.

The Unbreakable Glass Ceiling

Education in India, and more so women's education, as already discussed, is constrained by the socio-economic condition of our people, their attitudes, values and culture. Traditional structures of education that existed in the pre-British period were all dismantled during colonial rule to be replaced by a system of education best suited to the requirements of the colonial-ruler for their vested interest. The post-1857 period, marked as it was with the gradual rise of a Pan-Indian-consciousness, also saw the growth of local initiatives aimed at educating the Indian masses. The definitions of the mass varied from individual to individual but collectively the effort led to the setting up of a large number of regions, community and caste based institutions of learning.

The attitude of the social reformers of this period, at least in the initial phase, was at best marked by certain ambivalence if not by open hostility to the question of women's education. For most of them the goal of education for women was to make them more capable of fulfilling their traditional roles as mothers and housewives. Early marriage and early childbearing discourages or hindered schooling for the female.

Lack of hostels for women, shortage of lady teachers and lack of basic amenities like clean and hygienic toilets for females in schools and many colleges are not only factors that makes it difficult for them to study but are also reflective of social insensitivity to the needs of the female scholar. Add to this low entry, low retention and high dropouts and you get an idea of a system that continues to be heavily weighted against female education (Sudhakar, 2002).

A thorough examination of the status of women in higher education and related sectors all over the world and its comparison with the contemporary Indian scenario will show that by and large it is not very different. The differences that exist are only quantitative. Women have usually been marginalized not only in India but globally as well. The so-called advanced or developed nations have also failed in providing women their due share in this field (Wizarat and Arya, 2007). This however is no justification for our shortcomings, nor should this give us any reason to feel complacent.

Democracy is not only confined to making available a number of choices to its citizens; it is defined primarily through the protection it provides to its citizens in making free choices according to their own preferences. Viewed from this standpoint our system of education seems to be wanting on both these counts in as much as women's education is concerned.

Even a superficial survey of streams of study on offer for girl students will make this amply clear. Languages, Literature, Humanities and the Arts take the lion's share from among the disciplines available for women students.

A strange concoction of house keeping skills with small doses of nutrition related information and the like have been passed off as a science subject for women by calling it home science. This discipline of study, if one can call it that, ideally suits the educational requirements of a good wife and mother that most ninetieth century reformers wanted for women. Home Science thus ends up as the most favoured science stream for girls. This is followed by Biology and related disciplines. Mathematics, Physics, and Chemistry account for a far smaller representation of women both as student as well as faculty composition.

The status of availability and choices for the newer disciplines in the sciences like Microbiology, Biotechnology and Bioinformatics, Genetics, *etc.*, is no better. In Medicine, women are by and large confined to Gynaecology, Pathology, *etc.,* specializations like Cardiology, Neurology and advanced surgery continue almost exclusively as male preserves. It is well high impossible to come across women who have specialised in these areas.

The share of women in technical and professional courses like engineering has always been very low and continues to be so even today. Among the various engineering disciplines like civil, mechanical, electrical, chemical, electronics and computers, robotics, aeronautics, etc. whatever representation that women find is confined to certain branches in computer sciences.

The situation in the now increasingly preferred stream of management with choices in finance, human resource development, marketing, planning and administration, *etc.,* is no different. The glass ceiling ensures that most women opt for or have access either to finance or human resource development (HRD), the more lucrative and rewarding specialization of marketing is again cornered by males.

The over all picture of enrolment of women in higher education, during the years 1995-96 to 2005-06, shows the trend that 51 per cent of all women enrolled in higher education courses are concentrated within what is popularly known as the Arts stream. The Sciences and Commerce & Management related streams occupy the second position with around 19-20 per cent of young women enrolled in higher education opting for the former and about 13-17 per cent opting for the later. Courses in Agriculture, Veterinary Sciences, Law, Medicine, Engineering & Technology and education appear to be the least favoured with less than 5 per cent of those enrolled choosing these streams.

Table 4.1: Women Enrolled in Different Subjects as a Proportion of Total Women Enrolled in Higher Education in India

Year	Arts	Science Management	Commerce/	Education Technology	Engineering/	Medical	Agriculture Science	Veterinary	Law	Other #
1995-96	54.4	20.1	14.1	3.9	1.2	-	-	-	1.8	4.5
1996-97	54.4	20.1	14.1	3.9	1.2	-	-	-	1.8	4.5
1997-98	54.4	19.2	13.6	3.4	2.1	3.3	0.6	0.1	2	1.3
1998-99	54.4	19.2	13.6	3.4	2.1	3.3	0.6	0.1	2	1.3
1999-00	54.3	19	13.9	3.2	2.3	3.3	0.6	0.1	2	1.3
2000-01	51.1	19	16.7	2.4	3.6	3.9	0.4	0.1	1.8	1
2001-02	51.79	19.9	16.56	1.69	3.75	3.5	0.26	0.09	1.62	0.84
2002-03	51.13	19.94	16.48	1.81	4.17	3.63	0.25	0.08	1.68	0.83
2003-04	51.01	20.22	16.43	1.9	4.13	3.63	0.25	0.08	1.56	0.79
2004-05	51.07	20.08	16.45	1.86	4.15	3.63	0.25	0.08	1.62	0.81
2005-06	51.01	20.18	16.46	1.85	4.16	3.64	0.24	0.08	1.64	0.74

Note: # 'Other' in 1995-96, 1996-97 include Agriculture, Medicine, Veterinary Science, etc.
Source: UGC Annual Reports Various Years (1995-'96 to 2005-'06), New Delhi.

Although in terms of absolute numbers India may have more women scientists as compared to many of the western countries, their share as a proportion of total female population and as compared to their male counterparts is not very high. Most women scientists, doctors, engineers, *etc.,* in India belong to families that encourage education of women, and do not discriminate between their children on the basis of gender.

The overall picture tells us quite a different story. Despite the fact that a large number of girls opt for engineering, biological sciences and medicine at the under graduate level, very few continue with these subjects at the post graduate level and fewer still take it up as a career. Of the few who become professional engineers and doctors, most have been able to manage the dual responsibilities of home and work place successfully. This is also a clear proof that, despite assertions to the contrary, there is no need to make women choose between a profession and a family.

A large number of gender studies have shown that the most prestigious, euphemistically defined as more challenging areas of study that also turn out to be the most lucrative in terms of career options have all been monopolised by males and women end up receiving the left overs or the least rewarding options. This is unarguably the reality that confronts women who opt for higher education and the more rewarding post-educational careers for themselves. And this is as true in the Third World as it is in the First World.

Wenneras and Wold (1997) have conducted a study in Sweden that points to the shocking levels of nepotism and sexism in this advanced country where women are believed to enjoy a high status in society–62 men and 52 women appeared before the Medical Research Council to be interviewed for positions of post-doctoral candidates. While the success rate for men were 26 per cent, that for women was only 7 per cent. When the scores given by the review committee based on quality of publications, *etc.,* were analyzed there was a mismatch between this objective parameter of scoring and the rank given to judge competence. According to the authors, the females had to be 2.5 times more productive to get the same competence score.

Career Verses Family

The traditionally accepted role of women in India is to get married and to look after their family the rest of their lives. Even today a large number of women opting for careers do so not because of any innate desire to be independent; they do so because of the ever rising cost of living and a desire to contribute to the economy of the family.

Dominant social norms, especially among the middle classes, that prevents parents from even having a meal at their daughter's house make it almost a sin for them to take any part of their daughter's earnings for their household expenses. Parents, therefore, do not normally want their daughters to take up jobs and if they do so, the earnings are kept for purposes of the daughter's dowry. The jobs in any case are a stop-gap arrangement till the girl gets married.

Such arrangements fit in perfectly with the traditional role that a girl is expected to play after her marriage. Whether she will work or not after her marriage and if she does so, what kind of a job she will take up are issues that will be decided by her in laws and by her husband. These decisions are informed by the needs and the perceived self-image of the in-law's own social status.

For a large majority of young women higher education is not, therefore, linked to careers at all. The social roles expected of them and their own perceived notions of self worth affect the aspirations of a large number of women students who go to college, 'for time pass' as the expression goes, and to earn a degree that improves their marital prospects.

This may be the reason why a large majority are sent to courses in the arts and humanities, as they cost less, are perceived to be less challenging and do not require long-term academic commitments, for the girls are in a holding area so to speak and will leave the moment their future schedules have been finalised. All this combines together to create a situation where a large number of women in higher education system are not clear about their educational and post educational preferences.

A whole lot of far reaching societal changes will have to occur before we reach a situation when young women begin to make informed educational and career choices. Some thing that might help the process along will have to be put in place for education linked career guidance workshops for senior school students, especially girl students. Another step that will be of great help will be for girls to have greater access to education that gives them career-oriented skills.

The representation of women in higher education has increased considerably in independent India when compared to the pre 1947 days but they are still confined to a few selected fields and subjects as opposed to their male counterparts. Access to various branches of higher education at the under graduate level is not impartial across the gender divide and the same trend persists at the postgraduate and higher levels as well.

Choice of areas of study being subject to the requirements of the marital market will have to yield place to the requirements of a developing economy if the entire population has to be given a chance to contribute to, and be a part of, this growth and development that one hears so much about. Let us not forget that, despite well planned and efficiently executed schemes of killing millions of them even before they are born, women still constitute almost 50 per cent of country population and no meaningful growth in any field is conceivable without women being equal partners in such growth.

Young women enter higher education at a transitional stage of their lives and since there are no immediate returns from schooling, coupled with the heavy expenditure on marriage and dowry, daughters are less likely than sons to be sent to college. If women have to contribute as full members of our society, their potential must be harnessed especially when they have demonstrated their capability to succeed in the educational system. It is up to the colleges and universities to build their self-confidence, to harness their capacities and provide the opportunities and choices that they deserve.

While higher education is socially accepted and taken for granted among the upper and middle strata in urban India, it is also viewed more as an investment in the daughters' distant future rather than as an immediate goal. In other words, daughters are equipped with qualifications that are necessary for employment or work and that may be needed if they are deserted or widowed after marriage. This perception of education as deferred investment is quite strong (Chanana, 1998).

There is need to address this perception strongly for a number of reasons. One of the most important of these is the gradual breakdown of the joint family system and the increasing trend of newly married couples moving out to set up their own homes. In situations such as these the wife is both the breadwinner and the homemaker, all the more reason for her to be educated with a view of using her education and skills to contribute to the running of the house. The very fact that a woman 'earns' and is not dependent on a man for her basic needs is a concept not easily digested by a male dominated society and it will be quite some time before both the father and the husband will come to accept this change in the position of women.

The acceptance of the concept of gender equality and all that flows from it does not come easily. Attempts have been made through various quarters to pay lip service to the idea and to use the jargon of equality to try and reinforce traditional ideas of what is ideal for women. This attempt continues and Lord Denning is trying his level best to play the old game while appearing to speak for gender justice in 1980.

> "A woman feels as keenly, thinks as clearly, as a man, she in her sphere does work as useful as a man does in his own. She has as much right to her

> freedom - to develop her personality to the full - as a man has. When she marries, she does not become the husband's servant but his equal partner. If his work is more important in the life of the community, hers is more important in the life of the family. Neither can do without the other. Neither is above the other or under the other. They are equals". (Emphasis added)

All this talk of equality is just a façade, what the good lord is saying in essence is that women's work is looking after the family while the man contributes to the community. How is this qualitatively different from Manu or the Bigoted Mullah one fails to see? Entrenched and deep-rooted ideas take a long time to dislodge. It is crucial for all of us to recognise this and to continue our efforts, for without changing these attitudes the battle for women's education started more than a century ago cannot be won.

Areas with Visible Gaps in Higher Education

As noted earlier there is evidence of an increase in the share of women in higher education in the post independence era, it would have been most shocking had this not happened. A large number of government reports and census data points to this growth. A study of these figures also shows slight shifts in preferences over the last six decades and there is now some presence of women in areas that were earlier almost totally barred to them.

One must point out also that statistics dealing with higher education in India are not of a quality and reliability that one would wish them to be. The private institutions lack in transparency and do not provide any statistics. The public sector does no better. Even higher education regulatory bodies in India such as the MHRD, UGC, AICTE, *etc.,* do not provide enrolment statistics for men and women separately for institutions, levels of study and across disciplines.

There is as yet no separate information on private self-financed un-aided institutions. Moreover, pure sciences, social sciences, arts and humanities remain confined to the public institutions. It seems that the earlier trend of concentration of women in these disciplines is expected to have been reinforced. Additionally, even though women are enrolling in professional education in larger numbers, it is not clear which subjects and specializations do they take up. Which institutions are they joining and in what proportions (Chanana, 2004).

Over the years it has been observed that women's share in terms of enrolment to higher education is not increasing at a competitive rate. They are opting to join only the traditional, less challenging and less rewarding areas. Their participation in more rewarding and challenging technology and allied fields remains at levels that are abysmally low. The share of women in post education employment continues to be minimal as a result of withdrawals, both quantitative and qualitative, due to domestic responsibilities.

One can easily say that women who are qualified to contribute significantly to national development as a valuable asset are ending up as a liability under social compulsions and family responsibilities. These so called social compulsions and family responsibilities are a major stumbling block to the professional advancement and career promotion of women (Wizarat and Arya, 2007).

Any through and rigorous analysis of available data on education will show that the major contribution to growth of education and literacy among women is a result primarily of increases in enrolments registered among the urban population where they have resources and ready access to higher and quality education. There is no corresponding growth in rural areas.

There is no doubt that representation of women in higher education is growing, that it is growing in certain disciplines and there is no doubt that in certain subjects girls are out performing the boys. It is equally true that at least some of these subjects are no longer on the preferred list of male students or are subjects that provide lesser job opportunities than other subjects. It is also true that male students are opting for newer disciplines, for disciplines that offer more rewarding career opportunities. If representation of women is increasing in such areas, then this improvement is merely of a quantitative nature, what we need to see is qualitative improvement of enrolment; unfortunately there is little evidence of that.

There are several factors that inhibit access and disciplinary orientation of women in higher education. Factors that inhibit female access to higher education are non-availability of colleges and inadequate delivery systems, i.e., unsuitable infrastructure and absence of basic physical facilities. Other factors are qualitative and are rooted in the area specific socio-cultural context.

At times it is difficult to separate the former from the latter. For example, the presence of a co-educational college in Rajasthan does not mean that people will send their daughters to such a college. The young women may have given up the veil in the urban areas and may also move relatively freely in public places, yet separate colleges for women are considered desirable because prolonged interaction with men (students and teachers) is not socially desirable. Thus, physical access also becomes social access and it has policy implications (Chanana, 2000).

When planning for educational facilities for women, in a land as diverse and as traditionally rooted as India, one has to keep in mind the entire gamut of diversities, complexities and social proclivities. The gender divide, the social and regional divides, the culture divides, all come into play. If in Jammu & Kashmir and Assam militancy may be a reason, in Rajasthan and Haryana cultural and social barriers may become decisive while in Orrisa, Madhya Pradesh, Bihar, Rajasthan, Chattisgarh, Jharkhand, *etc.* poor financial state of the family may determine access to education. In states like Uttar Pradesh, Punjab, and West Bengal traditional education might be available but one may have to pay more attention to creating facilities for technical and professional streams whereas in states like Himachal Pradesh, TamilNadu, Uttaranchal, Andhra Pradesh, *etc.* the distance that students have to travel to get to college may be of crucial importance.

Getting rid of the baggage of the past to remove inequity

Women's education is one of the most powerful tools available for uplifting a nation. It is also a human right that too many women around the world have been denied. Perhaps the 21st century will be the Century for Women's Education Worldwide. It is a revolution long overdue (Louise, 2004).

The Commonwealth Secretariat (1995) focuses on a vision, which the Commonwealth works towards... *"A world in which women and men have equal rights and opportunities in all stages of their lives to express their creativity in all fields of human endeavours, and in which women are respected and valued as equal and able partners in establishing the values of social justice, equity, democracy and respect for human rights. Within such a framework of values, women and men will work in collaboration and partnership to ensure sustainable economic and social development for all nations."*

The simplest way to understand the gravity of any issue is by correlating it to the most basic existential questions of the time, because the importance of the issue can only be understood wholly when seen in its larger context. To understand the signal importance of women's education one must see it in relation to its impact on the welfare of their families and the impact of the welfare of all the aggregated families on the welfare of the nation.

From the foregoing, we need to address the essential question of the need of higher education for women. One could enumerate several justifications in support. Let us take one of them, not necessarily the most significant, but important nonetheless – Women as Workforce. If we consider them merely as a workforce, we would like to take full advantage of all the able bodied women in India; counting just the adult women we are looking at least at a work force of one quarter of a billion potential workers. Now if a workforce of this size was trained and equipped to be efficient workers, we could move high mountains.

After realization of importance of women in higher education there is a need to achieve it in terms of both quantity as well as quality. This issue may be addressed with reference to the problems during education and post education including careers options.

Try to imagine the impact of the collective contribution of this workforce to its immediate neighborhood and to the nation as a whole. Try now to imagine the impact they will make if they were all educated and the impact they would create if even one tenth of them had access to higher education. Should they not be allowed to reach their full potential?

If we need to compete globally then we must realise the importance of our large women's population. Unless this force is utilized judiciously we will not achieve our full potential as a nation and will lag behind in the race for higher targeted growth rates. A skilled workforce is always more productive and the demand for a skilled workforce never decreases. We cannot ignore the importance of this potential, it must be provided for at all costs and without any discrimination.

Indian economy has experienced a growth rate of about 8.1 per cent during 2005-06. The planned target for achieving above 8.5 per cent in the coming years needs to be addressed through a wide range of constructive efforts and one of these is to fully engage our available workforce in contributing its full potential to economic growth.

Exploring the full potential of the female workforce for rapid economic development is only a sub set of this larger subset called the Indian Workforce. A major boom in the economy has come from the expansion of the service sector and there is great scope for tapping its unexplored possibilities. There is a great need to equip our workforce for this sector and to gainfully employ all those who have the potential to be gainfully engaged in this enterprise but are still outside its reach for reasons of neglect by oversight or design (Wizarat & Arya, 2007).

Two sets of suggestions to overcome this gap between potential and realization are placed below.

The first set of suggestions deals with measures that would help in the creation of an environment that encourages women to begin to opt for the science stream in higher education in larger numbers than hitherto witnessed while The second set of suggestions are aimed at creating an environment that is more conducive and more consciously sensitive to the needs and requirements of working women.

The two sets of suggestions are being placed more in the nature of talking points for a discussion among those who are concerned about the exclusion of a large part of our population from processes that are crucial for the overall growth of our society.

It is hoped that a wider discussion on these issues will not only lead to greater sensitization of our own community of educational planners but will also eventually lead to the evolution of a national framework of action in this arena.

Table 4.2: Special Programmes to Encourage Study and Practice of Science by Women

Recommendations	*Implementing agency*
Special merit scholarship for girls studying in govt. schools to take up science. Science education is becoming increasingly expensive due to privatization, the axe will fall on girls.	NCERT
Travel support to girls from poor families and one escort when they come to the city to write competitive exams.	NCERT
Opportunities for placement for girls, especially from small towns & govt. schools to do summer projects in good labs.	DST, CSIR, ICMR, DBT, etc.
Opportunities for science teachers from colleges to do short-term research projects. Special leave with pay, for Ph. D.	UGC, DST, etc.
Role model programme. Fellowships to eminent women scientists to visit, give lectures, and interact with students and teachers in universities.	UGC, DST, etc. and Science academies
Website and directory of women scientists, giving their professional profile. This can be used to identify speakers for conferences, appointment to committees, etc.	DST, science academies
Opportunity for women who suffered a break in career to return to a career in science.	DST, Science agencies, academies
Articles on achievements of women scientists.	Journals like Current Science, etc.
Life histories of successful past and present women scientists to be chronicled.	NBT in Collaboration with science academies
Gender sensitization programmes in all institutions & schools.	Higher education institutions, schools

Source: Bamji (2005).

Suggestions for improving representation of women in the workforce

1. Flexible working hours and Part Time Jobs
2. Relaxing Recruitment Requirements of Age and option of Mid-Career Breaks
3. Assessment of performance on the basis of years spent in professional life, rather than biological age.
4. Systematic encouragement to inclusion of women in selection and policy making committees and giving them equal representation.
5. Transparency in selection process, reasons for rejection to be placed on record and not treated as confidential information.
6. Special schemes for career advancement for women including on the job training and orientations, etc aside from positive efforts for nurturing and rewarding talent at all levels.
7. Rigorous efforts to identify meritorious women, objectivity in selection for fellowships and awards, due representation to women at all forums including academic conferences, seminars, brain storming sessions and policy making fora.
8. Effective mechanisms for redressal of complaints of gender bias and harassment.
9. Both the Setting up of grievance cell for gender related and sexual offences at institution as well as at higher levels and equal representation to women on all such committees to be made mandatory
10. Ensuring gender neutrality in both illustrative and textual material in textbooks. Stereotypes of women engaged only in "womanly duties" like domestic work and men engaged only in "jobs fit for a man" in other occupations to be actively discouraged.
11. Transfers to enable wife and husbands to work in the same city and where possible freedom to work in the same institution.
12. Paternity leave for fathers to care for infants.
13. Facilities like crèche and day care centres at all work places.
14. Proper toilets and ladies rooms at all work places.

Conclusion

It is generally accepted now that the creative talent, manpower resources and intellectual potential of women in all its dimensions has barely been explored hitherto. Education in general and higher education along with its allied openings are no exception to this rule. Our entire society has suffered the consequences of relegating women to such utter neglect. It is, therefore, our collective responsibility as a society to evolve and put in place mechanisms that would do away with this entrenched system of discrimination against one half of our population. Determined action in this sphere carried out simultaneously on all fronts will open the doors to rapid economic growth for the nation and true progress for our entire population with all women and all men participating equally and contributing their mite in equal measure.

REFERENCES

Bamji, M. S. (2005), INSA Examines Indian Women's Access to and Retention in Science, *Current Science, Vol. 88, No. 9*, May 10, pp. 1361-1363.

Borcelle Germaine (1985), *Jobs for Women – A Plea for Equality of Opportunity*, UNESCO, Switzerland.

Chanana, Karuna (1998), 'Family Strategies, Gender Ideology and Education: The Impact of Partition on Punjabi Women of New Delhi', in Carla Risseeuw and Kamala Ganesh (eds), *Negotiation and social space: A Gendered Ananlysis of Changing Kin and Security Networks in South Asia and Sub-Saharan Africa*, Sage, New Delhi, pp 157-176.

Chanana, Karuna (2000), Treading the Hollowed Halls: Women in Higher Education in India. *Economic and Political Weekly*, March 18, 2000. Pp. 1012-1022.

Chanana, Karuna (2004), Gender and disciplinary choices: women in higher education in india. Paper prepared for the UNESCO Colloquium on Research and Higher Education Policy, *Knowledge, Access and Governance: Strategies for Change*, 1-3 December, 2004, Paris.

Commonwealth Secretariat (1995), Commonwealth Plan of Action on Gender and Development. London. Online at http://www.thecommonwealth.org/

Davies, S., Lubelska C., and Quinn J. (1994). *Changing the Subject: Women in Higher Education*, Taylor & Francis, London.

Komarovsky, Mirra (2004). *Women in the Modern World: Their Education and their Dilemma*, Altamira Press, USA.

Louise, W. Knight (2004). Educating Women Worldwide. *International Higher Education*, Fall 2004. Online athttp://www.bc.edu/bc_org/avp/soe/cihe/newsletter/News37/text008.htm

Pascall, G. and Cox, R. (1993). *Women Returning to Higher Education*. The Society for Research into Higher Education (SRHE) and Open University Press, Buckingham.

Patel K., Ahooja (1995). *Women and Sustainable Development: An International Dimension*. International Development Studies Series – 4. Ashish Publishing House, New Delhi.

Sudhakar Rohini (2002). Education of the Women. *University News, 40(35)*, September 2-8.

UGC (1995-96 to 2005-06) Annual Reports, Various Years, New Delhi.

Wenneras, C. and Wold, A. (1997). Nepotism and sexism in Peer review. *Nature, 387*: 341-343.

Wizarat, Kausar and Arya, Vijay Vrat (2007). Women in Higher Education: A workforce facing challenges and need for support and encouragement for national growth and development. *University News, vol. 45, no. 50*, December 10-16, AIU, New Delhi.

5.

GENDER INTERVENTION

The Factor Influencing Participation of Tribes in Higher Education

ANJANA PAIRA and RAJARSHI ROY

'...Education probably the most important medium of all because of its influential aspects. Education changes behaviour. People and nations are as they are because of their educative process.' [Hans, 1964]

Development, in its true sense, will be mere a utopia until and unless the population of any given nation is developed through appropriate education. Infact, education is the precondition for development. Homogeneity of development across the population is to be ensured in this context. Educational development in India is failing in this very direction, so far as the ethnicity and gender factors are concerned. Education among the Indian tribes is yet to reach the level of expectation. Among the ethnic communities, participation of the womenfolk in higher education is quite dissatisfactory due to varied socio-familial reasons. These actually hinder the ultimate goal of equality.

India has achieved multifaceted socio-economic progress since independence. However the task is not finished yet. Development of the vulnerable sections should be the necessary utopia at the present time, and for this purpose, proper and homogenous development of all sections and subsections of its population is essential. It is possible by the way of paying special attention to the 'education' which can further help to retain and also to enrich the existing cultural heritage of the country. In fact, education provides the necessary tools, skills, knowledge, values and attitudes required for the realization of the four cordinal values applicable for all humans, like survival, security, prosperity and progress, and thereby ensure sustainable development. The basic learning-needs and the way they are to be met will not be the same for all peoples and for all ages. They vary with time and space. Apart from this, education has always been considered as an instrument of and for social change [Gore, 1971].

In recent days, societies consider education as a sound economic investment because of which all the developing and developed societies are paying greater attention to education. Education has a fundamental role to play in personal and social development. It is one of the principal means available to foster a deeper and more harmonious form of human development and thereby to reduce poverty, exclusion, ignorance and oppression [Roy et. al., 2004]. Education emancipates social atoms from hangover of old time unreasonable social taboos, superstition and prejudices.

Development of a nation depends on the development of all sections of the society and development of a section, in its turn, depends on the progress of education among its members. According to the latest census report approximately one-fourth of the countrymen in India are disadvantaged, having an estimated population of around 190,000,000. It is difficult to get the cooperation of these populations in our cultural, social, political and economic programmes so long as we fail to carry the 'Education' within their reach. These disadvantaged sections include the people belonging to Scheduled Caste, Scheduled Tribes and some other backward classes. Among them the situation of the Scheduled Tribes is comparatively most distressing. Tribes suffers most from social disadvantage, oppression and economic deprivation, which co-existed with their educational backwardness [Elwin, 1960, Ambasht, 1970, Prashad, 1988 and Roy, 2002]. In fact, the higher rate of illiteracy among the tribes is the root-cause of their backwardness [Rathnaiah, 1977, Roy, 2005]. It is worthnoting in this context that the extent of backwardness differs between the gender-groups among the tribes, which reveals that women, as in other communities, are the most backward among the tribal communities, compared to their male counterparts.

Education among the Tribes vis-a-vis Constitutional Assurance

Six decades have already been passed since the constitution was drawn. The progress achieved so far in terms of tribal-development cast serious doubt whether the constitutional objectives are attainable even in distant future. A great majority of the tribal population in India is still shrouded in the darkness of illiteracy, except those in the Northeastern region. This is a brief perusal of the literacy supports to the above observation.

The Problem of Tribal Education

A brief perusal of the recommendations made by various committees, commissions and study teams claims another thought towards tribal education [*GoI, 1959, 1960, 1961, 1971, 1982, 1986,1989 & 1991*]. Irrespective of sufficient budget allotment, the expansion of education

***Table 5.1*: Literacy rates among General, Scheduled Caste and Scheduled Tribe Men, Women and Total Population in India.**

Year	General			Scheduled Caste			Scheduled Tribe		
	Total	Male	Female	Total	Male	Female	Total	Male	Female
1961	23.95	34.37	12.90	10.27	16.95	3.28	7.99	13.04	2.89
1971	29.48	39.52	18.70	14.67	22.36	6.44	10.89	17.09	4.58
1981	36.23	46.89	24.82	21.38	31.12	10.93	16.35	24.52	8.09
1991	52.21	64.13	39.29	30.06	40.24	19.03	23.63	32.50	14.50
2001 *(Estimated)*	65.38	75.85	54.16	38.34	49.63	27.04	32.40	40.00	24.80

Source: Primary Census Abstract for General Population, Scheduled Caste and Scheduled Tribes-1961-2001.

among the tribes did not reach up to the level of expectation. It is not due to the preconceived notion of the non-tribes regarding the lower level of cognitive ability of the tribes; rather it is the present approach of education, which is bringing 'a cultural shock' and thereby makes the process of educating tribals a tough task. Two consequences are commonly visible; where, either they are remaining illiterate and are alienated from education or among them, those who are educated even ignoring the post-traumatic stress, are alienated from their traditional community-life [*Roy*, 2005]. In this way, education itself is becoming a problem to them, which is breaking their family and community structure. Inferiority complex of the educated tribes, as observed by different empirical studies [*Ambasht, 1970 and Roy, 2005*], is a common phenomenon, caused by the cultural hegemony of the non-tribes. To get-rid of this problem they find an easier alternative to get them assimilated into a greater society or the majority community, which can be termed as a process of 'detribalization' [*Roy, 2005*].

The Feminine Issues of Tribal Education

The history of women's education in India is unwritten and less emphasized up till the end of the last century. Whatever scattered documentation is available and the general framework within which it is set, is a striking illustration of Simon de' Beauvoir's comment [1972] *"...The whole of the feminine history has been man-made"...*

The degree to which females are educationally, and as a consequence, economically deprived, exploited, or undervalued in various parts of the world can be illustrated by varied random examples. India in general and the eastern India in specific, is not an exception in this direction. In India,

Japan and other Asian countries, the average income of the women folk is varying from half to a quarter and sometimes even less than that, compared to their male counter-folk even in this new millennium. In various states in eastern and central India, almost five to ten times as many female infants die due to malnutrition and other allied causes in each year. In some of the eastern Indian states, even today, females can inherit only a fraction of their parental property, if compared to their male siblings and in some cases can't even inherit. Opportunity of women to participate in the workforce also advocates the fact of their deprivation in this civilized nation-state. A few of the professions are considered as the 'females' job' by the existing norm of the society; obviously most of which are less-paid occupations. The existing professional pattern still favours male.

Apart from these facts, excessive reproduction contributes significantly to the social disabilities and burdens of the great majority of the women throughout the world. Many women in India are unable to practice birth control, mostly due to lack of proper health education, and even if some of them are aware about the health-hazards, they are afraid of practicing the contraceptives until and unless their spouses agree. The century-long social customs consider abortion as a prohibition among various religious groups. Unhygienic abortion leads to major share of pregnant-mothers' death in various states in India in every year.

In India women are more likely than men to be illiterate, and to have fewer chances to be literate and educated even at the elementary level. Often they lack even the basic knowledge to keep themselves and their families healthy. In India women are less likely to receive higher education and don't acquire as many skills which have a high market value. Government(s), with varied political colour, also shows reluctance to prevent the effort to reinforce sex-role stereotypes. A sharp distinction is prominent between the male and female literacy rate in almost all the states across India.

Various surveys reveal that stereotyping of skills by gender usually begins in the primary school with manual work for boys and sewing for girls, and segregated sports [Punia & Sangawan, 1993; Prasad & Bhushan, 1993; Kumari, 1995 and Tewari & Joshi, 1996]. These differences become more pronounced at the higher levels. Subject specialization becomes apparent. For example, girls make up only a fraction of the advanced science and mathematics in the secondary enrolment. These sex-wise differences cannot be ascribed to a disparity in innate ability.

These problems of gender-biased education not only plague the mainstream population, but also the ethnic population. As a result, especially the women folks among them are more deprived of education.

In the context of an emerging democratic polity and the ideal of an egalitarian social order, the framers of the Indian Constitution were acutely conscious about the hierarchical nature of Indian society and the cumulative disadvantages suffered by certain sections and the collective nature of their social affiliation. In order to eliminate these disadvantages, education was viewed as an instrument of social change, individual mobility and social justice and equality and integration and mainstreaming. The Scheduled Tribes, the oppressed among the oppressed social groups require social justice and equality. Women folk among them need even far more.

The developmental strategy in independent India depends heavily on planning. For the sake of development, plans were prepared for each five-year span. They depict the development-priorities of the federal government. Inclusion or exclusion of an issue or dimension reflects its importance, or lack of it, within the national framework [*Roy & Biswas, 2004*]. The first two plans referred to the problems of women's education and sought to link professional education and occupations. The report of the committee on the education of tribes in 1959 made extensive recommendations, which lead to a more focused thrust in the subsequent plans [*Elwin, 1960*]. However the disparities in educational attainment between the men and women continued till today. These were amply substantiated by the report on the status of women [*GoI, 1971, 1974*].

These led to a broader perspective and the sixth plan linked education to the participation of women in the developmental process.

Dated back to 1964-66 the report of the education commission for national development, under the chairmanship of D.S. Kothari, emphasized the need of empowering women through education. National Policy on Education-1986 [*GoI, 1986*] *took an even broader view in underscoring the role of education in empowering women in order to overcome inequalities and disparities. The national perspective plan for women in India: 1988-2000 also reiterates this viewpoint* [1988]. *In other words, women themselves must overcome their handicaps. Have the ground realities changed due to this perspective? The answer is well known to us; how is it possible without raising their educational attainment?*

In this context, it is essential to be aware about their educational needs and also the problems, which hinder their education. Unfortunately problems and educational needs of the tribal women are not much known to us. What is mostly practiced is just guessing and proceeding on the plans over the guesswork. These gaps of knowledge require an immediate intervention for appropriate planning for the education of the tribal women-folk.

Gender Inequalities in Education

It has already been stated that in the countries with so-called developing economics, women are more likely than men to be illiterate, and to have fewer chances for education even at the elementary level. Often they lack even the basic knowledge essential to keep themselves and their families healthy. On the contrary, in developed countries, access towards elementary education is ensured; however women are less likely to receive education at tertiary level and hardly acquire as many skills as acquired by their male counterparts, which are having a high market value. Though an attempt was initiated since the mid of last century, even then textbooks and curricula tend to reinforce sex-role stereotypes.

Among the estimated illiterates across the globe, not less than 62 per cent are women [*UNDP, 2001*]. The situation in India reveals that out of each hundred illiterates, seventy-six are women. Among the Indian tribes, the figure is as high as eighty-four as reported by latest census reports. Dearth of literacy among the tribal women in eastern province-states of India is even more than that. A glance perusal over the *Census report-special tables on scheduled tribes* [GOI, 2001] reveals the fact.

Equality: The Ultimate Goal

Education for women is 'development' in the sense that education is vital for the self-fulfillment of the individual. Equal opportunity in education for women and girls needs to be seen therefore as vital to individual self-reliance and self-realization as well as a means of political, national and economic ends of the women groups.

More the women are educated, better they will be able to serve their respective families and the country [*Bhadauria, 2005*]. Uneducated women could be potential danger to their families. Knowledge about nutrition, first-aid, hygiene, economics and family planning is needed but is meagerly provided in the formal system of education up till date. Various studies reveal a close relationship between the levels of education of the mother with that of her family size.

In politics, better-educated women are more likely to participate actively and exercise an independent judgement rather than to simply casting a vote for a male candidate. The more women participate in public life, greater will be the resource given to the care of children and their upbringing, which will ultimately contribute to national development.

The Issue of Tribal Education

At the very outset of the independence of India, tribal-societies throughout the country drew the attention of the researchers and now at the eve of new millennium it is probably the most widely delved field of research where huge amount of research has already been carried out by the researchers from various disciplines. Anthropologists, sociologists, economists, historians, linguists, biologists, demographers, philanthropists and administrators carried out researches from their respective point of view, centering round their field. Educationists are not the exception in the spectrum and good number of research studies have already been carried-out by the educationists, which has helped to evolve a special dimension of 'Tribal studies', popularly known as 'Tribal education'. The studies on tribal education can broadly be classified under specific five contexts. These are *Institutional–context, Curricular–context, Psycho-educational–context, Teacher-denomination and Socio-educational–context.*

Irrespective of these different contexts, almost all the research-studies in education encompassed the 'student' in general as the basic factor of concern and till date only two studies have been carried out which considered the 'teacher' and hardly any study considered 'women' from the tribal communities as the basic factor in Indian context. Though very few in number, however some such studies have been reported from abroad. It is mostly the African–American countries where studies are in progress centering round the 'women's education' from the ethnic communities residing therein [*Roy & Mandal, 2004*].

On the other hand, 'women's-education', which entirely hinges on the 'feminine issues', is already an established dimension of academia. Surveys of research in education Vol. I-V [Buch, 1974, 1979, 1986 and 1991and NCERT, 2000], report only nine doctoral and post-doctoral researches on 'women-education' however none of those studies considered 'tribal women' as a factor.

All these studies reported in these surveys were carried out in between the extended period of early forties till late nineties of the last century (i.e., the twentieth century) with an uneven distribution over decades and most of those were taken up in recent past. That is why the retrospection reveals and considers women-education and tribal-education as two different and too different areas of educational research.

Participation in Higher Education

In spite of having a vast higher education system in india, only around six per cent youth of the relevant age group of 17 to 24 years is receiving higher education as compared to Canada (99.8 per cent), USA (81%) and France (50%) [*Roy, Chakraborty & Mandal, 2004 and UNDP, 2003*]. At the same time the system has failed to cater to the heterogeneity of the society. So far as the higher education of women is concerned, a large difference between male and female enrolment is found. No doubt, since independence, particularly in the last decade of the last millennium, higher education achieved tremendous quantitative expansion. It was expected that the changing attitudes in favour of gender-equity would contribute in raising the number of women from tribal denomination in higher education. But it had not happened.

***Table 5.2*: Participation of Women and Tribal Women in Higher Education (2001-2002)**

Sl. No.	*State*	*Total Enrolment*	*Women Enrolment*	*Women Percentage*	*Tribal Women Enrolment in Higher Education*	*Participation rate of Tribal Women in Higher Education*
1	*2*	*3*	*4*	*5*	*6*	*7*
1.	Andhra Pradesh	704075	275276	39.1	6584	2.391
2.	Arunachal Pradesh	5832	1732	29.7	1199	20.559
3.	Assam	194245	78602	40.5	8912	11.338
4.	Bihar	479035	110178	23.0	3925	3.562
5.	Chhattisgarh	143906	52526	36.5	–	–
6.	Delhi	166039	76046	45.8	426	0.56
7.	Goa	19245	11278	58.6	5	0.044
8.	Gujarat /Daman & Diu	488129	216241	44.3	13551	29.30
9.	Hariana	239217	96882	40.5	0	0
10.	Himachal Pradesh	86319	36858	42.7	1147	3.112
11.	Jammu & Kashmir	55603	26133	47.0	0	0
12.	Jharkhand	191413	8381	30.5	–	–
13.	Karnataka	537025	214272	39.9	6408	2.99
14.	Kerala	240038	144023	60.0	836	0.58
15.	Madhya Pradesh	450745	166776	37.0	7450	4.467
16.	Maharashtra	1220167	499048	40.9	7443	1.491
17.	Manipur	35424	15705	44.3	2299	14.639
]8.	Meghalaya	27271	13063	47.9	10470	80.15
19.	Mizoram	10345	4836	46.7	3102	64.144
20.	Nagaland	11460	4431	38.7	3263	73.64
21.	Orissa	341761	118249	34.6	1873	1.584
22.	Punjab	233745	123651	52.9	5	0.004
23.	Rajasthan	341198	111230	32.6	1985	1.785
24.	Sikkim	3808	1534	40.3	252	16.428

1	*2*	*3*	*4*	*5*	*6*	*7*
25.	TamilNadu	697343	313107	44.9	703	0.2245
26.	Tripura	19215	7840	40.8	492	6.276
27.	Uttar Pradesh	1100887	422758	35.4	1275	0.302
28.	Utaranchal	108594	43437	40.0	–	–
29.	West Bengal	620372	243806	39.3	3167	1.299
30.	A & N Islands	1943	1123	57.8	37	3.295
31.	Chandigarh	30882	17140	55.5	244	1.424
32.	Daman & Diu	536	252	47.0	15	5.952
33.	Pondicherry	15278	8036	52.6	14	0.174
TOTAL		8821095	3514450	39.84	3683	0.1048

Source: UGC Annual Report 2001–2002 & Selected Educational statistics, 2000–2001, Planning Monitoring and Statistics Division, MHRD, Table-5.*[Data for some newly created states are not available]

The table 5.2 shows the access of tribal women in higher education in various states in India. It is crystal clear that in national scenario, participation of tribal females at higher education is too meager (0.1048 per cent of the total female enrolled), which is not even coming at 1 per cent. On other hand it may be said that, among thousand women enrolled in higher education, there is just one belonging to tribal denomination, even when the eve of eleventh five-years plan is taken for consideration. The situation needs a second thought over the 'tribal education' and policy adopted so far. The participation rate, as per data, is not at all homogeneous. Where some states possess comparatively high participation rate of tribal women, in some states, it tends to zero.

Further, in three specific states, all of which are situated in northeastern region of India, the tribal women have a satisfactory access towards higher education. These states are Meghalaya (80.15%), Nagaland (73.64%) and Mizoram (64.144%). It is to be noted here that in all these states tribes comprise a dominant population. Therefore, in the last two decades, those quarters which are continuously raising question over expenditure on higher education in the seven sister states (which apparently reflected by increasing number of newly established universities in these states), should realize that such investment in that region was not at all wastage.

In contrast, the situation in the so-called progressive states and such states, where tribes comprise a sizable proportion in central and south-central India, produces serious doubt over the state-initiatives for the development of the tribal women. Obviously, it is a fact that participation in higher education of certain section/community goes in consonance with the proportional size of that very section/community in the state.

It should be accepted that participation of tribal population in general, and that of the tribal women folk in particular, in higher education needs to be enhanced. To ease the task, unitary universities need to be established in the midst of natural habitation of the tribal population. As an alternative, the affiliating universities may think of developing 'campuses' is such zones.

***Table 5.3*: Faculty-Wise Enrolment of Women and Tribal Women (2001-2002)**

Sl. No.	*Faculty*	*Women Enrolment*	*Percent-age*	*Tribal Women Enrolment in Higher Education*	*Participation rate of Tribal Women*
1.	Arts	1820134	51.79	59592	3.274
2.	Science	699376	19.90	9648	1.38
3.	Commerce & Management	581993	16.56	7580	1.302
4.	Education	59394	1.69	1755	2.954
5.	Engineering & Technology	131792	3.75	–	–
6.	Medicine	123006	3.50	1928	1.567
7.	Agriculture	9137	0.26	–	–
8.	Veterinary Science	3163	0.09	–	–
9.	Law	56934	1.62	–	–
10.	Others	29521	0.84	–	–
	Total	3514450	100.00	80503	–

Source: UGC Annual Report 2001-2002 & Selected Educational statistics, 2000 – 2001, Planning Monitoring and Statistics Division, MHRD, Table-5.

The faculty-wise participation of tribal women in higher education establishes the fact that they are less represented in various subjects and rarely represented in the subjects like technical education, veterinary science and law. As such, the planners and the curriculum-developers need to think of incorporating appropriate curricular-components in such disciplines. Indigenous technology and medicine, with which tribal people are acquainted across ages, need to be tagged with formal education, obviously after exploring the scientific bases behind such knowledge, most of which is 'oral' in nature. Unfortunately such initiatives are yet rare in India. Sooner the planners of higher education in India concentrate over such issues, easier it will be to enhance the participation of tribal women in such disciplines.

REFERENCES

Ambasht, N.K. (1970). *A critical study of tribal education.* New Delhi: S. Chand and Co.

Bhadauria, M. (2005). Access of women to higher education. *University News,* 43(06), 13-15.

Buch, M.B. (1974,1979,1986 & 1991). *Surveys of research in Education – First, Second, Third & Fourth.* Baroda: MS Univ.; SERD; New Delhi: NCERT.

De Beauvoir, S. (1972). *The second sex.* Harmondsworth: Penguin.

Elwin, Verrier (1960). *Report of the committee on special multipurpose tribal blocks.* New Delhi: Ministry of Home Affairs.

Gore, M.S. Cited in, Desai, A. R. (Ed.) (1971). *Essays on modernization of under-developed societies.* Bombay: Thacker Publication.

Government of India. (1959). *Report of the study team on social welfare and welfare of the Backward Classes (Renuka Roy Committee Report).* New Delhi: Ministry of Home Affairs.

Government of India. (1960). *Report of the committee on special multipurpose Tribal blocks, (Elwin Committee Report).* New Delhi: Ministry of Home Affairs.

Government of India. (1961). *Report of the scheduled areas and scheduled tribes commission (UN Dehbar Committee Report). Vol.1.* New Delhi: Ministry of Home Affairs.

Government of India. (1971a). *Education and National Development, Report of the Education Commission (DS Kothari Committee Report)* 1964-66. New Delhi: NCERT.

Government of India. (1971b). *Report of the committee on the status of women in India (Phulrenu Gugh Committee Report)* New Delhi: Department of Social Welfare, Ministry of Education and Social Welfare.

Government of India. (1974). *Towards Equality: Report of the committee on the status of Government of India.* New Delhi: Ministry of Education and Social Welfare.

Government of India. (1982). *Report of working group on Tribal Development during sixth plan (1980-85).* New Delhi: Ministry of Home Affairs.

Government of India. (1986). *National Policy on Education.* New Delhi: Ministry of Human Resource Development.

Government of India. (1989). *Draft Report of working group on development and welfare of scheduled Tribes during eighth five-year-plan (1991-95),* New Delhi: Ministry of Welfare.

Government of India. (1991). *Report of the Working group on Tribal Development during seventh plan (1986-90).* New Delhi: CSCST.

Kumari, Kanta (1995). Political orientation of Women students, *Bharatiya Shiksha Shodh Patrika,* 14(1), 11-23.

National Commission on Women. (1988). National Perspective Plan for women, 1988-2000: A perspective from the women's movement. New Delhi.

NCERT.(2000). *Fifth Survey of Research in Education, 1983-1988.* New Delhi.

Hans, Nicholas (1964). *Comparative Education*. London: Routledge and Kegan Paul Limited.

Prashad, R. (1988). *A Study in Cultural Ecology and Tribal Dynamics*. New Delhi: D.K. Publications.

Prashad, Rambha & Bhushan, L.I. (1993). Age and Employment differences and educated womens' concern for status, *Perspectives in Psychological Research*, 17-18(1-2), 30-32.

Punia, S; Balda, S & Sangawan, S (1993). Mental Perception of Girls' status, *Prachi Journal of Psychocultural Dimentions*, 9(1), 33-38.

Rathnaiah, E.V. (1977). *Structural Constraints in Tribal Education: A Regional Study.* New Delhi: Sterling Publishers.

Roy, R (2005). Religious status of Ethnic Teachers in East and Northeast India. *JNEIES*, VIII (I), 1-7.

Roy, R (2005). Rethinking Teacher Education: Need of the Day. *University News*, 43(51), 12-16.

Roy, R. & Biswas, N. B. (2004). *Planning Inclusion in Education in Indian Social Fabric*. Cited in the post-seminar proceedings of National Seminar on Inclusion in Education: A Matter of Right to Education for all, 116-120.

Roy, R., et. al. (2004). Education, Technology and Development: An Approach. *Indian Science Cruiser*, 18(4), 36 – 44.

Roy, R. (2005). Society, Culture and Education. *Indian Science Cruiser*, 19(2), 29 –36.

Roy, Rajarshi, et. al. (2004). Technology and Education for Human Resource Development in Asia and Pacific, Cited in the *Post-conference proceedings of International Conference on New challenges in Technology Education for HRD in Asia and Pacific Region,* 114 - 125.

Tiwari, Jyoti & Joshi, J.K. (1996). Identity status of graduate female students in relation to socio-familial and educational factors, *Journal of Psychological Researches*, 40(1 &2), 44-47.

UNDP. (2001). *Human Development Report*, 2001. Oxford: OUP.

6.

BRIDGING THE GENDER GULF IN EDUCATION FOR WOMEN EMPOWERMENT IN INDIA

SHOBANA NELASCO

'If you educate a woman, you are educating a family
If you are educating all women, you are educating the whole world'

Food, water and shelter - the basic necessities are dreams alone for many in India. Higher Education is continuing to be a luxury even for the middle class. The dual-status of men and women is continuing. The literacy-gap among male and female is continuing to exist. Women's education in India plays a very important role in the overall development of the country. It not only helps in the development of half of the human resources, but in improving the quality of life at home and outside.

In 2001, Indian literacy rate for male was 75.96 per cent whereas the female literacy was just 54.28 per cent. UNESCO defines a literate as one 'who can with understanding both read and write a short simple statement on his everyday life'. Considering the definition, this rate is a poor state of affair for any country. It is a well-known fact that education is the foundation stone for the future economic and social development of any country. It is also a fact that 'If you educate a woman, you are educating a family'. In such a case, if we educate the female population, the whole country will be educated.

Considering Indian environment, constitutionally and legally women enjoy the unique status of equality with men. Women are given special reservations other than the open quota in many areas, including in the elections. Special tax deductions are permitted for women, so as to promote women employment. Priorities are given for the sprouting women's colleges and schools. We have separate women's universities and not men's. In sports, lesser standards are fixed for women. Special schemes and extra incentives are provided by the government of India for the development of women. Eighth of March is celebrated as the international women's day. The year 2001, was declared by the Indian government as the women's year. Innumerable women movements, women institutions and organizations are working hard for women empowerment and upliftment.

In spite of all the above attractions and incentives given for women, the female population ratio, the female literacy ratio, female employment ratio, female school or college enrolment ratio, etc., continue to be at a lower rate.

According to Mohan M. Mathew(2001), the Indian average female-male ratio (FMR) of 0.93 (2001 census) is the second lowest in the world (after Pakistan) lower than the FMR of sub-Saharan Africa. As per the reports of Sukumar Basu (2000), the percentage of female labour force compared to the total labour force is just 28.5 per cent in 1991. India is ranked 125th in the Gender Empowerment Index, as per the UNDP database.

Education is the basic tool to tap the 50 per cent potential of our human resource.

Oxford Dictionary defines the word education as 'training a person mentally and morally'. Starting from the Seargent plan of 1944, many efforts are taken by the government and other statutory organisations like UGC and NCERT to promote female literacy. Article 45 of the constitution emphasizes compulsory universal education up to the age of 14 years. All five year plans have emphasized education. In 1996, the Kothari Commission recommended that 6 per cent of the GDP be allocated for education. But, this has not materialized even today.

A comprehensive purpose of education is given by Dr. Adiseshiah (1972), 'The government should take steps to meet the increasing demand with adequate supply of educational services. 'It (education) must itself be a factor of social change and technological progress while continuing to transmit a cultural heritage. It must be more and more closely linked to preparation for an employment market where competition is ever more ruthless, training more diversified and specialized skills obsolete before they can be fully mastered. And it must reconcile the rapidly evolving social and economic requirements of society with the awakening aspirations of the individual. At the same time, education must continue to fulfill its age-old role: to build character; to combine and balance scientific and technological knowledge and training, and humanistic, ethical and cultural values; to help the student achieve an idea of purpose, a sense of underlying unity and permanence in the midst of extremities and accelerating change'[1]

Gender Differences: Caste-Religion Interface

It needs to be recognized as given in the report of Dr.Sukhadeo Thorat (2008), that although the enrolment ratio is generally lower for the female compared to the male, the females belonging to the lower caste and some religious groups suffer more in access to higher education than others. For instance in 2000, as against the overall average of 9.4 per cent for the female, the Gross Enrolment Ratio (GER) was 2.4 per cent for ST female followed by 4.7 per cent for Scheduled Caste (SC) females, 7.6 per cent for Other Backward Classess (OBC) females and 17.2 per cent for other females. Thus the GER for Scheduled Tribes (ST) females was seven times less compare to the higher caste female. Similarly, the GER of the SC females was lower by about four times compared with higher caste females.

In the case of religious groups, the Muslim women suffer the most. The GER of Muslim females was 6.3 per cent compared to 10.8 per cent for Hindu females, 12.7 per cent for Sikh/Buddhist females, 20 per cent for Christian and 48 per cent for Jain females.

In the case of Enrolment Ratio for Eligible (EER) the inter-caste disparities among the females are particularly significant. The EER for SC/OBC female was the lowest with about 50 per cent compared to 57 per cent for ST /other higher caste females.

Similarly, the EER was the lowest for the Muslim female compared to the females belonging to other religion. The EER was 48 per cent for Muslim females -about 54 per cent for Hindu/Buddhist females, 56 per cent for Sikh and about 69 per cent for Jain/Christian females.

Female Dropouts from Education

It is estimated that 45 per cent of girls drop out of school between classes 1 and 5. Of the literate women in India, 59 per cent have only a primary education or less. Only 41 per cent of the literate population, or 13 per cent of all Indian women, have more than a primary education. Although literacy levels are low, there has been progress in improving educational attainment in India over the last several decades. In 1971, only 22 per cent of women and 46 per cent of men were literate. By 1991, 39 per cent of women and 64 per cent of men were literate. Thus, there has been a large increase in the proportion of women who are literate in just 20 years. Despite the improvements in literacy, there continues to be a large gap between the literacy levels of men and of women. In 1991, the urban female literacy rate was more than twice that of the rural rate, 64 and 31 per cent, respectively.

Male-female Literacy Gap in various States of India

It is miserable to see that in all the states the female literacy is low when compared to male literacy. This female-male literacy gap is the lowest in Mizoram in 1991 (7.01) and in 2001 (4.56). The table shows few states like Mizoram, Megalaya and Kerala are having low literacy gap, whereas Rajasthan, Utharanjal, UttarPradesh and Jharkhand are the states having large of Male-Female literacy gap in 1991.

Table 6.1: **Male –Female literacy gap in various states of India between 1991 and 2001**

States	*1991*			*2001*		
	Male Literacy	*Female Literacy*	*Gap in Literacy*	*Male Literacy*	*Female Literacy*	*Gap in Literacy*
India	64.13	39.28	24.85	75.96	54.28	21.68
Andhra Pradesh	55.13	32.72	22.42	70.85	51.17	19.68
Arunachal Pradesh	51.45	29.69	21.76	64.07	44.34	19.83
Assam	61.89	43.03	18.84	71.93	56.03	15.90
Bihar	51.37	21.99	29.38	60.32	33.57	26.75
Chattisgarh	58.07	27.52	30.54	77.86	52.4	25.46
Goa	83.64	67.09	16.55	88.88	75.51	13.37
Gujarat	73.39	48.92	24.47	80.5	58.6	21.90
Haryana	69.1	40.47	28.62	79.26	56.31	22.94
Himachal Pradesh	75.41	52.26	23.16	86.02	68.08	17.94
Jammu & Kashmir				75.96	54.28	23.93
Jharkhand	55.8	25.52	30.28	67.94	39.38	28.57
Karnataka	67.26	44.34	22.93	76.29	57.45	18.84
Kerala	93.62	86.17	7.45	94.2	87.86	6.34
Madhya Pradesh	58.54	29.35	29.19	76.80	50.28	26.52
Maharashtra	76.56	52.32	24.24	86.27	67.51	18.75
Manipur *	71.63	47.6	24.03	77.87	59.7	18.17
Meghalaya	53.12	44.85	8.27	66.14	60.41	5.73
Mizoram	85.61	78.6	7.01	90.69	86.13	4.56
Nagaland	67.62	54.75	12.87	71.77	61.92	9.85
Orissa	63.09	34.68	28.41	75.95	50.97	24.98
Punjab	65.66	50.41	15.26	75.63	63.55	12.08
Rajasthan	54.99	20.44	34.55	76.46	44.34	32.12
Sikkim	65.7	46.76	18.94	76.73	61.46	15.27
Tamil Nadu	73.75	51.33	22.42	82.33	64.55	17.78
Tripura	70.58	49.65	20.93	81.47	65.41	15.06
Uttar Pradesh	54.82	24.37	30.46	70.23	42.98	27.25
Uttaranchal	72.79	41.63	31.17	84.01	60.26	23.75
West Bengal	67.81	46.56	21.25	77.56	60.22	17.35

Source: Census of India Report

This gender literacy gap is a major stumbling block for the development of any country. It means that one gender is favoured for education. Another major issue of this analysis is that between 1991 and 2001 the literacy rate of male and female gender is improving but the disparity continues. The differences in literacy rates among the states are also extreme. Kerala has the highest female literacy rate both in 1990-91 and 2000-01.The state with the second highest female literacy is Mizoram. And Goa is standing third in the row. On the other hand, the order of women literacy is reshuffled in the year 2000-2001. Rajastan is ranked first, Bihar, the second, U.P., Jharkhand are the successors in 1990-91. Wheras in 2000-2001, the order is Bihar, Jharkhand, U.P. and Rajastan. In other words, while Rajastan was topping the list of female literacy in 1990-91, in 2000-01 Bihar is pushed back to top the list.

Looking at the gender gulf, in 1990-91 the Rajastan, Uttaranjal, U.P. and Jharkhand are having the wider gender literacy gap; in 2000-01 the order is changed as Rajastan, Jharkhand U.P. and Bihar. In both periods the gender literacy gap is very high in Rajastan. Following is a photograph taken in Jaipur, where children are seated under the hot sun without any infrastructure at the mercy of one teacher. This picturises the real status of education in Rajastan, where the gender literacy gap continues to be the highest.

A School in Jaipur, Rajasthan

Photograph courtesy: Cherly (2004)

As with India as a whole, many states have large rural-urban differences in female literacy. In 6 of the 24 states, 25 per cent or less of the women in rural areas is literate. In Rajasthan, less than 12 per cent of rural women are literate. In 1992-93, 75 per cent of boys and 61 per cent of girls aged 6 to 10 years were attending school. There are large differences in school attendance by state. In six states, over 85 per cent of girls aged

6 to 14 were attending school. Not surprisingly, these states also had female literacy rates that were above the national average. In all states except Bihar, Rajasthan, and Uttar Pradesh, more than half of the girls aged 6 to 14 were attending school.

Area wise Male-female Literacy Gap

The following table shows the percentage of literacy among men and women among various types of areas.

***Table 6.2*: Area wise male-female literacy gap in 1991**

Place / Status	*Men*	*Women*
Cities	81.09%	64.05%
Villages	57.87%	30.62%
Scheduled	49.91%	23.76%
Tribal	40.67%	18.19%

Source: Women's links, Cyril & co, Human Rights Education, Vaigarai Publishing

In villages, the literacy gender gap is very high, whereas in cities it is not so. In tribal areas the literacy gap is extremely wide among men and woman.

***Table 6.3*: Literacy Gap between 1950-51–2000-'01**

Year	*Male literacy*	*Female Literacy*	*Total Literacy*
1950-51	27.16	8.86	18.33
1960-61	40.40	15.35	28.3
1970-71	45.96	21.97	34.45
1980-81	56.38	29.76	43.57
1990-91	64.1	39.3	52.2
2000-01	75.85	54.16	65.38

Source:www.indiabudget.nic.in

Figure 6.1. ***Male-Female Literacy Gap in India from 1950-51 to 2000-01***

The bar diagram and the table shows clearly that Indian literacy rate is going on increasing. But the female literacy rate is the lowest in all the periods. It is also below the total literacy rate.

Relationship between Literacy and Other Factors Deciding Women Empowerment

An analysis is done to relate the female literacy with few other indicators of women empowerment. Female literacy, female sex ratio, female work participation and female enrolment at university level are considered as the indices of women's positive growth position. The percentage of women suffering from anaemia, female drop outs and crimes against women are the indicators of women oppression. The variables in the 5th table were correlated with the literacy rate to find out the degree in which literacy affect these factors and to prove that literacy could only be the targeted solution for women empowerment. The results are as follows:

Table 6.4: Correlation between literacy and other factors deciding women empowerment

Relationship bet. Literacy and factors	*Correlation*
Literacy and Female sex ratio	0.401
Literacy and Female work participation	0.113
Literacy and Female enrolment at university	0.743**
Literacy and Percentage of women with anaemia	– 0.565**
Literacy and Female dropout rate	– 0.537**
Literacy and Crime rate against women	0.093

Source: computed values based on table is given as an appendix
* Significant at 5 per cent level & ** Significant at one per cent level

Female sex ratio in the population is correlated with female literacy at a co-efficient of 0.401. The literacy and female work participation rate are correlated at a co-efficient of 0.113. The literacy and female enrolment at university level are correlated positively with a co-efficient of 0.743** And hence female literacy surely improves the female work participation, female sex ratio and female enrolment at university level. In other words the states having more literacy are having better female work participation, female sex ratio and female enrolment at university level.

And it is also proved that literacy and percentage of women with anaemia are correlated at a rate of - 0.565 with 1 per cent level of significance and literacy and Female dropout rate are correlated a rate of - 0.537 and is significant at 1 per cent level. Therefore female literacy reduces percentage of women with anaemia and female dropouts though not much of crime rates.

It is paradoxical to see that, the crime rate against women does not have any relation with literacy. The correlation between literacy and crime rate against women is nearing zero that is 0.093. So whether *the women are educated or not, they are exploited by the society*. Educated women suffer in a different way and uneducated suffer in a different way. The reason could also be that the women become more aware of their rights and hence their sufferings are brought to any platform for discussion.

The literate states have proved themselves with more female population ratio, more female work participation, and more enrolment for higher education, good health records and less female drop outs. And hence the literacy could only be the solution for women empowerment.

Factors Responsible for the Slow Growth of Woman and Woman Literacy

In the process of development, the contribution of women towards the growth of the country is ever increasing. But their social status, educational status, economic status and political status continue to remain below their counterparts. The lower status of women in the society does not give them confidence to come out of their shells. Hence it is necessary to identify the factors responsible for this serious issue.

Our cultural history & Political history have proved that women were considered as secondary human beings. It is considered that the birth of a son is bliss incarnate, while that of a daughter is the root of family misery. Only the sons are the heirs of their parents and they are eligible to do the final rites of their parents.[2] India is ranked 128th (0.424) in the world Gender Development Index (GDI) in 1995 and is ranked 95th (0.228) in the World-Gender Empowerment measure (GEM) in 1995[3] .

Social Constraints

The serious social evils like sati, ill treatment of widows & divorcees, ban on widow remarriage, dowry system, polygamy, child marriage, denial of property rights, denial of women education, temple prostitution, custom of *purdah*, abortion of female feotus, female infanticide, wife battering, bride burning, rape, abduction and sexual harassment are the special unpleasant features of Indian women's social environment. These serious evils do not permit them to come out for education

Women with higher qualification and higher earnings are generally secluded from their society. The social practice of marrying highly qualified and highly earning bridegroom discourages the parents to permit their girl children foe education. The overall Indian social structure, which constitutes religion, caste, custom, tradition, culture, family structure and other social institutions remind every one that woman, is inferior.

The naturality of childbirth and child rearing makes women's life hectic. The psychological trauma and the physical pains undergone during the menstruation, menopause and childbirth, etc. are constraints for the women to flourish. The diseases associated in all these process also add to the trauma. Pregnant Indian women have the world's highest levels of anemia.[4] Child psychology books say that girls mental I.Q level is high when compared to boys up to the age of 10 to 12. After 10 to 12 the boys I.Q exceeds girls IQ. This may be due to the natural constraints.

Unpleasant School Atmosphere

The pattern of education is promoting rote learning, where there is less scope for overall personality development. The curriculum does not permit us to use the full potentials of the students. Children, especially the rural children, lack encouragement and support from the school. Their creativity is not encouraged. Corporal punishment given by the teachers is one of the major reasons for dropouts and child labour is the result of this practice. Inefficient teachers do not promote the creativity and self-confidence of the students by their attitude and words. If education is made more attractive, dropouts will be reduced considerably. Many of the rural schools could not provide water, toilet and such facilities for the girls. Due to these basic reasons, there are heavy dropouts among girls. There is less awareness about the schemes, scholarships, financial incentives and programmes available for women.

Ragging and Eve Teasing are the major problems faced by female children, while going for education.

The role conflict of the women also makes them psychologically inferior. Women have to play a dual role if they opt for career life. Priority cannot be given for any of these roles. And hence the psychological and emotional pressures lead to lots of trauma.

The most conspicuous failure of the Indian educational system is that it has failed to implement the directive of Article 45 of the Constitution which had recommended that the state should provide free and compulsory education for all children until they complete the age of 14 years by 1960. Political priorities and defence priorities overpower the educational priorities in financial resource allocation. If this is made a reality, there is no question of female literacy.

India and China put together form 2/5 or 40 per cent of the world population. In 1950, India's literacy level in the age group of 16-40 was 16 per cent while of China was 20 per cent where as India's literacy rate stood at 36 per cent in 1981 and that of China was 66 per cent in the same year.

Suggestions

Several measures are taken to bring parity between both sexes, to bridge the gender gulf in education. Government has to take some serious steps to solve this problem.

- Trainings, workshops and courses may be organised, so as to raise the self esteem and self development of women, irrespective of their literacy. Career women also should be trained to perform their dual roles.
- Personality Development of Women: The various dimensions of women personality have to be developed so that their confidence is raised to face any situation.
- Uniqueness of every gender has to be taught to women so as to make them accept the realities. The awareness of their uniqueness will be their weapon to defend themselves from various social evils.
- Women should have a separate curriculum for their development. They should not try to imitate men. Both formal and informal education should be tried.
- More focus should be given on women role models. The elite among the woman should come forward to help the fellow women to come out of their professional jealousy and unhealthy competitions.
- To reduce the female drop-outs, following efforts may be taken.
    - Girls' schools and girls' colleges should be promoted.
    - In all schools & colleges, especially which are in rural area, toilet with proper facilities for ladies should be provided.
    - In lieu of the household responsibilities flexible timings may be fixed.
    - For the security of girl students, ladies special buses should ply from all villages to various schools according to the school timings.
- The educational pattern followed should promote the women students originality. Overall personality development should be the target of education. Individual science projects and exhibitions should be made a part of curriculum.
- All school and college teachers should be trained to be effective guides, counsellors and communicators.

- Services like crèches, door delivery of food, mobile health care, etc should be promoted.
- Gender sensitivity camps should be organized in backward and remote areas to develop the right attitude towards women.
- Significance of mother's presence for the infant's healthy growth be realized by the government and it can permit 1 year or 2 year unearned leaves for the women employees.
- Extension education, and distance education should be promoted for women in a user friendly manner with a high scope for their overall development.
- Compulsory education has to be accompanied by legislative and social action.
- The overall economic development of the country will help the women to prosper. Oostendorp (2004) investigated the impact of trade liberalisation on the gender wage gap in 158 countries, both developed and developing. Regression analysis shows a negative relationship between trade integration (i.e. ratio of trade to G.D.P) and occupational wage gaps. And hence the labour market gender discrimination falls with increasing trade. And therefore increase in trade will reduce gender gap.
- Higher education has become a global market commodity. Globalization or internationalization of education will bring about a bright future for women.

If the current situation continues, India will have to face a gloomy future. Till we reach the day of compulsory primary education, we cannot imagine a bright future for Indian women. To quote Jawaharlal Nehru, "The level of democracy in a country, thus can be measured by the standard of education of its residents". To conclude, a good social environment has to be enabled by the government to promote women to participate in various fields. More efforts should be made to bring about good self-development among women right from their childhood. If the lord of creation in any family, the mother, is empowered, the whole family is empowered and if all women are empowered, we will surely have a bright future for the whole world.

REFERENCES

'Women Education: Continuing Neglect', *Economic and Political Weekly*, July, 20, 2002.

Archana Kumari Sahu (2000), 'Women Empowerment: Challenges & Prospects' *Competition Refresher*, May, 2000

Dr. Rengacharyulu, S.V., (ed), *Rural Development Statistics 1999*, National Institute of Rural Development, Hyderabad, 2000.

Economic Survey 1999-2000, Economic Division, Ministry of Finance, Governement of India.

Gurushri Swamy (2004), 'International Trade and Women', *Economic and Political Weekly*, Nov 6, 2004.

Michaela Martin, Antony Stella, 'External Quality Assurance in Higher Education: Making Choices', International Institute for Educational Planning'

Mohan Mathew (2001), 'Women & Gender Empowerment India: Facts and Figures' Sterling, New Delhi, pp.75-90.

Mohan. M.Mathews (2001), *India; Facts and Figures*, Sterling New Delhi, pp. 75-90.

Preeti Rastogi (2004), 'Significance of gender related development indicators', *Indian Journal of Gender Studies*, Volume II, No-3, Sep-Dec 2004

Prof. R. Jeyegopal (1984), Students in Extension Activities, Indian University Association for Continuing Education, New Dellhi.

S.R.P. Bakshi and Kiran Bala. *Social Status and Role of Women*, Deep & Deep Publications.

Select Socio-Economic Indicators for all states and India, Statistical Hand Book (2004), Department of Economics and Statistics, Government of Tamil Nadu.

Shalu Nigam, 'Women's Empowerment - A myth or a reality', *Legal News & Views*, May, 2001.

Sukhadeo Thorat, (2006), 'Higher Education in India, Emerging Issues Related to Access, Inclusiveness and Quality', Chairman, University Grant Commission, New Delhi, Nehru Memorial Lecture, University of Mumbai, Mumbai, November, 24.

Sukumar Basu, Role of Women in Economic Development. p. 102, Edited by Anita Banerji,

Sunita Kishore, Kamala Gupta, (2004), 'Women's Empowerment in India and its States', *Economic and Political Weekly*, February 14.

Veena Poonacha, 'Higher Education of Women in the Era of Globalisation & Privatisation', *Samyukta*, vol. 4, No. 1.

END NOTES

1. Adiseshiah, *It is time to begin,* Paris, UNESCO, 1972., p. 91-92.
2. S.R.P.Bakshi & Kiran Bala – Social status and role of Women (Deep & Deep Publications).
3. Sukumar Basu, 'Role of Women in Economic Development', p. 102, edited by Anita Banerji, Rajkumar Sen in 'Women and Gender Empowerment, Facts and Figures.
4. India Facts & Figures page 19

APPENDIX

Inter-State Position of Women

Name of State	*Female literacy*	*Female sex ratio*	*Female work Participation*	*Female enrolment at university*	*Percentage of women with anaemia*	*Female dropout rate*	*Crime rate against women*
Andra Pradesh	51.17	978	40.2	31.8	49.8	41.23	143
Arunachal Pradesh	44.24	901	45.0	22.9	62.7	50.81	123
Assam	56.03	932	24.9	33.5	69.7	42.20	130
Bihar	33.57	921	23.5	18.9	63.4	58.64	54
Chattisgarh	52.40	990	48.0				
Chandigarh				51.5		– 66.17	
Delhi		821		45.3	40.5	6.03	
Goa	75.51	960	24.8		36.4	11.51	61
Gujarat	58.60	921	30.9	40.1	46.3	28.10	139
Haryana	56.31	861	32.1	39.3	47.0	12.78	152
Jammu & Kashmir	41.82	900	25.7	40.6	58.7	47.39	184
Karnataka	57.45	964	36.6	34.6	42.4	27.19	74
Kerala	87.86	1058	17.2	53.6	22.7	-5	153
Madhya Pradesh	50.28	920		30.5	54.3	22.97	206
Maharashtra	67.51	922	40.1	37.0	48.7	21.72	151
Manipur	59.70	978	46.2	43.4	28.9	42.90	39
Meghalaya	60.41	975	43.7	40.1	63.3	57.22	33
Sikkim	61.46	875	45.5	36.3	61.1	56.35	75
Mizoram	86.13	938	56.8	40.1	48	51.27	171
Nagaland	61.92	909	44.8	40.1	38.4	46.68	18
Orissa	50.92	972	28.6	32.7	63.0	44.38	121
Punjab	63.55	874	21.2	51.5	41.1	20.15	53
Rajasthan	44.34	922	41.0	33.0	48.5	62.68	231
Tamil Nadu	64.55	986	35.1	40.1	56.5	39.19	83
West Bengal	60.22	934	21.0	36.3	62.7	58.48	8.9
Uttar Pradesh	42.98	898	20.0	27.0		62.16	103
Uttaranchal	60.26		31.9				

Source: 1. Preeti Rastogi, 'Significance of gender related development indicators', Indian Journal of gender studies, Volume II, No-3, Sep-Dec 2004

2. Mariama A. Varghese – Women's Education, Educational Policies in India edited by K.Sudha Rao, Published by National Institute of Educational Planning and Administration, New Delhi.

7.

WOMEN IN ASSAM
Conflict, Human Development and Decentralization

SUJATA DUTTA HAZARIKA

North East India, especially Assam with its traditional geopolitical characteristic has somehow found itself at a conjunction of tribal and caste Hindu social formation. It has thus often taken pride in its self-proclaimed egalitarian social setup vis-à-vis the ruthless segmentation of caste and gender in other parts of India. While the myth of a casteless society here today has been demystified by instances of success and failures in the various attempts of proselytization of tribal, who in this specific case were the 'constructed untouchables', Gender and its different ramifications however went totally unnoticed and sometimes even glorified as the only instance in Indian society where women enjoyed equal status . It is a fact that Assam has traditionally been devoid of practices such as dowry, child marriage, bride burning, female infanticide, that are rampant in most other parts of India. Moreover mobility of women in Assam is also far more due to factors like the absence of *purdah, and* occupational caste-groups which also resulted in a higher degree of caste flexibility. A long standing influence of the tribal work pattern where the village economy at times revolves primarily around women's labour and female entrepreneurship has also led to greater physical freedom. This argument however can be contested on grounds of tribal and caste differences. All these have to a large extent augmented opinions of a higher social status for women, which should have then logically ensured higher and adequate degree of political participation and representation for women here. A historical and contemporary analysis of different political mobilization of Assam will show inadequate 'representation' for women at every instance, which is not to say that women did not endeavour to create spaces for their own empowerment. These organized movements created political spaces with a sexist bias , using women to mobilize only to contribute in numbers, but ignored and marginalized them when they voiced their own agenda. Thus in Assam too ,the limitations in the very language of defining women and *representing* the category adequately in both the spheres of formal politics and the informal domain of struggles and movement makes their *representation* within a political process that seeks to legitimize women as political subjects vastly over-ambitious. Participation in the politics will thus have to be traced within individual experiences of negotiating the private and the public issues in day to day life and within voices, sometimes single, sometimes collective, which have gone unnoticed and unarticulated within the male dominated public sphere but nevertheless present . Hence Feminist discourse in Assam deserves the same attention and weightage and has to be seen as part of a wider and the more universal feminist discourse of Indian idealism. Although stealthily and sometimes very emphatically gender relations here do deviate from the more traditional theoretical framework within which Indian women as a whole can identify, especially due to its proximity to tribal ethos and a vaishnavite tradition, but nevertheless absence of theoretical identifiable traits such as absence of caste disabilities should not be taken as absence of a need to identify other more significant variables such as the patriarchal and gender-bias exhibited by the *Vaishnavite* cults or Sattras in the region, local customary laws or the lack of political participation of women in traditional bodies of local governance.

'Participation of Women in Local Self Governance in Assam' a Project funded by Action Aid India, was carried out on three districts of Assam, viz., Sonitpur, Cachar and Nalbari. The districts were selected on the basis of dynamics ranging from economic backwardness to insurgency, from cross-cultural and linguistic homogeneity to patriarchal social relations. The Project, which evaluated the efficacy and functioning of the Panchayat Raj Institutions in Assam, especially after the 73rd and 74th Amendment of the Indian Constitution, had clearly identified Panchayat Raj Institution in India as the most viable and effective means of grassroots participation in Governance. This chapter uses the same argument in the context of Assam, a state in North East India, marred by insurgency and conflict within its multiethnic myriad, in order to ensure sustainable peace and human development in the region. This chapter focuses on the linkages among governance, peace building and decentralization as the central theme, with a particular interest in women's capacities in democratic institutions. It proposes Peace Through Development (PTD) as a viable approach to be taken by the democratic institutions to make these linkages, and assesses the capacity and willingness of governance and institutions to address conflict prevention and peace building in Assam through improved governance that is gender sensitive, after identifying the specific governance areas that could contribute to peace building based on stated needs and priorities of civil society representatives. The purpose of this chapter is to undertake a scooping exercise to provide recommendations on strategic options for strengthening local democratic governance and peace building in the conflict-affected regions in Assam through effective implementation of the 73rd amendment of Indian constitution.

Almost all the states of Northeast India have, at some time or the other, experienced political mobilization and organized violence against migrants, anti-outsider movements leading to victimization and expulsion of the communities of migrant origin and at times even ethnic cleansing of the non-indigenous groups. This 'identity politics', which became the defining theme of postcolonial Northeast Indian political agenda, laid an exclusive claim to a land that had emerged as a shared homeland since the earliest times. The anti-outsider politics came sharply into focus by the 'Son of the soil' agitation in Assam (the famous Assam Movement, 1979-'85), which became a point of reference for many of the subsequent nativist movements in the rest of the Northeastern region. These tensions, overtly organized against illegal immigrants, also spilled over to some Indian citizens because the categories were never clearly defined and perhaps intentionally left hazy, and these soon came to include tribals and descendants of migrants in the various states of Northeast India. What began as ethnic strife between 'indigenous' and 'foreign' groups turned into ethnic clashes between populations that had essentially become local to the area? There are three key grievances that led to the push for secession or movements for political autonomy in North East. First, a refusal to recognize the distinctive ethnic and cultural traditions of the region; second, the exploitation of its resources without due compensation or development; third, dismantling the local land rights. As a consequence, all seven states in Northeast experienced some type of militant movements; and unrest and repression spread wider.

A substantial proportion of the current proliferation of armed groups representing various tribal and ethnic identities in the Northeast is the result of the demonstration effect of the 'success' of other such groups in the past. Such 'success' is not necessarily measured in terms of any political gains but, increasingly, in terms of the financial gains of widespread criminal operations that are undertaken by all militant groups in the Northeast (as in other theatres of conflict in India). The collusive character of many of the terrorist movements in the region, in terms of their linkages with overground organizations, legitimate businesses, the State bureaucracy and the political leadership, enormously reduces the actual risks of militant activity and also provides secondary incentives for the creation and operation of armed gangs.

According to Dr Ajay Sahni from the Institute for Conflict Management, the Internal conflicts in India's Northeast are overwhelmingly conceptualized within the framework of unique ethnic identities that are threatened by and in confrontation with the nationalist state, which is often seen as a representative of an inchoate cultural 'mainstream'. While some of the conflicts in the region certainly fit into this general framework of interpretation, few, if any, are completely explained by it; others, moreover, are entirely unrelated to this reductionist scheme of 'freedom struggles' by ethnic minorities against the 'homogenizing state'. Indeed, even where militant groups direct their rhetoric and their violence against the symbols of the state, the underlying motives and ideologies are more correctly interpreted in terms of conflicting tribal identities and histories of internecine warfare based entirely on tribal, sub-tribal, or tribal-outsider rivalries and corresponding competition over limited resources, especially land. It is, consequently, appropriate to analyze and assess conflicts in the Northeast in terms of three basic 'fault lines': Tribal groups verses the state, Tribal verses tribal (Internecine), Tribal verses non-tribal.

Human Development

'The basic purpose of development is to enlarge people's choices. In principle, these choices can be infinite and can change over time. People often value achievements that do not show up at all, or not immediately, in income or growth figures: greater access to knowledge, better nutrition and health services, more secure livelihoods, security against crime and physical violence, satisfying leisure hours, political and cultural freedoms and sense of participation in community activities. The objective of development is to create an enabling environment for people to enjoy long, healthy and creative lives.'

Mahbub ul Haq, Founder of the Human Development Report

In Assam the key obstacles to Human Development, poverty eradication and achieving the Millennium Development Goals (MDGs) (Details of the Millennium Development Goals are available at http://www.undp.org/mdg/.).is the general ambience of dissent among the contending ethnicities and the resulting voices of autonomy and secession through insurgency, counter insurgency and ethnic conflict. The most basic capabilities for human development in order for choices to be available and opportunities in life to be accessible is a peaceful environment where one can lead long and healthy lives, choose to be knowledgeable, have access to the resources needed for a decent standard of living and be able to participate in the life of the community.

According to India's National Human Development Report 2001 (NHDR), which is the latest in a series of publications that are linked to, but independent of, the annual, global Human Development Report issued by the UNDP (United Nations Development Program) (While India's NHDR derives its conceptual moorings and methodology from the UNDP's Human Development Reports, it incorporates ideas from elsewhere, including the Reports on Human Development in South Asia published by the Human Development Centre, Islamabad.) The relative rankings of the States on the Human Poverty Index stayed unchanged over the 1980s and 1990s, with HPI in Bihar, Arunachal Pradesh, Assam and Uttar Pradesh ranging between 55-60 per cent while the better-off States like Kerala, Punjab and Himachal Pradesh have a HPI of 32-35 per cent. Most of conflict-affected districts in Assam had poverty rates double and GDP growth less than the national average according to the same report.

Although NHDR authors note that there is no direct relationship between the economic attainments of a society, and the quality of life of an individual and an even less direct connection between economic development and social development; or the distribution of benefits between various regions of the country and different social groups but in case of Assam the overall presence of violent activity presupposes a fallen standard of HDI even if we choose to emphasize its paradigm shift that material attainments or means of development needs to be substituted by a concern 'to outcomes that are either desirable in themselves or desirable because of their role in supporting better opportunities for people'.

The paper emphasizes the NHDR report and reiterates governance approach to human development, adopting the UNDP's concept of governance. Further, it views governance as a continuous interplay between (a) institutions, (b) the delivery mechanism and (c) the supportive and subordinate framework of rules, procedures and legislation. This conception of governance, sanitized of political content, instead of offering a framework for governance in any holistic sense, merely suggests small structural and procedural changes at the national level. It proposes an alternative model of governance in which the institutions of decentralized governance - Panchayats, (statutory, democratically-elected, self-governing local authorities in rural areas) and civil society actors - are seen to have a central role. However, no correlation is made between decentralization and its impact on human development.

Democratic institutions vis-à-vis Traditional Governance

Northeast India consists of seven states of Indian Union, viz. Assam, Arunachal Pradesh, Manipur, Meghalaya, Mizoram, Nagaland and Tripura covering 8 Per cent of the total geographical area and 3.78 per cent of the total population of the country. A large part of the Northeast India is governed by the fifth and sixth schedules of the Constitution of India. The *Panchayats* (Extension to the schedule areas) Act, 1996 extends the 73rd Amendment: to the fifth schedule areas. Three states, viz. Mizoram, Nagaland and Meghalaya, which are governed by the sixth schedule, are exempted from the purview of the 73rd Amendment. The sixth schedule envisages establishment of Autonomous district councils. These councils have been given legislative, administrative and judicial powers under the sixth schedule. No law of the centre or the state in respect of the legislative powers conferred on the Autonomous District Councils could be extended to those areas without their prior approval. The councils are responsible for looking after the social, economic and minor criminal and civil matters of the tribal people. More specifically these councils are empowered to make laws with respect to: a) Land; b) Forest; c) Water source; d) Shifting cultivation; e) Establishment of village and town and its administration; f) Appointment of, or succession to chiefs or headmen; g) Inheritance of property; h) Marriage and divorce and matters relating to any other social customs. The district councils are also empowered to constitute Village councils and also Village courts. While the Autonomous District Councils have the advantage of legislative powers, the PRIs are exempted from it, moreover the Autonomous District Councils do not make provision for reservation for women, backward classes. Thus in Northeast India we find two simultaneous democratic institutions at work, a modern democratic system vis-à-vis a traditional system among the hill tribes. The traditional system has never recognized the rights of women as primary decision and makers in matters of community concerns like inter-ethnic conflicts, crisis management, social sanctions. In Assam, out of twenty-three districts only two fall under 6th scheduled areas. These are North Cachar Hills and Karbi Anglong; the other twenty-one districts fall under the modern democratic institution of Panchayati Raj.

The call for autonomy and the formation of autonomous councils was shaped by the Indian example of granting territorial autonomy to resurgent minority peoples in Northeast India. However autonomy does not seem to be feasible solution to ethnic conflict when the claimed territory is shared with other ethnic groups and immigration leads to numerical minoritization and the areas dominated are not contiguous as in the case with Bodo. The mismatch between demographic reality and the vision of territorial autonomy is the main reason for the relative intractability of the Bodo conflict. The territorially claimed area of Bodo Autonomous Council (BAC) and Bodo Territorial Coucil (BTC) has less than 50 per cent of tribal Population. And is also inhabited by other tribals such as the Rabhas, the Mechas, Miri's, Hojais, Deoris, Saraniyas, and Non-Tribals such as Koch Rajbanshis, Scheduled castes and Caste Hindus, and Muslims (Original and immigrants), and Santhals, Mundas, Nepalis, Biharis, Marwaris, forming a substantial portion of the populations. Census of India 1991 showed that this area had an approx tribal population of 34.41 per cent which had been further reduced to below 30.5 per cent in 2001. It is considered to have about 2494 villages in which 300 villages are pure tribal villages (100 per cent tribal), 821 tribal dominated villages (more than 50 per cent Tribal Population) leaving 1313 villages where tribal population is less than 50 per cent (Nunthara, 2006). Barpujari (1998) wrote *'It is in vain to expect that the grant in autonomy will keep the unity and integrity of the state. What is the guarantee that the Karbis and the Bodos (Even accorded full autonomy) will not clamour for full fledged statehood? How can the Union and state government resist legitimate and forceful claims of Koch Rajbanshis and Tai ahoms........ Will the tea tribes and Muslim immigrants remain silent spectators for long'*?. Keeping the different ramifications of autonomous councils it has been suggested that probably the political aspirations of tribal homogenous groups could be appropriated by amendments to 6th schedule and 73rd amendment provisions for devolution of power at the local level and bringing the entire issue of local governance within the ambit of Panchayati Raj Institution.

Panchayati Raj and Assam

This portion begins by engaging with the details of the Panchayat system and its operations in order to facilitate a perspective of good governance that can successfully address issues of human development and sustainable peace in Assam. Schedule XI of the Indian Constitution defines the functional items for which states may devolve responsibility to Panchayats. While states vary in the extent to which they devolve policy powers to gram Panchayat, most gram panchayats have responsibilities of civic administration in the village together with limited independent taxation powers. On an average roughly 10 per cent of a GP's total revenue comes from own revenues with the remainder consisting of transfers from higher levels of government. While the ambit of Gram-Panchayats policy influence varies across Indian states, Gram Panchayats perform two distinct policy tasks. The first is beneficiary selection for central and state welfare schemes. These are low spillover public goods because the benefits are likely to accrue to individual households. These include a variety of transfer programmes such as schemes that provide beneficiary households with funds to acquire housing, water supply and private electricity. Eligibility for these schemes is usually limited to households below the official poverty line, with a minimum fraction of beneficiaries between scheduled casts and tribes. Thus an important part of panchayat's job is also to identify households which are 'below poverty line' or BPL households. Possession of a BPL-card makes the household eligible for an array of government schemes ranging from subsidized food through the public distribution system to free hospitalization. The Gram Panchayat in collaboration with state government officials is supposed to identify via a census household with income below the poverty line and prepare the list of BPL households. The lis and subsequent selection of beneficiary households under different schemes (from among BPL households) are supposed to be ratified in gram sabha meetings Since all BPL households are eligible for a BPL card provided by the government, the procedure makes the allocation of BPL cards highly political where the success or failure in targeting needy household is a key issue.

The second area of gram Panchayats' policy activism is the construction and maintenance of village public goods such as streetlight, roads and drains. These are 'high spillover public goods' since the benefits accrue more broadly across members of the village. The Gram panchayat decides the distribution of these public goods and the quality of provision both within the village and across villages within a gram panchayat.

Two Important institutional features of the gram panchayat which are specific to decentralization in India are political reservation and village meetings (gram sabhas). The 73rd and 74th constitutional amendment mandated political reservation in favour of scheduled caste and tribes and women, and required that the extent of such reservation in a state reflect the scheduled caste and tribes population share in the state. It also required that no gram panchayat reserves for the same group for two consecutive elections. The most viable methodology for conflict resolution embedded in the panchayat system is that the panchayat legislation requires that the *Pradhan* (elected panchayat leader) consult the villagers and ward members in deciding the choice of beneficiaries and allocation of public goods, which is done via village meetings or (gram sabha) called by elected local government to discuss resource allocation decisions in the village.

The other most vital area for grassroot level intervention for peace-building in Assam can be ensured through the gram sabha, which is the lynchpin of the panchayat system. Citizen participation at the village level can improve workings of democracy primarily by improving the flow of information into the political process beyond that available by electing representatives. In the case of Assam PRI not only has the potential to improve information flows and structure democratic institutions to ensure fair and efficient allocation of funds but also can facilitate arbitration between conflicting parties in the presence of a governing body where membership is determined by a legitimate universal and constitutional mandate that cuts across different ethnicities and communities. According to a study made by Besley, Rohini Pande and Rao on 500 villages in four south Indian states of Andhra Pradesh, Karntaka, Kerala and Tamilnadu, the main ways in which Gaon Sabha can improve the workings of the government is firstly relative to elected representatives, these meetings may better reflect citizens preferences on issues such as how to target resources to the most needy groups and secondly by providing a forum for monitoring the actions of elected representatives they may reduce agency problems in politics and the extent of corruption.

According to a recent article by Gulshan Sachdeva 'Demystifying Northeast' in *Dialogue* (January-March, 2006, Volume 7, No. 3) besides certain areas of maybe political or psychological neglect, facts about devolution and transfers of resources from the Centre to the North East reveal a entirely different story. Between 1990-'91 and 2002-'03, the region received a grant amount of about Rs 1, 08,504 crores. Assam received about Rs 43,000 crores from the Centre. Arunachal and Manipur received about Rs 9,900 crores and Rs 11,500 crores respectively. Meghalaya received about Rs 9,000 crores and Tripura's share is about Rs 14,000 crores. Similarly, figures for the same period for Nagaland and Mizoram are about Rs 12,000 crores and 9,000 crores respectively. These are gross figures. A portion of that money is also given back to the Central government as repayment on loans and interest payments. Still, the cumulative net devolution from the Centre to the Northeast for the period between 1990-'91 and 2002-'03 is about Rs 92,000 crores. Only grant portion to the region during these 13 years is about Rs 65,000 crores. So the lack of development could not be because of shortage of funds. In fact, as economist and Congress leader Jairam Ramesh has recently argued that this kind of public expenditure has become very much part of the problem of the Northeast.

If lack of devolution of funds for development and infrastructural growth through effective democratic structures is seen as one of the primary sources of conflict in this region, it can be easily argued that Panchayat Raj Institutions (PRI) has all the institutional safeguards at least theoretically to deal with effective fund allocation and distribution of resources ensuring universality and legitimacy. Permeation of Centre funding into the grassroot can be effectively ensured by structures in the PRI, through both distributive justice and equitable distribution of

Table 7.1: **Devolution & Transfer of Resources from the Centre to NER, 1990-'91 to 2002-'03**

	1990-91	*91-92*	*92-93*	*93-94*	*94-95*	*95-96*	*96-97*	*97-98*	*98-99*	*99-00*	*00-01*	*01-02*	*02-03*	*1990-2003*
Arunachal														
Gross Devolution	351	415.5	472.3	485.2	553.5	702.9	780.5	822.1	907	954.3	1049	1246.9	1172.6	9912.85
Net Devolution	329.2	385.8	452.9	459.8	543.8	675.9	748.1	782.9	859.4	899.4	985.48	1173.5	1095.6	9391.83
Assam														
Gross Devolution	1955.9	1873.13	1874.2	2756.5	2512.1	3002.8	3211.5	3734	3522.4	4261.6	4047.2	4781.2	5541.5	43073.8
Net Devolution	1399.4	1256.8	1236.8	2046.8	1730.5	2298.5	2416.4	2789.3	2910	3076.4	3207.1	3679.6	4383.8	32431.32
Manipur														
Gross Devolution	413.8	430.8	494.3	604.5	541.2	641.9	768	919.5	981	1080.1	1198.3	1753.2	1648.7	11475.32
Net Devolution	388.6	393	418.7	513.6	575.7	613.4	714.3	804.8	849.6	1012	1063	1342.1	1274.8	9964.59
Meghalaya														
Gross Devolution	326.1	359.3	388.4	529.3	472.9	571.6	634.15	632.8	741.8	807.6	971.2	1177.6	1281.1	8893.79
Net Devolution	307.2	330.5	363.8	423.6	441.3	537.1	595.99	590.6	694.5	752.9	911.17	1109	1210.2	8267.75
Mizoram														
Gross Devolution	355.3	380.3	400.2	487.3	519.1	607	644.3	700.8	726.5	951.4	1084.5	1096.4	1003.5	8956.62
Net Devolution	191.1	366.7	384	471.2	500.3	588.3	621.4	673	694.5	913.5	1046.7	1051.9	951.13	8453.85
Nagaland														
Gross Devolution	446.07	509.88	659.09	712.5	596.44	754.9	835.33	955	1170.5	1245.7	1394	1569.9	1598.6	12447.78
Net Devolution	402.06	438.8	444.1	585.8	560.9	725.86	796.6	912.2	940.2	1140.7	1331	1402.9	1502.7	11183.83
Tripura														
Gross Devolution	519.5	551.8	592.8	614.3	709.6	883.8	987.8	1065.4	1260.4	1419.3	1499.5	1748.2	1892	13744.32
Net Devolution	477.98	506.2	540.6	563.2	656.1	833.9	932.7	1001.1	1183.3	1325	1392.1	1627.4	1756.7	12796.27
NER Total														
Gross Devolution	4367.7	4520.7	4881.3	6189.6	5904.8	7164.9	7861.6	8829.6	9309.6	10720	11244	13373	14138	108504.5
Net Devolution	3495.5	3677.8	3840.9	5064	5008.6	6272.9	6825.5	7553.9	8131.5	9119.9	9936.5	11386	12175	92489.44

Source: Author's calculations based on Reserve Bank of India and CMIE data.

resources. If well-intended, decentralization of governance through democratic institutions like PRI can ensure constitutional homogeneity and equality within multiethnic myriad of tribal and non tribal identities in Assam. Considering this fact we have to now protect and nurture this institution by cleansing it of the discrepancies that plague the system. Both policy tasks undertaken by the panchayat 'high spillover public goods' and 'low spillover public goods' through reservation of socially deprived categories like scheduled caste, tribes and women are effective means of ensuring distributive justice that can permeate grassroots at large without triggering sensitive sentiments of ethnicity and identity. The feature of constitutional universality in democratic governance provides panchayat institutions a powerful weapon to mediate in sectoral crisis. Although knowing that the scars of identity formation experienced by Assam have larger political issues that need to be resolved like state border concerns, land ownership and immigration but, as a first step, to intervene in the present conflict situation would be to strengthen local governance through Panchayat. It is a viable means for the Indian state to establish its credibility and regain the trust of the common people. The 2001 panchayat election in Assam implemented 73rd and 74th amendment for the first time in Assam and saw increased participation but unfortunately functionally at least most categories seem to be mere filling up of numbers of the reserved seats. The study highlights the fact that the elected members (Both men and women in the areas where the study was conducted) has had very little or no knowledge whatsoever of either 73rd amendment or 33 per cent reservation in favour of women as a mandatory inclusion in the Panchayati Raj Act. This is a result of the ignorance at every level about the Panchayat act, and the resulting duties and functions of the institution as a whole.

Towards Good governance: Perspectives of Panchayat in Assam

Ensuring peace and human development are in a larger perspective dependent on each other and a synthesis of both is essential pre-requisite for economic growth. At the same time, unless we try to ensure a sustainable and durable economic growth both Peace and human development will elude us. Based on the study conducted, it has been ascertained that the primary impediments to the realization of the full potentials of Panchayat system in Assam are Bureaucratic Red-Tapism, Fund transfer through DRDA (Directorate of Rural Development Assam) which is extremely cumbersome and time consuming, Transparency of fund transfer and percolation of incentives to BPL households. Scheme benefits most of the time do not filter down to those who actually need them but get diverted to those with connections, highhandedness and condescending attitude of BDO's (Block Development Officer) in their dealings with women members, finally party affiliation of candidates which today is an important criterian, so much so that powerful parties sideline deserving candidates who are either independent or from other parties. Besides these factors, indifference of mainstream politics towards marginalized section not only impede political participation of women but more generally of the whole community,

Moreover major government policies for overall development and capacity building of common people at the grassroots like microcredit, literacy, infrastructural development, reproductive healthcare, etc. have more or less suffered due to lack of sensitization of these developmental programmes. In this context it is worth mentioning that though women put in equal and more often extra hours of work, there exist gross disparities in remuneration. In case of tea-garden women labourers, in spite of the provision of equal wage for equal work, women were discriminated in work allocation. Heavier and thus more paying works were not given to women, making an alibi of her physical limitations. In plucking too the permitted weight of tea leaf plucked by women was less than that allowed by men, in spite of the fact that women are still considered quality pluckers than men. The discriminations were carried out more commonly on a latent rather than manifest level.

The chapter strongly recommends effective implementation of 73rd amendment to increase women's participation in the local governance, with the objective of autonomous participation rather than numerical participation. This alone can change governance at the local level because women bring their experience of governance of civil society into governance of the state. In this way, they make the state sensitive to issues of poverty, inequality and gender injustice. Every issue of governance taken up by women is ideally influenced by two sources of self-perception. First, three prevails own sense of shared experience; and secondly, from attitudes and imagery imposed on them by the men. It appears that gender can supersede class and party lines. Women can open up the possibility for politics to have not only new faces but also a new quality.

However increasing the representation of women alone may not automatically lead to a more gendered analysis of the issues confronting local government. Nor will it necessarily raise the profile of women's needs and interests in the policy agenda, given that elected women often act as proxies for men's views at the councils, being advised by their male relatives. In spite of this there is always this slight possibility that a small minority of women who are in politics because of their own leadership qualities or feminist consciousness may exhibit different priorities and values in politics someday.

Some of the ways in which women, through PRI, can change governance are evident in the issues they would choose to tackle (as was evident in course of the presently referred work), e.g., water, alcohol-abuse, education, health and domestic violence. Women also express different values. Women value proximity, whether it is a drinking water source, a fuel source, a crèche, a health centre, a court of justice or an office of administration. The enormous expansion of women's representation in decentralized government structures most of the time highlights the advantages of proximity, namely the redress of grievance and (most important of all) the ability to mobilize struggle at a local level where it is most meaningful. Thus women can help to radicalize local government towards the building of a peaceful society. But this can only happen if steps are taken to ensure that the basic awareness is generated to improve the quality of life of women in particular by eradicating poverty, illiteracy, entrenched socio-cultural values and patriarchal ideologies through sensitization and capacity building. PRI and its democratic spirit will always be out of common peoples' grasp unless civil society ensures equal access to resources irrespective of gender-difference. This will only be possible when there are other such accompanying constitutional rights to ensure this. On the other hand these measures cannot be effectively achieved without proper functioning of the local self-government. The author thus faced with a situation where the number-game in the politics of democracy is not subsumed to the democratic spirit of panchayat system .A democratic autonomy of women is only possible by developing social capital and human resource at the same time. Proxy representations many a times have proved that reservation is not an end in itself but a means to an end, which is to ensure participation of women. Women who need to be brought forward are not those who are puppets and mouthpieces of powerful and unscrupulous male influences but those who are themselves capable of making a difference to the lives of other women like them. The Tussle between muscle and money power also makes it difficult for honest and dedicated leaders and participants both male and female to come forward in order to ensure effective functioning of the Panchayat system.

Thus the obstacles to the realization of PRI's transformative potential are many, especially for Assam given its political instability, identity movements and a multi-ethnic paradigm susceptible to ideologies of dissent and conflict. There continues to be a resistance to the real devolution of power and funds from centres of (male) power to the periphery. Women as we have seen still face considerable handicaps to their involvement in politics; for example, inadequate education, the burden of reproductive and productive roles, a lack of self-confidence and the opposition of entrenched cultural and religious views. Urbashi Bhutalia has contributed an article '*Confrontation and Negotiation: Women's movement response to violence against women*' in the Karin Kapadia [Ed.] *The violence of Development: Politics of Identity Gender and social inequalities in India* (2002, Kali for Women Delhi). In the article Bhutalia has articulated the understanding of violence by women's group as we started with the basic insight that violence is inherent in all social structures of society like class, caste, religion, ethnicity and in the way the state controls people. However within all those general structures of violence, women suffer violence in a gender specific way and patriarchal violence permeates and promotes other forms of violence

Given that women have always been the first victims of a violent society, a transformative feminist politics in India is only possible when politics directly and frontally engage in caste discrimination, communalism, class based inequalities and state repression which are the basic structures that create a subordinated and tyrannized identity for women. In Assam the transformative potential of 73rd amendment for feminist politics has to be fully exploited in order for women to evolve as the most important actor in peacemaking. Accordingly, Professor Sajal Nag in his article 'His masters voice: Women, Peacemaking and genderizsation of Politics' utters: *"In an otherwise doomed situation in India, women in North East India have played a very important role as Peacemakers and not just between families, clans, and tribes but underground insurgents called national workers and Government of India as a unique and unparalleled instance in entire South Asia."*

Experiences of Naga mothers Association,(The only group in South Asia to have participated in a ceasefire negotiation), The Mothers Union of Tura(Meghalaya), Meira Peibes of Manipur and Naga Womens Union of Manipur and Mizo Womens Federation are indicative of the evolving of feminization of the civic space beyond ethnic identity and imposed subjectivity for women in societies marked by extreme militarism and insurgency. The Peace building activities of Naga Womens Groups have produced a social consciousness in Naga society that upholds womanhood, human values and rights, recognizing Peace as the prerequisite for any human development. It validates women as making a difference especially in reaching out to bitterly divided Naga armed factions and fostering reconciliation and healing. It has persuaded the top leaders of the armed groups to recognize women as significant resource for peace building and legitimized their identity as stakeholders in a plural peace process. Accordingly, Professor Anuradha Dutta voiced, *'The Bodo women, in spite of being the victims of violence once are working for sustainable peace today'*.

'These women in particular were strong supporters of the movement for identity in the Bodoland areas organized by the students under the leadership of Upendra Brahma. The Bodo women organized under the banner of the All Assam Tribal Women's Welfare Federation (AATWWF) joined the movement for the adoption of the Roman Script way back in 1974. Later when the Bodo movement established a military wing to conduct an armed struggle, it trained the womenfolk in arms and from 1989 onwards, some women did join the arms wing. The AATWWF was not in favour of this decision. And in 1993 the AATWWF changed its nomenclature to All Bodo Women's Welfare Federation (ABWWF). Since All Bodo Students Union, abbreviated as ABSU could not reach the nooks and corners of the Bodoland, they took the help of women group to mobilize people in support of the movement. These women's organizations explained the programme of the ABSU to the people from time to time, convincing people about their demands and taught people to remain alert about army and police raids. They approached people to help the ABSU with food and shelter. Thus this group of women activists had unique characteristics. They as victims also protested against frequent police and army raids in the villages leading to arrest of innocent people. The Bodo women group has had a very good network in every nook and corner of the different Bodo dominated areas'.

The Bodo women in spite of being so active in the Bodo movement have not been a part of the formal peace process. In post reconciliation also, ABWWF has failed in finding for itself a political space. In the election to the Bodoland Territorial Council (BTC), the Bodoland People's Progressive Front (BPPF) which was formed in April 2005 was bifurcated in May. One faction comprised the BLT leaders and surrendered cadres, while the All Bodo Students' Union (ABSU) took the lead in formation of the BPPF that comprised the other faction. In Kokrajhar, several leaders of the disbanded militant outfit filed nominations against the BPPF President Rabiram Narzary. The BTC Chief Hangrama Mahillary supported former comrade Manoj Kumar Brahma. Though initially the ABWWF, a key player in Bodo politics lent its support to the new party BPPF, it withdrew from the party as not a single woman candidate was nominated. The influential women's body extended support to the former BLT leader instead, who stood as the rebel candidate against the official BPPF candidates.

If we see the lack of effective political leadership of Bodo women in the Bodo movement as a crisis of participation and motivation, we will overlook the latent structure and the fruitless effort in fighting an institutional governance, where women's political potentials have never been recognized traditionally. Being ethnically bound, these women have never been exposed to the constitutional universality of democratic governance of decentralization as in the Panchayati Raj institution. The true potential of women's political participation can be explored when fearless and sensitized women like them are provided with specific kinds of institutional support which go beyond technical training. They need support to build solidarity amongst women through strengthening links between women's organizations and elected bodies. They need information about innovative organizations which enhance women's lives such as health providers and credit institutions. It is also necessary to strengthen women's sense of common identity by articulating the elements of a feminist consciousness and presenting it as the special quality of women's leadership. There has been insufficient elaboration of what that leadership has to offer which distinguishes it from men's leadership and which commends it as something special. Such an elaboration through feminist discourse and action is essential for this revolution to deliver the promise it holds for peace making. On the basis of the study, the author has chalked out a possible area of intervention where self-help groups, NGO, and government institutions could intervene to generate political awareness of citizenship rights and democratic electoral process of Panchayat Raj System.

1. Any plan of intervention should highlight the following seven categories:

- A Gaon Sabha Mobilization through Street Plays and Theatres
- Communication Workshops
- Media workshops
- Block Elected Women's Representatives Forums (BEWRF)
- Women Leadership Workshops
- Public Opinion Building and Awareness Generation on PRI
- Gross Participation in National Level alliances and Networking

2. Training on Panchayat system, its functions and modules of Activity have to be organized for everyone, may be for general public or elected members. Issues that need to be sensitized are:

- Complete right over the subjects mentioned in 11th schedule
- Compulsory elections
- Immediate transfer of power

- Quorum in Gaon sabha meeting should not be substituted with quorum of Panchayat meetings

3. Accessibility of Information networks on health service providers and credit institutions

4. Strengthening Links between women's groups and elected bodies through effective networking, in order to smoothly facilitate lobbying to accrue to panchayats.

5. Capacity Building of women through awareness and sensitization of vital issues without depending solely on reservation.

6. Formation of self-help-groups, which aim at savings and thrift to collectively raise economic concerns before panchayat justifiably.

7. Last but most important is Infrastructural Development, like ensuring basic facilities of Health, Sanitation and Education for women and other weaker sections that cut across ethnicity, tribe, caste or religion, in order to boost their confidence and morale. In case of women, infrastructural support can combat the burden of entrenched cultural and socio-religious values which has for generations subjected them to a dual structure of exploitation, one in her domestic domain and the other as part of a wider male-centric value system.

8. Forming women's organization or other such groups as supervisory bodies for

- Ensuring that the women are not marginalised in the revenue and expenditure committee structures that will emerge to manage the development in these bodies;
- Ensuring the devolution of project design and monitoring powers from central government to the elected bodies, so that the **people** can develop their own policies, reflecting the views of their own representatives rather than those of central government, and be held accountable for them;
- Strengthening the identity and feminist consciousness of women representatives, for example, by leadership training;
- Building global coalitions through the activist, as distinct from the academic mode. This includes bringing women into political structures and supporting the backward and forward linkages of women's presence in politics, linking household and family priorities with macro-planning processes;
- Pressing for South Asian regional economic cooperation amongst women to be based on regional support to empower woman's role in local and national governance;
- Campaigns and training programmes to prepare the women both as electors and elected; and

- Urging multi- and bi-lateral agencies to revise their own patriarchal structures.

Proposed Strategic Framework: Peace Through Human Development (PTHD)

Panchayati Raj Institutions and decentralization of Rural governance in Assam can be seen as the most viable means for sustainable peace in Assam, provided we can use them to build a strategic framework for peace through development (PTD) which encourages conflict sensitivity in development. The study highlights an undeniable fact that with better access to the Knowledge of the Panchayat act, its rights and duties, training and capacity building of men and women alike, the institution alone can facilitate rural upliftment and bring the marginalized rural society closer to mainstream development. In the specific context of Assam economic deprivation and a grueling human development, crisis manifests in cultural alienation, persecution complex and an identity-crisis leading to conflict.

It is proposed that the strategic framework provided by PTD approach be channelized through the participatory governance embedded in PRI focusing on the building of partnerships on long-term development, governance and peace building among government actors, local civil society groups and the public. The key strategic approaches recommended for incorporation in the design of PTD as a program in Rural Assam are:

a) ***Government Leadership*** - Government ownership is vital for the success of the program. The program strategy is based on strengthening existing government mechanisms and the application of existing regulations.

b) ***Area-based Approach*** - Within the context of decentralization in Assam, PTD can be an area based program focused on the districts. An area-based approach allows capacity building and the experience of hands on delivery to be combined within an existing institutional framework targeted at areas with significant conflict risk. PTD can initially work in selected core districts in which it will provide comprehensive support. The selection of districts can be based on specified criteria and aught to be agreed by a National Committee. The provincial level needs to be supported is its mandated role of managing cross-district initiatives, oversight of district PTD performance and establishing and monitoring minimum service standards.

c) ***Multi-stakeholder Processes and Collective Benefits*** - Effective multi-stakeholder processes are of great importance in rebuilding trust and confidence in conflict and post-conflict contexts. PTD can achieve this through effective program mechanisms, management arrangements and assistance aimed at strengthening processes and the skill of those involved. The effectiveness and performance of multi-stakeholder processes will be monitored and reviewed by those involved. PTD will link multi-stakeholder processes with the delivery of collective benefits for the community that can strengthen social cohesion.

d) ***Building Capacities for Peace and Development*** - The main emphasis of the program will be on capacities for building long-term peace and development. Capacity building should be demand-driven with careful identification of needs and formulation of capacity building responses. Capacity has been defined as 'the ability of an individual, organization or a system to perform functions and meet objectives effectively and efficiently'. Capacity-building therefore concerns support to achieve performance and produce outcomes focusing on three interrelated levels. These are:

I. ***The systems level***, which sets the policy, legal and regulatory framework that includes management and accountability systems, resource allocation and broad system level processes such as planning and evaluation;

II. ***The organization (unit) level*** including its core business and strategy; culture, organizational structures and competencies; internal management processes and procedures; its human, financial and information resources; and its infrastructure;

III. ***The individual level,*** including general and specific skill, such as initiative, judgment, values, professional competencies, motivations and work attitudes. Capacity building to support decentralization highlights the need to build the capacity of a variety of stakeholders including government, non-government organizations and local communities. It includes four key stages: (i) comprehensive identification and formulation of capacity building needs within the context of regional autonomy, (ii) formulating priorities for capacity building initiatives, (iii) determining comprehensive plans for capacity building and (iv) allocation of technical and financial resources to capacity building plans including donor and government sources. The program can focus on developing sustainable mechanisms for capacity development through the local and national institutions responsible for supervision and capacity building support.

The essential capacities for long-term peace have been identified through the PDA as those relating to governance and social cohesion. Social cohesion refers to the crosscutting social and economic relations within society, including the trust, intergroup associations, networks of communication and cultural patterns of interaction – that bond a society together, promote harmony, a sense of community, and a degree of commitment to promoting the common good. The concept of social cohesion emphasizes the importance of horizontal equity between groups and places the responsibility for minimizing disparities, avoiding polarization and facilitating balanced development

a) Capacities for Local Governance – PTD will support the executive and legislative arms of local governments (Panchayats), civil society and the community through enhanced public awareness and participatory planning mechanisms to strengthen the capacities for local democratic governance to promote peace and human development. Although the rule of law and the role of the judicial arms of government are essential, there are limitations to the extent that work can be done within the context of PTD as a decentralized program for example, AFSPA in Assam.

b) Capacities for Social Cohesion – Social segregation and prejudice need to be overcome in the promotion of peaceful and equitable development. PTD will strengthen the capacities of government and civil society to promote social integration and harmony. The PDA when implemented in Conflict torn countries like Indonesia has shown that opportunities for strengthening inter-community networks and relations exist and are a priority in these provinces. PTD will focus its support to organizations and networks that promote social cohesion through meeting priority development needs across community divisions. In particular there is scope to address the issues of currently or previously displaced people which, in some areas, are the main barrier to sustainable peace. In all cases there is a need to analyze the issues at local level, link them to the broader environment and create the conditions within which local solutions can be found or advocacy activities supported to resolution at a higher level.

In India for local government to be both representative and accountable both in form and practice, the PTD approach through PRI need to be sensitive to the fact that Governments generally create institutions that are upwardly accountable to the central state. For reaping the theoretical benefits of community participation, however, accountability needs also to follow downward transmission, aiming towards the local population. Elected local representatives are not always downwardly accountable. If political parties can only choose candidates, they may be more accountable to the parties than to the local populations that elect them (Hesseling, n.d.: 17; Ribot 1999). Further, even when independent candidates are admitted to local elections, there are many ways that local elite or political parties are able to capture the electoral process, bringing the local accountability of leaders into question. Nonetheless, elected representatives are one important building block in the construction of accountable local government. Crook and Manor (Parker 1995:27) indicate that locally elected representatives can make central government more responsive to local needs. In order for PRI to effectively facilitate PTD it will require power, downward accountability, and durable institutional forms.

It is thus proposed, as Hadi does in his study of Indonesia, that we accommodate a possible shift from Integrated Rural Development to Integral Local Development (ILD) through representation, eentrustment and accountability, which is possible by moving away from forms of PTD orchestrated from the outside or 'above' (joint management, stakeholder approaches, participatory rural appraisal, etc.—see World Bank 1996; Chambers 1983), to forms that are built into local government. PTD can merge with decentralization and democratization to become one—participation through rural democracy. Integral Local Development (ILD), rural or otherwise, is an appropriate and timely approach that is based on allowing rural communities to integrate across community differences through decisions made by locally accountable local authorities—representative bodies who are downwardly accountable to the local population. It is integral rather than integrated since it depends on authority that is integral to the community, rather than being the product of outside agency, integrated before delivery. It is also integral because in this model of rural development, ecology and environment are not separate from other matters of local government; rather they are part of a more organic or integral whole. That whole is the realm of decision making under the jurisdiction of locally accountable authorities. It is integral since all sources of community revenues (taxes, stumpage fees, central government grants, loans, financial development assistance) are pooled and are allocated not according to their origins, but according to the needs and aspirations of the community as expressed through locally accountable representative government. ILD is the creation of a domain of local autonomy in which local representatives can act on the integrity of local resources and local needs and desires. Integrated Rural Development is based on providing an array of interventions at multiple levels supporting the productivity of the farm household and the development of agrarian economies and thus the approach became cumbersome quite quickly, leading to large, costly, top-down projects, given the name 'Christmas tree projects' since there were always more components that could be hung on the Integrated Rural Development frame to assure success. It was the mechanism of integration that was wrong. Integrated Rural Development is based on a farm-systems model of local needs, usually designed in far away places to be flown in and set up around rural communities who had little influence on the process.

While Participatory approaches to rural development as in Panchayat system have improved the situation, mostly by soliciting local input into decision making processes but still they have not systematically increased local control by representative local authorities. ILD, on the other hand integrates through local representative bodies. This is its principal difference from the Integrated Rural Development approach.

Finally PTD through PRI, unlike other participatory approaches to development which have avoided the state and tried to approach development by avoiding state and going directly to the people, can avoid certain impending risks involved in state alienation While the ideal of many practitioners of state alienation has been greater inclusion and justice, the choice of this approach is part of a larger global narrative that pits people against government rather than seeing government as an effective partner in development.

The growing conflict situation of Assam has led to mobilization of various movements in order to address this contradiction between the individual and the state. This complexity while at a manifest level presents itself as a contradiction of cultural reproduction, social integration and socialization of neglect at a more pragmatic and latent level can be viewed as democratic response to the Human Development deficit in the region. It is the call of the hour to demystify the neglect theory of cultural reproduction, integration and abhor the Indian example of granting territorial autonomy to resurgent minority groups which has aggravated not only ethnic conflict and competition for limited resources both political and social but has also led to increasing contradictions between the individual and state. In a situation where people face great economic hardships through loss of livelihoods and withdrawal of investment funds from the region as a result of economic crisis and conflicts, reliance on government is even higher and community self reliance is very low. Years of so called 'bottom-up' approach of planning have resulted in few real welfare gains for communities or specific groups. Poor coordination between district and provincial governments results in duplication of development programs within villages or very poorly targeted support that does not match community needs. Women's status has not improved and educated young people are unable to find employment and the presence of internally displaced persons remains a challenge for social cohesion and human development (especially in health, education and economic empowerment).The lack of coordination among village, sub-division, district and provincial levels of government means that problems emerging at the village level hardly even reach district let alone provincial government and, vice versa, policies at the provincial and district levels hardly reach people in villages (particularly to women and poor). The solutions to inherent problems range from extreme inhumanity of army anti-insurgency acts like AFSPA and suspension of democratic rights to a liberal and soft-peddling by granting of autonomous councils, promise to solve almost nothing. Decentralization of governance and local level participation through democratic constitutional measures like Panchayati Raj Institutions can facilitate a Peace Through Development Approach (PTD), which appears as a viable means of establishing trust and good governance in the region.

REFERENCES

Adamolekun, Ladipo. 1991. 'Promoting African Decentralization,' *Public Administration and Development*, Vol. 11, pp. 285-91.

Agrawal, Arun. 1997. 'Community in Conservation: Beyond Enchantment and Disenchantment,' Conservation and Development Forum Working Paper No. 1, University of Florida, Gainesville. March 18 Draft.

Agrawal, Arun and Jesse C. Ribot. 1999. 'Accountability in Decentralization: A Framework with South Asian and West African Cases,' *Journal of Developing Areas,* Vol. 33, pp. 473-502.

Allen, Chris. 1997. 'Who Needs Civil Society?' *Review of African Political Economy*, No. 73, pp. 329-337.

Baland, J. 1996. *Halting Degradation of Natural Resources: Is there a Role for Rural Communities?* Oxford: Clarendon Press.

Berry, Sara. 1989. 'Social Institutions and Access to Resources', *Africa*, 59(1).

Bhagwati, J N. 1982. 'Directly Unproductive, Profit-seeking (DUP) Activities,' *Journal of Political Economy* Vol. 90, No. 5, pp. 988-1002.

Blaikie, P. 1985. *The Political Economy of Soil Erosion in the Third World.* London: Longman.

Blair, H. 2000. 'Participation and Accountability at the Periphery: Democratic Local Governance in Six Countries' *World Development* 28(1):21-39.

Blair, H. 1998. 'Spreading Power to the Periphery: An Assessment of Democratic Local Governance,' Program and Operations Assessment Report No. 21, Washington DC: USAID.

GTZ, USAID, Ministry of Home Affairs and Bappenas (2001) Capacity Building for Local Governance: A Frameworkfor Government Action and Donor Support. See http://www.gtzsfdm.or.id/cb_nat_fr_work.htm for further details

Bordieu, P. 1977. *Outline of a Theory of Practice.* Cambridge: Cambridge University Press.

Cernia, M (ed.) 1985. *Putting People First: Sociological Variables in Rural Development.* New York: Oxford University Press.

Chambers, R. 1983. *Rural Development: Putting the Last First.* Essex: Longman Scientific & Technical.

Dahl, R A. 1993[1961]. 'Who Governs?' ch. 13, pp. 104-119 in Philip Green (ed.) *Democracy.* Atlantic Highlands, NJ: Humanities Press.

Echeverri-Gent, J. 1992. 'Public Participation and Poverty Alleviation: The Experience of Reform Communists in India's West Bengal,' *World Development* 20, no. 10 (October 1992): 1401-22.

Granovetter, M. 1985. 'Economic Action and Social Structure: The Problem of Embeddedness,' *American Journal of Sociology*, Vol. 91, No. 3, pp. 481-510.

Hadi, S. 2005, Enhancing Local governance through decentralization policy in managing conflict –Affected regions in Indonesia. presented at the International Conference on Engaging Communities; UNDESA/UNCRD Workshop on Decentralization: Poverty Reduction, Empowerment and Participation, Brisbane, Australia, 14-17 August, 2005. http://unpan1.un.org/intradoc/groups/public/documents/UN/UNPAN020695.pdf

Mawhood, P . 1983. 'The Place of Traditional Political Authority in African Pluralism,' *Civilisations*, Vol. XXXII, No. 2 1982-Vol. XXXIII, No. 1 1983, pp. 209-37.

Manor, James. 1999. *The Political Economy of Democratic Decentralization*. World Bank: Washington, DC.

Mazonde, Isaac Ncube. 1996. 'The Basarwa of Botswana: Leadership, Legitimacy and Participation in Development Sites,' *Cultural Survival Quarterly*, Fall 1996.

Mehta, A S. 1996. 'Micro·Politics of Voluntary Action: An Anatomy of Change in Two Villages,' *Cultural Survival Quarterly*, Fall 1996.

Mkandawire, T. 1995. 'Beyond Crisis: Toward Democratic Developmental States in Africa,' paper presented at CODESRIA's Eighth General Assembly, Crises, Conflicts and Transformations: Responses and Perspectives, 26 June - 2 July 1995.

Oyugi, W O. 2000. 'Decentralization for Good Governance and Development' *Regional Development Dialogue* 21(1):3-22, Spring 2000.

Ribot, J C. 1999a. 'Integral Local Development: Authority, Accountability and Entrustment in Natural Resource Management,' Working Paper of the Africa Region RPTES program, Thc World Bank, April 1999.

.Sen, Amartya. 1981. *Poverty and Famines: An Essay on Entitlement and Deprivation*. Oxford: Clarendon Press.

Shiva, V. 1989. *Staying Alive*. Atlantic Highlands, NJ: Zed Books.

Dutta Hazarika S . 2007 Examining Autonomy and 73rd Amendment in Assam .in Paula Bannerjee and Samir Das (Ed) Autonomy Beyond Kant and Hermeneutics, Anthem Press New Delhi.

World Bank. 2000. *Entering the 21st Century: World Development Report 1999/2000*. Oxford: Oxford University Press.

World Bank. 1996. *The World Bank Participation Sourcebook*. Washington, D.C.: The World Bank.

8.

BEING A FEMALE INDUSTRIAL ENGINEER: A Portuguese Case

CELINA P. LEÃO, CARINA PIMENTAL and
CRISTINA S. RRODRIGUES

'One of the most striking characteristics of work organizations in the 20th century is the hierarchical status gradient in favour of men and gender segregation in the world of work'. (Lawthom et al. 2006, p. 3).

Introduction

The increase of women engineers' participation in a profession established as masculine changes the traditional understanding of engineering. In Portugal, the available data refers that only 4 per cent of female students are enrolling in engineering courses, representing no more than 19 per cent of total engineering students, suggesting the existence of the largest gender imbalance of all the university degree levels. The Industrial Engineering course of the *University of Minho* is an exception: 44 per cent of female graduates during the last 30 years. Knowing that this course has a primary focus in the Portuguese manufacturing industry, with a strong male culture, how these female engineers face and respond to their career challenges? The paper intends to explore the main variables that influence career progression of Portuguese female industrial engineers. A questionnaire was developed to identify the paths of career progression of these professionals. Then, some interviews to female industrial engineers working in manufacturing industry were performed. They highlighted, among others, a major consensus that this area of specialization implicates a strong commitment not compatible with family demands. A different questionnaire was applied to female students (2nd year), in order to identify and perceive their expectation about their future professional career.

In Portugal, engineering degree is the second most popular student option (13%), following business and administration courses (15%). Despite the fact that there are more students of the feminine gender enrolled at university and high school education, only 4 per cent are following engineering degree courses. By comparison with their male counterparts, female students represent no more than 19 per cent of engineering students (INE, 2003). Since women tend to earn better grades than men in both high school and college (Brown, 2005), it can be stated that in Portugal a large amount of professional potential is being lost because those women are not being attracted to the engineering field. Data also confirm that engineering represents the largest gender imbalance of all the Portuguese university degree levels. This gender imbalance in the engineering field is reported in others countries. Despite the definition of active policies to gender equity, Shackleton et al (2006) study supports the need for a change in culture. Therefore it will be important to track these "brave" women engineers as they move through their professional life cycle. The literature research also indicates a lack of studies concerning this Portuguese reality – women in engineering. Nonetheless, there are several exploratory gender studies concerning other professional occupations (see for instance Santos and Cabral-Cardoso, 2003).

We identify several opportunities for research, namely (1) a closer look at the engineering industry level in respect of women (Auster & Ekstein, 2005), (2) a deeper interpretation of factors affecting the career growth (Ismail, 2003), and (3) a discussion of practices and curriculum in Higher Engineering Education (Powell et al., 2004).

In this paper, the EGI-Woman study main results are presented and discussed. This study intends to comprehend the career path and the major variables that distinguish the feminine *alumni* of industrial engineering experience from their male counterparts. To accomplish that, a self-administered and mail survey was implemented, together with the development of an exploratory case study based on audio-visual interviews. Simultaneously, a questionnaire was applied to the students of 2nd year of an Engineering course with the objective to identify and to recognize the students' expectation about their future professional career.

Engineering and Gender

It has been said that the history of civilization is the history of engineering. Through times, the use of precision techniques and mathematical knowledge played an important role in highly developed civilizations. Nevertheless, the central role of engineering is not necessarily evident to public (Powell et al., 2004) and current research suggests that how an engineer is viewed often depends on cultural, social and economic context (Newman, 1998). If we define engineering as the design, construction and operation of structures and machines, then it will be straightforwardly perceived as a technical work in an industrial environment. "Tough", "heavy", and "dirty" are the words that compose the popular image of engineering profession (Powell et al., 2004; Ismail, 2003; Evetts, 1998). Nevertheless, engineering has undergone a profound change in recent years (Newman, 1998; Evetts, 1998). First, the computer technology and its advances have "softened" the engineering field (Ismail, 2003) and also improved the engineers' analytical skills. Second, the concept of subject integration emerged as an important requirement for engineering practice (Newman, 1998) and therefore the engineering field evolved to new areas of specialization.

Nowadays, engineering has to face two difficult challenges. The first is to overcome low student's interest. Even though engineering degree courses still seem popular (Newman, 1998), it is important to acknowledge that its choice by students requires a mathematical background. It is possible to identify an increased negative attitude towards high motivation in scientific and analytical skills. The study of mathematics and science faced an attitude of being worthless or "uncool", and therefore, it can be stated that if that tendency is not reversed, less students will have mathematical knowledge and skills in a nearby future.

The second challenge is to retain the 'best and brightest' professionals. Engineering graduates have not been pursuing conventional careers in engineering industry, and many are moving to different disciplines (Newman, 1998). There are evidences that the lack of appropriate motivation results in a higher rate of turnover among engineers than with non-professionals (Petroni, 2000). One motivational factor is related with engineer's career expectations. Ismail (1998) identified four relevant engineering career routes: (1) technical, (2) managerial, (3) project to project, and (4) technical transfer. The managerial route is the path most usually described as successful and highest prestige (Ismail, 1998) and corresponds to moving from the engineering work to managing others who are doing the work (Evetts, 1997). The research of Petroni (2000) highlighted the need for improved management understanding of the concept of career planning of engineers and considered diversity as a critical ingredient in ensuring a fulfilling engineering career. Otherwise dissatisfaction will arise and as Newman (1998, p.399) stated "graduates will, more often than not, look long and hard at engineering as a profession and prefer to seek their fortune elsewhere".

Since 1960s and following the women's liberation movement, women have increasingly entered the professions and careered options. Based on the concept of equal opportunities defended in Western societies, women's occupational aspirations have become more similar to those of men (Powell and Butterfield, 2003). Young women became more disposed to aspire to occupations more high paying, prestigious, and male dominated. One of which is the engineering. The less emphasis on heavy engineering and machinery, and more focus on computers, mathematical models and electronics combined with adequate guidance counselling prior to entering university contributed to attract women to engineering degree courses (Powell et al., 2004; Evetts, 1998).

Being a woman engineer is an exception rather than the rule. Despite the graduate levels change, the cultural image of engineering is perceived as a masculine profession (Evetts, 1998). That image has a significant impact on society and contributed to engineering to be perceived as unsuitable for women (Powell et al., 2004; Evetts, 1998). Ismail (1998) confirmed the notion of engineering as a male dominated job. Results indicated that both men and women engineers perceived only some areas of specialization in engineering as suitable for women: instrumentation, chemical, process and design engineering and electric and electronics engineering. Research also suggests that this masculine culture is not exclusive to the engineering workplace, the engineering classrooms has an analogous culture with courses designed for male students (Powell et al., 2004).

Despite the fact that women who entered engineering have been seen as unusual, Preston (1994) realized that the exit rates from science and engineering occupations were approximately two times superior for women, and that women were much more likely than men to shift for other occupations. The study also concluded that marriage and children explained only a part of the male-female difference in labour-force exit, and that women are more likely than men to leave the labour force for reasons other than family within every age group. 'Why are women with highly marketable and socially valuable skills leaving the labour force with very low probabilities of re-entry?' (Preston, 1994, p.1460).

Evetts (1998) concluded that women enjoyed the practice of engineering, and the problems experienced by some are not related with theirs technical skills as engineers. The problems arose because of gender aspects in work organization, and the solutions to solve such gender problems focus on the women themselves. Women assimilate into the engineering industry by attempting to become "one of the boys" and knowing how to conform to the masculine engineering culture and doing it well are critical to women's success in the workplace (Powell et al., 2004).

Even so, Ismail (1998) concluded that women engineers face some limitations in terms of career growth due to traditional demand on family responsibilities. Women engineers' performances are affected most when they got married and their job performance slow down mostly because of pregnancies and taking care of young children. Auster and Ekstein (2005) confirmed that women engineers feel that a supportive work environment for women, interesting and challenging work, and help with balancing work and family are some of the key levers facing women in engineering that will help improve their retention rates.

The growing women's labour market participation changes the composition of the labour force and the traditional understanding of work (Hansen, 2002). This is the case of engineering workplace with a very high numerical preponderance of men. Research suggests that women engineers are looked at as a variation of the male work and that is necessary for a broader understanding of the engineering work. As stated by Hansen (2002, p.200) "the integration of a gender perspective will influence the foundations of the tradition, the theoretical framework(s) and the concept building".

Industrial Engineer

A distinct field in engineering is the Industrial Engineering which integrates and organizes all intervenient on the production process, namely the workers, machines, energy, materials and information and optimize their performance by using the available resources in the most efficient way.

The University of Minho (UM), http://www.uminho.pt, was the first portuguese university to have a curriculum with those characteristics, since 1976. Nevertheless, due to the experience during these years the course has been adjusted to the technological developments and to the world market requirements, in order to graduate competitive engineers. The Engineering and Industrial Management course (EIM), http://www.dps.uminho.pt, firstly denominated Production Engineering, has thirty years of experience, being an important contribution in the identification of an area in expansion and so excellent in the intention of increase in the Portuguese productivity and competitiveness. The first Production Engineer finished his course in 1982 and up to 2005 there were a total of 703 Production Engineers. Of these, 56 per cent are men and the others 44 per cent women. These indicators show a high predominance of the female gender in this course, which is not very usual, considering the Portuguese reality. The available data of the Portuguese Census 2001 (INE, 2001), refers that in the fields of Architecture, Engineering and related professions there are 78 per cent of men and only 22 per cent of women. However, engineering degree is the second most popular university student option. By comparison with their male counterparts, female students represent no more than 19 per cent of engineering students, according to data from 2002/2003 (INE, 2003). When considering the total number of female students in the same period, only 4 per cent of them were enrolled in engineering degree courses. These statistics suggests the existence of the largest gender imbalance of all the Portuguese university degree levels.

We conclude that in Portugal a large amount of professional potential is being lost because woman are not being attracted to this field, perceived as a male profession with high reputation. Although the Engineering and Industrial Management course of University of Minho is an exception to the rule, we consider that it will be important to track these "brave" woman engineers as they move through their professional life cycle in order to answer questions like: Where are these graduate women? What functions they have or had? What is their actual professional situation? Are they doing additional courses? What reasons or motivations make them change work? If the industry has male culture predominance, what challenges face the industrial engineers?

EGI-Women Study

To understand and to identify the importance of this study, it was necessary to know the evolution of the number of female students who completed engineering studies in the EIM course of the University of Minho (UM) from the first engineer. All the data was collected and summarized in Figure 8.1, where the number of male and female engineers, since 1982, the year of the first master, up to 2005, is presented. The first EIM female engineer concluded her course in 86/87. The number of male engineers was in general higher than the number of female ones, with exception in 90/91, 93/94, 94/95 and 95/96 with gender equilibrium. In 96/97, exceptionally, we observed the highest gender balance difference, having a superior percentage of female engineers. This situation was considered as casual, since it was not persistent. The data of Figure 1 strengthened the interest and importance of our study, since they show a high rate of the feminin sex in the course, *i.e.*, 44 per cent opposed to 56 per cent of the masculine sex, opposing to the Portuguese reality: only 4 per cent of female students are enrolling in engineering courses, representing no more than 19 per cent of total engineering students. Notice that these values only concern the students that conclude their degree and receive their diploma. It is known that some of the students, as they join the industry work placement, do not have time or even motivation to finish their degree. The present study did not consider those cases.

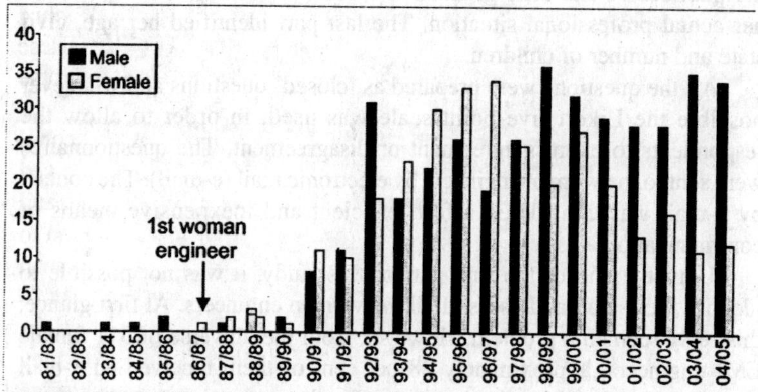

Figure 8.1. ***Evolution of the EIM - UM from the beginning up to 2005, separated by gender***

Knowing that this course has a primary focus in the Portuguese manufacturing industry, with a strong male culture, how these female engineers face and respond to their career challenges? Can we not speak about Industrial Engineering in Feminine? The engineers in this area of activity 'live' or 'survive'?

To get the answers to these questions and many others, a study was performed and denominated EGI-Woman study to be described in the following sections. This study was divided into three parts: (1) development and application of an exploratory questionnaire to identify the professional path of the industrial woman engineers of the UM, (2) performing interviews to some industrial engineers and, (3) development and application of an exploratory questionnaire to all the second year EIM students.

Female Industrial Engineers Survey

The tool developed and applied in the EGI-Woman study first part was a survey to *alumni*. The questionnaire had allowed the identification of the professional path of the industrial women engineers of the UM. The results obtained were presented and discussed highlighting the importance and pertinence of this subject (Pimentel et al., 2006a, 2006b; Leão et al., 2007). The questionnaire was divided into three parts: (1) secondary and academic data, (2) professional path data and, (3) personal data. In the first part, the woman engineer identified her first and last year of registration as an engineer student, her final graduation mark, if she was or not a full time student, and if she had done postgraduation. The second part identified her path before and after graduation course, with a special emphasis to her actual professional situation. The last part identified her age, civil state and number of children.

All the questions were prepared as 'closed' questions and whenever possible the Likert five-point scale was used, in order to allow the respondents to express agreement or disagreement. The questionnaires were sent to the women engineers by electronic mail (e-mail). The contact by e-mail was considered a fast, efficient and inexpensive means of communication.

Until the end of the first part of this study, it was not possible to identify the e-mail addresses of all the women engineers. At first glance, this realy seemed a problem. However, from the universe of 311 female EMI engineers, approximately 38 per cent of them received an e-mail invitation to participate in the study. The invitation letter included the questionnaire and a presentation of the EGI-Woman Study. A total of 62 answers were received, considered as being representative to the study since corresponding to around 54 per cent of response.

The analysis of the answers allowed creating an average profile of the EIM-UM woman engineer: 33 years old, with a professional experience of 8.7 years, married and with 0.61 children, working in the manufacturing industry, namely working in the quality or production department.

Summary of the conclusions: It can be identified a strong investment in Professional Formation (78%) in detrainment of advanced formation (Postgraduation, Master or PhD degrees), as illustrated in Figure 8.2a. None of the respondents had decided to carry out an MBA.

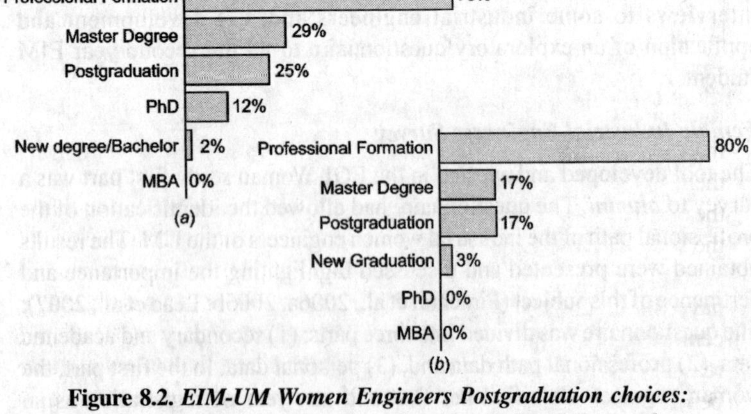

Figure 8.2. ***EIM-UM Women Engineers Postgraduation choices: (a) All Respondents and (b) Manufacturing Industry Respondents***

For the female engineers that are working in the Manufacturing Industry, the predisposition of a lower perceive in advanced formation as previously mentioned (Figure 8.2a), in particular the MBA is more evident: 80 per cent choose to take a Professional Formation in opposition to a Postgraduation or Master degree (34 per cent), see Figure 8.2b. In the manufacturing industry group, none of the female engineers decided to carry on a PhD degree. In other words, from the 12 per cent of the female engineers that have or are taking a PhD degree, no one are working in the manufacturing industry.

Figure 8.3 demonstrates that only 45 per cent of the respondents work currently in the manufacturing industry, 15 per cent in Science and High Level Education (CES), 14 per cent in Commerce and Services (C&S), 9 per cent in Formation and Consulting (F&C) and the remaining in others areas such as Health, Education and Social Services.

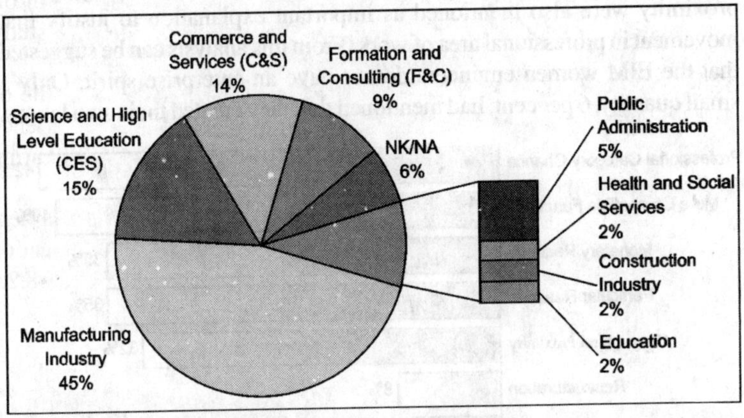

Figure 8.3. ***Actual Sectors of Activity of the EMI female Engineers of UM***

At this point, although 45 per cent of the respondents work currently in the Manufacturing Industry, it was possible to verify that 74 per cent of them already have experience in this area (Figure 8.4). This can suggest the existence of a rate of abandon. This was discussed in more detail during the second part of the EGI-Woman—the interviews (see next section).

Returning to the observed reality that 74 per cent of our respondents have worked in the manufacturing industry, and knowing that only 45 per cent work currently in this area, it is essential to understand the reason or reasons of that behaviour. When asked to identify the possible reasons beneath these changes, 42 per cent mentioned the change of professional category to a better one as the principal reason, followed by the need of more compatible functions (40 per cent), as illustrated in Figure 8.5.

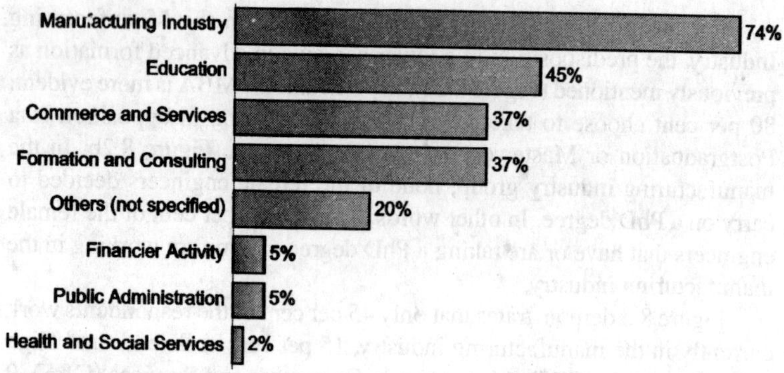

Figure 8.4. ***Experience, by activity areas, of the EMI-UM Female Engineers***

Monetary and particular reasons, 35 per cent for each, and graphical proximity were also mentioned as important explanation to justify that movement in professional area of work. From this analysis can be suggested that the EIM women engineers do not have an enterprise spirit. Only a small quantity, 6 per cent, had mentioned that they created their own labour.

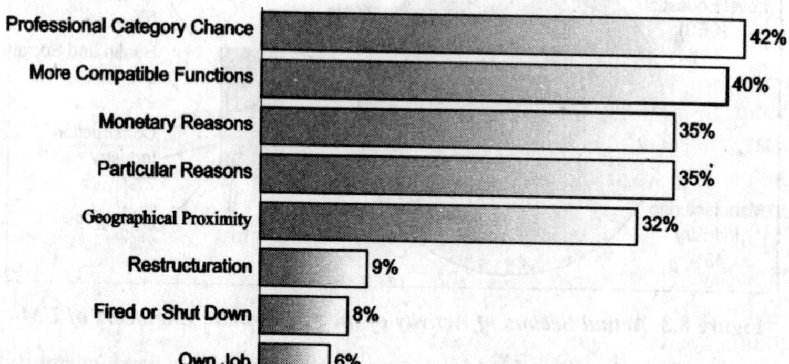

Figure 8.5. ***Professional changes: Reasons of the EIM-UM Women Engineers***

It was also possible to identify the privileged areas of activity of the EIM-UM women engineers that are in the industry: quality (44 per cent) and production (34 per cent), as illustrated in Figure 8.6. All others areas of activity (22 per cent in total) can be considered with lower importance.

Interviews

After identifying the paths of career progression of the female industrial engineers from University of Minho with the help of the developed survey,

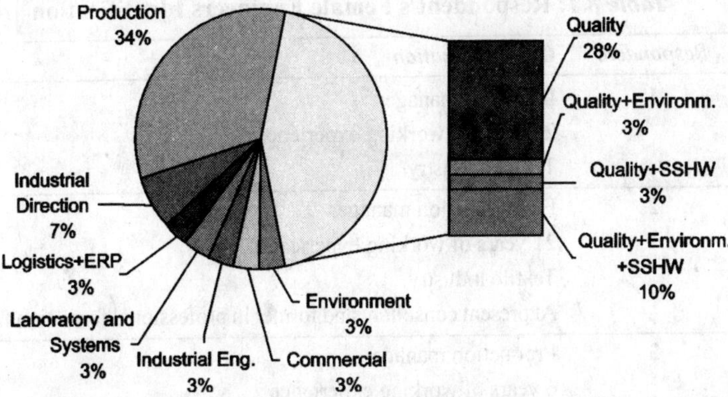

Figure 8.6: *Privileged areas of activity of the EIM-UM women engineers*

several in-depth interviews were performed. These interviews regarded only female industrial engineers working in manufacturing industry (45%, as illustrated in Figure 8.2b). The interviews were the second part of the EGI-Woman Study.

Knowing that there has been a progressive increase of female engineers becomes essential to understand how these woman engineers, firstly, have been attracted to engineering and secondly, understand their careers perspectives and progression. The main aims of the in-dept interviews were: (1) to identify how a woman engineer is accepted and perceived in the manufacturing industry, for example in terms of recognition, support, credit, influence; (2) to understand their career progression opportunities; (3) to identify the main differences between them and a male industrial engineer; (4) to identify the main challenges and opportunities they face; (5) to collect some advices from experienced women engineers to new-graduates and (6) to collect evidences of the professional experience of some industrial engineers working in the manufacturing industry.

In the sample selection we tried to select engineers working in different areas related with industrial engineering, in order to collect an illustrative sample. The professional areas of the interviewed engineers are: quality, production, logistics, commercial, product development, and provision. A group of seven engineers were taken as the study respondents. Two of them are engineers of large industrial textile companies, with more than twenty years of working experience; other two with nine years of working experience and the remaining three with six years of working experience as engineers. In Table 8.1 the characterization of each of the seven respondents is presented: the occupation in the organization, the number of years of working experience and the area of activity.

***Table 8.1*: Respondent's Female Engineers Identification**

Respondent	*Characterization*
1	Industrial manager 24 years of working experience Textile industry
2	Ex-Production manager 21 years of working experience Textile industry At present consultant and former in professional formation field
3	Production manager 6 years of working experience Metallomechanics industry
4	Logistics and ERP support manager 9 years of working experience Systems and electronic industry
5	Industrial and provision manager 6 years of working experience Tyre retreading industry
6	Administrator and industrial manager 6 years of working experience Wooden industry
7	Production manager 9 years of working experience Textile industry

Respondent 2, that have more than twenty years of working experience, had recently left her job–a position of Engineer Production Manager. Respondents 6 and 7 are single and respondents 1, 2 and 3 have children.

The interviews were conducted at the offices of the respondents, with exception of three of them due to professional constrains. Each of the interviews was audio-video taped. The interview was divided in four main themes: (1) individual identification and personality characterization; (2) understanding of what is being an industrial engineer; (3) family *vs* profession and (4) final balance of industrial engineer in the feminine. Each of the four themes was divided into several sub-themes and in each sub-theme one or more questions were performed. In Table 2 are presented the sub-themes associated with each theme.

Table 8.2: **Themes and Sub-themes of the Interview**

Themes	*Sub-themes*
1. Individual identification and personality characterization	Individual identification Personality
2. What is being an industrial engineer?	Course choice: reasons for choosing engineering First experience Professional recognition: factors that influences respondents in career advancement Working relations in the organization.
3. Family *vs* profession	Family responsibility and career progression Maternity
4. Industrial engineer–final balance	Personal realization women and engineering: advices to new-graduates in industrial engineering

In the following/sub-sections in-depth analyses of some of the themes/ sub-themes of the interviews are performed, emphasizing some of the obtained answers.

First Experience

In this topic two questions were developed: (1) "when and what you felt the first time that you entered a factory?", and, (2) "can you describe your first experience as an engineer?"

The majority of the respondents have seen a factory the first time in their last year of the graduation, during a graduate training. Almost all of them faced some adaptation problems and felt some fear of failing. In Table 3 it is summarized the main parts of the answers obtained for these two questions.

Professional Recognition: Factors that Influences Career Advancement

This part starts with the reason or reasons behind the EIM engineering course preferences. It must be pointed out that the University of Minho is one of the youngest Universities of Portugal. The School of Engineering had its first's students in 1973/74. Two of the respondents (1 and 2) were the only girls in a class of 60 engineering students. In that time, the choices of engineering areas were limited, being the production and management the most appealing choice. All of them chosen to follow EIM engineering because of its management area of application and because of the opportunities of career.

***Table 8.3*: First Experience of the Respondents**

Respondent	*Related Citations*[5]
2	"It was amazing... it was something really special...into the bargain I went to a huge factory."
	"I had such a great satisfaction...the moment when I got to the factory to do a graduate training realized me, and I felt such an extraordinary satisfaction, because I knew that from that moment on I will have the opportunity to deal with papers, informations... on that moment I felt that I really had done the best and right choice for me."
6	"hey! It was very bad..."
3	"I was practically born here..."
1	"I felt a great will of coming back home (laughs)... and I had lots of times will of returning to home "
	"When I started it was not very easy because the technical staff was not abundant, especially in terms of women."
5	"I felt the fear of couldn't solve the problems...but I was already advised."
	"(...) life at industry is not easy..."
7	"The first time I saw a factory was in my graduate training."
	"After a week of graduate training, I remember of being in the lift and think: oh my Good, what I have myself in for! In addition a woman in the middle of lots of mans... It was complicated..."
	"(...) everyone started looking at me, as if they are saying: Who is she? What is she doing here?"
4	"(...) one thing is theory, and another is practice... and we cannot always apply what we learn in theory in practice."

Another's aims of this topic were related to the understanding of the type of relationship the respondents have with their counterparts, if they feel equal to a man in terms of work recognition and work opportunities and if they feel themselves favoured or disfavoured for being women. Table 4 summarizes the opinions of all the engineers concerning these issues.

Nowadays to be a woman engineer seems not to be an issue as it was twenty years ago, as the responses of respondents 2, 3, 4 and 6 indicate. Based on the answers we can say that almost all of the respondents feel some differences in treatment between a man and a woman. That difference feeling is more obvious for the engineers with more work experience. Another notorious thing seems to be the understanding that if a woman has a high performance she will certainly have the opportunity to get a better position, although she will have to give much more evidences to obtain it.

***Table 8.4*: Professional Recognition Factors**

Respondent	*Related Citations*[6]
2	"I would have liked to follow chemical engineering..."
	"There is a great difference between what people say to us and what it is in reality...I have faced serious problems for being a woman."
	"When I went to the factory there was the expectation of me or another colleague of me, that was a man, to become working in the spinning section of the factory. By that time, one of the man's of the section went to the manager of the section and told him: no woman tells me what to do, if you want to put here a chief, it must be a man."
1	"I would have liked to follow chemical engineering, maybe due to my father influence..."
	"Apart from the initial trajectory of affirmation, that is always difficult, I would say that it is easy for a woman to be recognized. I say that if the performance is high the fact of being a woman or a man is not important."
	"In the time of evaluating and measuring the performance of an engineer, I think people are much more exacting with a woman than with a man."
	"Mans have much more opportunities, namely in the attainment of management positions, sometimes having less capacities."
7	"Well, ...I would have liked to be a doctor (smiling) (...) but engineering was my choice due to the management component."
	"At the beginning I certainly would have had more career opportunities if I was a man. By that time I was rejected in an interview for being a woman."
6	"I would have liked to be a ballerina (...) however that does not proportionate, and then Economy was my choice."
	"I don't think I am favoured nor disfavoured... more than being a woman or a man, is the professionalism we have in work that can let us be recognized or not."
5	"Well, ...I would like to had been a doctor (smiling)."
	"I think that nowadays there are still some prejudices around the woman engineer."
4	"I like the industrial environment (...) due to the career opportunities."
	"I feel myself equal to a man engineer....but they see us in a different manner..."
3	"(...) I'll never know what I would like to be. (...) my options were in areas of management due to job opportunities."

"When we get to the work, we are not taken serious because of being young."

"I never felt any difference in the way people treat me in the factory because of being a woman."

Working Relations in the Organization

Knowing that the engineering world has a great influence of male engineers, it is important to: (1) understand how a woman engineer deals with this, and (2) to identify the differences and limitations a woman engineer faces to do her job.

In this sub-theme some of the questions posed were: (1) how is your relationship with your counterparts? do you try to be more "one of the boys?"; (2) which strategies do you use to assert your ideas? do you have a special way to dress or a special way to talk with your male colleagues?; (3) how do you describe your relationship with your direct chief (men/woman)?; (4) do you have subordinates? If so, which difficulties do you face in the role of chief? Is it easy to be a woman chief in an industrial environment?

The answers to those questions, which are presented in Table 5, make evident that all the respondents use some type of strategy to deal with their subordinates and with their chief. A very important thing seems to be the way a women engineer talks either to their subordinates or with the leader. More than one of the respondents emphasized the importance to get close to the subordinates. The main characteristics/adjectives highlighted by the respondents to describe the working relations were: persistence, humility, trust, team work, talent, spirit of negotiation and sincerity.

Table 8.5: Working Relations in the Organization

Respondent	*Related Citations*[7]
7	"As I am very persistent, I think that fact makes people respect me... and I am too humble. I think we must have humility..." "I try to talk to my subordinates...we must get close to them, because if they trust us we can get everything from them." "Although I have faced more difficulties at the beginning for my subordinates being mans, and I already had chiefs of line women in another company, I have obtained results more quickly with mans than with women's."
1	"I give my subordinates the opportunity to tell me they agree or not agree with me..."

	"I can not work close with nobody, if the relationship is not good."
5	"The relationship with my chief is not perfect. I have some problems with him, but I can survive with that person. I can relate myself with him in order to carry out my duties."
6	"I work very much in team, and one of the things that I am worry with is to work in team."
	"Our subordinates must recognize us (as being their chief) competences. We should not impose us as the fact of being the chief, but, above all we are a person who the others must recognize talents, and if people recognize our capacities, to be woman or men makes no difference."
2	"We must join our knowledge with the experience of people, and the best thing is to get close to them....we must not impose the situations. The situations are negotiated."
3	"I try to do things with much naturalness, and the way I am in everything, is too the way I am in my work."

Family Responsibility and Career Progression

This sub-theme was devoted to the identification of barriers in the career progression and in family responsibility. The respondents were invited to answer to the following questions: (1) how do you conciliate your professional career with family demands?; (2) how many hours do you work per day? Do you have the flexibility to arrange your working hours? Do you feel any fault feelings for the moments of unavailability and incompatibility, either in professional or personal terms?

All the respondents consider that it is very difficult to manage both career demands and family demands. All of them have or had responsibility jobs, which makes it difficult to have a regular working time. Above all they consider that it is necessary to establish an equilibrium between both demands and with that balanced it is possible to do both things quite well, although they have to do an extra effort to make the best use of their sparse time. In Table 6 the main ideas collected in this sub-theme are summarized.

Table 8.6: Family Responsibility and Career Progression

Respondent	*Related Citations*[8]
7	"I have a hour to start working, but I do not have hours to return home. The earlier that I leave work is about 8 p.m.."
1	"It does not exist super men's but it also does not exist super women's. I do not punish me...every day we take options in our life."

"It's impossible to think, that a woman engineer can have a professional career without any familiar assistance."

"Working ten to eleven hours a day, leaving home at 8:30 a.m. and returning to home at 8 p.m., without considering the foreign tours, I would say that it is not easy to manage all these requirements..."

"I wasn't a mother one hundred per cent present (...) I do not punish me. Every day we make options in our life... I think that my children have had the enough support, although we can always do more..."

5 "We do not have enough time to ourselves and to take care of our family. It is not easy..."

3 "(...) it is not easy..."

4 "We talk lots about our profession. My husband talks too about his profession. Our work never interfered in our relationship."

2 "Unfortunately the family life is much more for the women's than for the mans. My parents helped me a lot, but it was very complicated."

"Now that I left industry, I have more time to the family demands, but I have lots of longing from the industry."

"(...) we have to find a balance between the career demands and the family demands."

Personal Realization

In this topic it is pretended to recognize what the respondents like more and less in the industrial engineering profession. The thing most focused by the respondents to express what they like less to do in their job was the difficulty they have to manage the personal relationships with their counterparts. Despite this, one of the respondents appointed the people management as being the thing she likes more in her profession. Some other things pointed to express what they like to do were: the diversity of work, the team problem solution and the fact of being with people. The conflict management was pointed out to express the things they don't like to do.

Women and Engineering: Advices to New Graduates in Industrial Engineering

In Table 8.7 attempt has been made to present a summary of the main advices the respondents provided to a young industrial engineer.

***Table 8.7*: Advices to Newly-graduates in Industrial Engineering**

Respondent	*Related Citations*[9]
1	"(...) one of the teachings my mother used to say to me was: to know how to command, you must know how to do it."
	"The advice I give to a newly engineer is to begin by studying the processes (...) they must be familiar with the business, they must know what the company they work for does and what the company can do..."
	"(...) they cannot forget to study continuously..."
7	"They must have an open mind, they must be humble and they must get socialized either with the top managers or with the factory workers."
2	"To never give up studying and to keep herself up-to-date."
4	"They have to be persistent and they have to make every days efforts in order to be victorious in their professional life."
3	"To do not want to do lots of thing just to show work done, because it will be a better choice to do less things well done."

Second Year EIM Students Survey

The last part of the EGI-Woman Study until now was the development and application of a questionnaire to the students of 2nd year of EIM-UM. The main objective was to identify and recognize the students' expectation about their professional future career.

The questionnaire was divided in two parts: (1) personal and secondary academic data, and (2) reasons and perceptions. The second part of the questionnaire tries to identify the students' small academic path and their expectation about their future as EIM engineers.

The questionnaires were distributed during May of 2007, to a group of 28 second year students. The questionnaires were conducted in a traditional classroom where each student wrote his answer directly in the questionnaire paper sheet. In the group, 36 per cent were female students and 70 per cent of them with age around 19 years. Most of the female students, 31 per cent, are in the EIM course as a first choice and similar percentage of male students, however as a second choice (Figure 8.7).

Most of the students, independently of gender, have already been in contact with the industrial environment: 70 per cent and 78 per cent for female and male students, respectively. The studying visit during the secondary was the reason mentioned for 57 per cent of the female students. For male students different reasons were mentioned: 36 per cent because they have family relatives that work in the industry and 36 per cent for others reasons mainly because they work in the industry (Table 8.8).

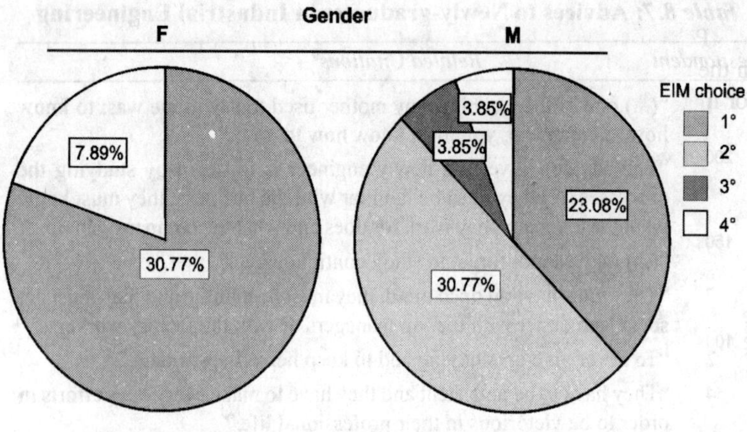

Figure 8.7.*Choice order percentage by gender: (M) male, (F) female, 2nd year EIM students*

***Table 8.8*: Contact with industrial environment: (M) male, (F) female, 2nd year EIM students**

Reasons	*Gender*	
	F (%)	*M (%)*
Studying visits during the Secondary	57.1	28.6
Visit with relatives that work in factory	42.9	35.7
Others reasons		35.7

It was asked to the students to identify the order of reasons behind the choice of the course of Engineering and Industrial Management (1st, 2nd and 3rd order, higher order means a less important motive) from a list: (1) personal and professional achievement; (2) qualification to work in an engineering profession; (3) acquisition of new knowledge in the interest area; (4) professional choices; (5) familiar pressure; (6) working in the area; (7) secondary teachers influence; (8) course status; (9) possibility to work in a profession that will personally fulfil them; (10) high percentage of graduated; (11) influence of friends and secondary colleagues; (12) course curriculum; (13) well remunerated profession; (14) mean grade.

Despite gender, the attitude and motives, behind the choice of the EIM course, follow similar choice order. The summary of the obtained results are printed in Figure 8. Notice that parents' pressure in the course choice presents insignificant influence, 14.3 per cent for female students and 6.2 per cent for male students (Figure 8b). The same opinion was recognized concerning the secondary teachers' pressure on the choice of students' graduation course.

Personal and professional achievement was the most important motive in the course choice: 66.7 per cent for female students and 76.5 per cent for male students (Figure 8.8a).

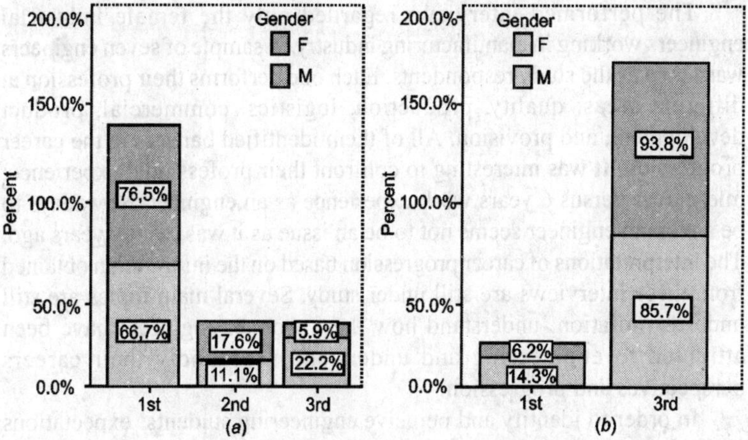

Figure 8.8: *Obtained results for: (a) personal and professional achievement and (b) familiar pressure*

Comments and On-Going Work

Engineering degree is the second most popular Portuguese university course. A distinct field in engineering is the Industrial Engineering with a crucial focus in the Portuguese manufacturing industry with a strong male culture. The Engineering and Industrial Management course of University of Minho is an exception and not the rule: 44 per cent of female graduates during the last 30 years. This paper intends to explore the main variables that influence career progression of Portuguese female industrial engineers and on the other hand, understand the actual engineering 2nd year students expectations.

The presented results are a part of a project work named EGI - Woman Study whose main goal was to contribute to a gender-specific perspective concerning Portuguese woman engineers' career progression. It was possible to identify the average profile of the female EIM of UM: 33 years old, with professional experience of 8.7 years, married, with 0.61 children. At the present time, only 45 per cent of the female engineers work in manufacturing industry, namely SME'S traditionally characterized by familiar management, with a strong investment in the Professional Formation in opposition to Post-graduation and Master degree. These results are part of a preliminary questionnaire.

Guided interviews helped and promoted a discussion of how woman engineers perceive their career progression and a conscience that, in some way, this implicates a strong commitment not always compatible with family demands.

The performed interviews regarded only the female industrial engineers working in manufacturing industry. A sample of seven engineers was taken as the study respondents. Each one performs their profession at different areas: quality, production, logistics, commercial, product development, and provision. All of them identified barriers in the career progression. It was interesting to confront their professional experience: mid-career versus 6 years work experience as an engineer. Nowadays to be a woman engineer seems not to be an issue as it was twenty years ago. The interpretations of career progression based on the information obtained from these interviews are still under study. Several main topics are still under exploration: understand how these woman engineers have been attracted to engineering and understand profoundly their careers perspectives and progression.

In order to identify and perceive engineering students' expectations about their future professional career, a questionnaire was developed and applied to the 2nd year EIM students. From the analyses of the 2nd students' answers, we can say that female students are not familiarized to the industrial environment in opposition with male students. To mention that of the male students, 36 per cent already work in an industrial environment. This can be an opportunity for the university teachers in order to fill this gap, increasing the contact with the industrial environment through the students.

Acknowledgment

The authors are grateful to R&D Centre Algoritmi for funding.

REFERENCES

Auster, E. R. & Ekstein, K. L. (2005). Professional women's mid-career satisfaction: an empirical exploration of female engineers. *Women in Management Review*, 20 (1), 4-23.

Brown, S. (2005). Communication and Women in Engineering. *Orange Journal*, 6, 4.

Evetts, J. (1997) Women and careers in engineering: management changes in the work organization. *Woman in Management Review*, 12 (6), 228-233.

Evetts, J. (1998). Managing the technology but not the organization: women and career in engineering. *Woman in Management Review*, 13 (8), 283-290.

Hansen, L. L. (2002) Rethinking the industrial relations tradition from a gender perspective: an invitation to integration. *Employee Relations*, 24 (2), 190-210.

INE (2001). Censos 2001, Instituto Nacional de Estatística, Lisboa (*in Portuguese*)

INE (2003). Anuários Estatísticos Regionais 2001-2003, Instituto Nacional de Estatística, Lisboa (*in Portuguese*)

Ismail, M. (2003). Men and women engineers in a large industrial organization: interpretation of career progression based on subjective-career experience. *Women in Management Review*, 18 (1/2), 60-67.

Lawthom, R., Petterson, M., West, M. & Staniforth, D. (1996) Women managers' views of manufacturing nice work?. *Women in Management Review*, 11 (6), 3-10.

Leão, C. P., Pimentel, C., & Rodrigues, C.S. (2007). Being a Female Engineer Student: Lessons from the Industrial Engineering. In Furtado, C. S. et al. (Eds.), *International Conference on Engineering Education – ICEE2007* (6 pp.). Universidade de Coimbra: iNEER.

Newman, S. (1998) Where have all the engineers gone?. Education & Training, 40 (9), 398-404.

Petroni, A. (2000) Myths and misconceptions in current engineers' management practices. Team Performance Management: An International Journal, 6 (1/2), 15-24.

Pimentel, C., Leão, C. P., & Rodrigues, C. S. (2006a, Outubro). A Engenharia Industrial no Feminino, *I Workshop de Engenharia Industrial da UMinho*, 1, 16-17. (*in Portuguese*)

Pimentel, C., Leão, C. P., & Rodrigues, C. S. (2006b). A Mulher e sua Carreira na Engenharia Industrial: estudo piloto, In Ayala Calvo, J. C. et al. (Eds.), *Conocimiento, Innovatión y Emprendedores - Camino al Futuro*, (pp. 187-199). Universidad de La Rioja. (*in Portuguese*)

Powell, A., Bagilhole, B., Dainty, A., & Neale, R. (2004). Does the engineering culture in UK Higher Education advance women's careers? *Equal Opportunities International*, 23, (7/8), 21-38.

Powell, G. N. & Butterfield, D. A. (2003). Gender, gender identity, and aspirations to top management. *Women in Management Review*, 18 (1/2), 88-96.

Preston, A. E. (1994). Why have all the women gone? A study of women from the science and engineering professions. *The American Economic Review*, 84 (5), 1446-1462.

Santos, G. G. & Cabral-Cardoso, C. (2003) Career and work-family relationships among academics: an exploratory study. *Comportamento Organizacional e Gestão*, 9, 2, 213-229.

Shackleton, L., Riordan, R. & Simonis, D. (2006). Gender and the transformation agenda on the South African higher education. *Women's Studies International Forum*, 29, 572-580.

9.

DOMESTIC VIOLENCE
A Violation of Human Rights of Women

VIBHUTI PATEL

'Violence against women is perhaps the most shameful human rights violation. And it is perhaps the most pervasive. It knows no boundaries of geography, culture or wealth. As long as it continues, we cannot claim to be making real progress towards equality, development and peace.'

Kofi Annan, Secretary-General of the United Nations

Introduction

The concept of human rights evolved largely from ideas of western political theory about rights of individuals to autonomy and freedom. Thus the international human rights law evolved to protect individuals' autonomy vis-à-vis the state. And, it held states responsible for individual rights and accountable for abuse of those rights.

The development of human rights has been expressed in terms of 'generations': The civil and political rights, as the first generation rights; economic, social and cultural rights as the second generation rights; and the group or people's rights, which are recently defined as the third generation rights.

Indeed the development of human rights movement, right from the Universal Declaration of Human Rights (1948), and the three generations of rights show that rights are defined as 'belonging to all human beings' irrespective of gender. However, though international law is gender neutral in theory, in practice it constituted men and women into separate spheres of existence—public and private, respectively. Thus men exist as public, legal entities that enjoy civil and political rights and in a way define the nature of rights discourse. Women's existence, on the other hand, is 'privatized', thus, seen as existing outside the purview of the state's obligation. Often women's exclusion from the human rights practice and discourse, their relegation to the private, has been justified on grounds of social and cultural specificity of region or a group. Thus, social and cultural norms, which become grounds for respective states' consistent relegation of women to private sphere, results in international law being either reinforcing or replicating exclusion of women's human rights abuses from the public sphere. The effects of this public/private divide in the international law are more evident in domestic violence, which literally happens in the private. Many laws are gender neutral; however, their application is gender biased. (Agnes, 1988).

Moreover the economic and social context of its (laws) application had not been considered seriously by both the governmental and at the same time non-governmental organizations, all over the world.

Harms suffered by women at the hands of private individuals or within the family had been placed outside of the conceptual framework of international human rights. Feminists have argued that a failing of international human rights norms is in not recognizing the 'gendered' consequences of their application they render invisible, particularly problems suffered by women.

Moreover, in addition to holding states responsible for taking action against the human rights abuses occurring in the private sphere, feminist human rights thinkers argued that domestic violence should be conceived as a form of torture. They aver that though torture with cases of disappearance and murder, is widely recognized as a core violation of human rights, that inequality on the basis of sex is widely condemned, why is torture on basis of sex in the form of rape, domestic battering and pornography not seen as a violation of human rights?

The feminist analysis examines characteristics of domestic violence, in the light of international legal understanding, of what constitutes torture and cruelty, the inhuman and degrading treatment it entails. They affirm that process, purposes, and consequences of torture and that of domestic violence are startlingly similar. That whether torture committed in domestic context or that inflicted officially, does not reduce its intensity of violence, nor does it demand different standards of judgments and actions on part of state.

The existing international human rights instruments, has both a separate provision for women's rights (i.e. Convention on the Elimination of All Forms of Discrimination against Women, CEDAW), and other general mechanisms which stress formal equality of women and men. While this development is important, it is not adequate to address issue of women's subordination. Recently, non-governmental organizations have begun to document women's abuse within the context of traditional human rights law. (Mathur, 2004).

These efforts are based on and addressed within that framework of whose 'very structure is built on the silence of women'. The fundamental problem women face is not discriminatory treatment vis-à-vis men. Rather it is necessary to raise a larger problem: that, women are in inferior position because they have no power either in public or private worlds, or in international human rights law. Thus problem of domestic abuse as a human rights issue will have to be seen as a part of larger reality of subordination of women—their powerlessness in terms of defining the human rights discourse.

What are the Signs of Domestic Violence?

Destructive criticism and verbal abuse: shouting/mocking/accusing/ name calling/verbally threatening.

Pressure tactics: sulking, threatening to withhold money, disconnect the telephone, take the car away, commit suicide, take the children away, report you to welfare agencies unless you comply with his demands regarding bringing up the children, lying to your friends and family about you, telling you that you have no choice in any decisions.

Disrespect: persistently putting you down in front of other people, not listening or responding when you talk, interrupting your telephone calls, taking money from your purse without asking, refusing to help with childcare or housework.

Breaking trust: lying to you, withholding information from you, being jealous, having other relationships, breaking promises and shared agreements.

Isolation: monitoring or blocking your telephone calls, telling you where you can and cannot go, preventing you from seeing friends and relatives.

Harassment: following you, checking up on you, opening your mail, repeatedly checking to see who has telephoned you, embarrassing you in public.

Threats: making angry gestures, using physical size to intimidate, shouting you down, destroying your possessions, breaking things, punching walls, wielding a knife or a gun, threatening to kill or harm you and the children.

Sexual violence: using force, threats or intimidation to make you perform sexual acts, having sex with you when you don't want to have sex, any degrading treatment based on your sexual orientation.

Physical violence: punching, slapping, hitting, biting, pinching, kicking, pulling hair out, pushing, shoving, burning, strangling.

Denial: saying the abuse doesn't happen, saying you caused the abusive behaviour, being publicly gentle and patient, crying and begging for forgiveness, saying it will never happen again.

Domestic Violence in India

NFHS II data on domestic violence are quite revealing.

***Table 9.1*: Percentage Beaten or Physically Mistreated since Age 15**

India / State	*Percentage beaten or physically mistreated since age 15 by:*		
	Husband	*In-laws*	*Other Person*
India	18.8	1.8	3.1
Andhra Pr.	21.2	2.8	2.0
Kerala	7.5	0.2	3.2
Uttar Pr.	20.8	1.9	2.2
Bihar	24.9	2.4	3.1
Rajasthan	9.8	1.5	0.9
Madhya Pr.	19.7	1.9	1.6
Orissa	22.9	3.0	7.9
Punjab	11.7	1.3	4.4
Haryana	10.8	2.3	3.4
J & K	15.4	4.8	7.1
Tamil Nadu	36.0	0.5	9.0

Source: NFHS, 1998-99, IIPS, Mumbai, 2000.

A nationwide survey shows that 52 per cent of women suffer at least one incident of physical or psychological violence in their lifetime (ICRW, 2004).

Voilence Against Women (VAW) in the personal life—manifested in the form of pre-birth elimination of girls, female infanticide, dowry murders, forced polyandry, trafficking of girls and women and incest is increasingly accepted as a serious social problem (Mathur, 2004).

The Indian feminists have asserted that the pillars of patriarchy—namely family, kinship and community organizations, religious and cultural organizations and state—covertly and overtly glorify widow burning and witch hunts of widows, divorcees and deserted women, all in an effort to exercise total control over women's sexuality, fertility and labour, and also to usurp their property and land rights (Lohia, 1998).

A study by the Centre for Women's Development Studies says every hour five women face cruelty at home. (CWDS, 2002). Other studies reveal that every six hours, somewhere in India, a young married woman is burned alive, beaten to death, or driven to commit suicide. (ICRW, 2004). The NFHS (II) reported one in five married women in India experiences domestic violence from the age of 15. It is estimated that more than 15,000 women suffer from dowry-related violence every year. Analysis by the National Crime Records Bureau shows that in 1999, cruelty by husbands and dowry-related violence together accounted for 36 per cent of the total crimes against women (Jagori, 2003). According to the Indian National Crime Records Bureau's unique 'crime clock 2005' which tracked criminal activities over 2004, the country reported one molestation every 15 minutes; one crime against women every 3 minutes; one dowry death every 77 minutes; one rape every 29 minutes; one murder every 16 minutes; and one sexual harassment case every 53 minutes. Recent studies show that even in the most progressive state in the country, Kerala, crimes against women have risen four-fold in the past seven years. Foeticide is on the rise — there were 967 girls for every 1,000 boys in the 0-6 age group in 2001 as opposed to 976 in 1971 (Patel, 2006). 75 per cent of women who are victims of domestic violence do not seek help due to concern for family 'honour' (ICRW, 2004). Data from NFHS (II) show that 56 per cent women justified beatings by husbands.

What came to be known in India as 'dowry deaths' – the killing of young married women for the 'dowry' or money/goods they brought with them at the time of marriage. This was also the beginning of a process of learning for women: most protests were directed at the State. Because women were able to mobilise support, the State responded, seemingly positively, by changing the law on rape and dowry, making both more stringent. (Ghaswala, 1998). This seemed, at that time, like a great victory. It was only later that the knowledge began to sink in that mere changes in the law meant little, unless there was a will and a machinery to implement these. And that, the root of the problem of discrimination against women lay not only in the law, or with the State, but was much more widespread.

In the early campaigns, groups learnt from day to day experiences that targeting the State was not enough and that survivors also needed support (Patel, 2002). So a further level of work was needed: awareness raising or conscientisation so that violence against women could be prevented, rather than only dealt with after it had happened. Legal aid and counseling centres were set up, and attempts were made to establish women's shelters (Dabir, 2000).

The Constitution of India guarantees the following Fundamental Rights that guide us to challenge domestic violence.

Article 14 - equal rights and opportunities for men and women in the political, economic and social sphere

Article 15 - prohibition of discrimination on the grounds of sex, religion, caste etc

Article 15(3) - empowers the State to take affirmative measures for women

Article 16 - provides for equality of opportunities in the matter of public appointments

Historical Background to Campaign for Protection of Women and Children from Domestic Violence Act

In 1983, domestic violence was recognised as a specific criminal offence by the introduction of section 498-A into the Indian Penal Code. This section deals with cruelty by a husband or his family towards a married woman. Four types of cruelty are dealt with by this law:

- Conduct that is likely to drive a woman to suicide,
- Conduct which is likely to cause grave injury to the life, limb or health of the woman,
- Harassment with the purpose of forcing the woman or her relatives to give some property, or
- Harassment because the woman or her relatives is unable to yield to demands for more money or does not give some property.
- What are the forms of "cruelty" recognised by the Courts?
- Persistent denial of food,
- Insisting on perverse sexual conduct,
- Constantly locking a woman out of the house,
- Denying the woman access to children, thereby causing mental torture,
- Physical violence,
- Taunting, demoralising and putting down the woman with the intention of causing mental torture,
- Confining the woman at home and not allowing her normal social intercourse,
- Abusing children in their mother's presence with the intention of causing her mental torture,
- Denying the paternity of the children with the intention of inflicting mental pain upon the mother, and
- Threatening divorce unless dowry is given.

What is A "Matrimonial Home"? What Rights do Women have in their Matrimonial Home?

The matrimonial home is the household a woman shares with her husband; whether it is rented, officially provided, or owned by the husband or his relatives. A woman has the right to remain in the matrimonial home along with her husband as long as she is married, though there is no definite law regarding this right. If a woman is being pressurised to leave the matrimonial home, she can ask the Court for an injunction or "restraining order" protecting her from being thrown out.

This can usually be obtained quite easily. It is generally advisable not to leave the matrimonial home; it is easier to get a court order preventing a woman being thrown out than to get an order enforcing her right to return to it once she has left or been thrown out.

What is an 'Injunction' and How Does it Apply to Domestic Violence Cases?

An injunction is a court order directing a person to do or not to do something. A woman has a lot of flexibility regarding what she can request the Court to order. For instance, if she is being stalked by somebody (including her husband), she can obtain injunctions against the person coming near her home or place of work, or even telephoning her.

What can be Done in the Case of Dowry-related Harassment or Dowry Death?

Section 498-A of the Indian Penal Code covers dowry-related harassment. As with other provisions of criminal law, a woman can use the threat of going to court to deter this kind of harassment. The Indian Penal Code also addresses dowry deaths in section 304-B. If a woman dies of "unnatural causes" within seven years of marriage and has been harassed for dowry before her death, the Courts will assume that it is a case of dowry death. The husband or in-laws will then have to prove that their harassment was not the cause of her death. A dowry death is punishable by imprisonment of at least seven years. When filing an FIR (First Information Report), in a case where a woman is suspected to have been murdered after a history of torture due to dowry demands, the complaint should be filed under section 304-B rather than under section 306, which deal with abetment to suicide. Section 306 should be invoked when a woman commits suicide because of dowry-related harassment.

Can You Refuse to Have Sex with Your Husband? Is there a Law on Marital Rape?

- Since India does not have a law on marital rape, even if a woman's husband has sexual intercourse with her without her consent, he cannot be prosecuted for rape. However, excessive and unreasonable demands for sex, or demands for unnatural sex have been considered forms of cruelty and may entitle a woman to a divorce.

- If a woman is judicially separated, her husband cannot have sexual intercourse with her without her consent. If he does, he can be prosecuted under section 376-A of the IPC. Note that consent under pressure (e.g. because of threats to injure or to stop paying maintenance) is not considered valid.

What can A Woman do to Prevent Domestic Violence?

- One option is to get the woman's husband to execute a "bond to keep peace", or a "bond of good behaviour "through the Executive, Magistrate who can order the husband to put a stop to domestic violence. The husband can also be asked to deposit securities (i.e. money or property) that will be forfeited if he continues to act violently.

Protection of Women from Domestic Violence Act, 2005

- Recognition of the right to residence
- Provision for the appointment of Protection officers and the recognition of Service Providers
- Trainings for Protection Officers and Judges
- Awareness creation
- Budgetary allocation

Distinction between Civil and Criminal Law

- The distinction between civil and criminal law is a basic part of the Indian legal system. Civil laws deal with the rights and obligations of people and what is needed to protect them, while criminal law deals with offences and their punishment. In a criminal offence, the State takes upon itself the responsibility to investigate and collect evidence (through the police), to fight the case in court (through a public prosecutor) and enforce the punishment. Robbery, murder and kidnapping are examples of criminal offences. Criminal offences are dealt with by the Indian Penal Code (IPC).
- The procedure by which a criminal trial is conducted is quite different from the processes involved in a civil trial. An important difference is that the "standard of proof" required in criminal cases is much higher than in civil cases. Since criminal law is centrally linked with issues of punishment, allegations and facts must be proved "beyond reasonable doubt", so that innocent people are not punished. In civil cases, the courts scrutinise the "balance of probabilities" before deciding in whose favour to make a judgment.
- Both civil and criminal laws apply in case of DV.

- Inflicting physical violence on a wife or daughter-in-law as well as subjecting her to cruelty - physical, mental, sexual or emotional and economic - in a marriage is not only a civil offence and provides ground for divorce (a "matrimonial offence"), but is also a criminal offence under the Indian Penal Code, for which a person can be imprisoned. The laws dealing with marital abuse have been made very stringent through amendments in the Indian Penal Code and the Evidence Act (Jaising, 2001).

Implementation of Laws

To make the laws concerning women the state needs to strengthen the machinery for their implementation. Important steps in this regard are:

- Appointment and empowerment of statutory authorities at the central and state levels.
- Preparation of policy statements by such statutory authorities enclosing clear guidelines on the manner of implementation of the law such as code of conduct to be followed by functionaries, provision of best practices, etc.
- Evaluation and auditing the effectiveness of particular laws and the periodic publication and submission of compliance reports with a central statutory authority.
- Upgrading the quality of statistics maintained on women. Each statutory body to conduct yearly surveys in their particular field.
- Building capacity of the functionaries appointed under the law such as statutory authorities, police personnel, health personnel, counselors, etc by conducting regular trainings on the law including aspects of gender sensitisation as well as improving practices followed by them.
- Introducing mechanisms to ensure quicker and simpler procedures for women to obtain legal redress to their problems. This would include the provision of legal aid, assistance at the time of registering complaints, making applications, provision of information on the legal options available to the women, etc.
- Raising awareness of the services and support available to women facing discrimination, from both governmental and non governmental sources.
- Ensuring adequate representation of women in statutory advisory bodies/ policy making bodies.
- Sustained interactions between different governmental agencies to promote multi agency working.

- Allocation of adequate budgets for the proper functioning of the statutory authorities.
- Constant monitoring and auditing of accounts by a central authority.
- Submission of financial report to the Auditor General for it to be placed on the floor of the Parliament or State Legislature as the case may be.

Dilasa-crisis Centre for Treatment and Counseling of Women Victims of Violence in a Public Hospital

With the aim to sensitize the public health system to gender and violence issues, CEHAT and the Public Health Department of the Brihanmumbai Municipal Corporation have established Dilaasa at K B Bhabha Hospital, Bandra West. Dilaasa means Reassurance and it seeks to provide social and psychological support to women survivors of domestic violence.

This Centre has been set up in a peripheral public hospital in collaboration with Brihanmumbai Municipal Corporation (BMC). CEHAT will continue to provide support in terms of counseling and allied services to survivors of domestic violence for the next 3 years. The crisis centre model is being replicated in two other hospitals in Mumbai and one district hospital. In addition the activities will focus on prevention of violence against women; community based support system for women survivors of violence, research on violence faced by health care professionals and the violence which exists within the system. It will also upscale the training function through regular 'Training of Trainers' programme and a course for nurses on 'Gender Based Violence and their Role in Responding to the Survivors of Violence'. (Deoshali, Maghnani & Malik, 2005).

Dilaasa believes that every woman has a right to a safe home, right to a life without violence. There is no excuse to domestic violence.

Objectives

1. Provide social and psychological support to women coming to the centre.
2. Sensitize the hospital staff to gender and violence issues.
3. Train the hospital staff of the casualty and various out-patient departments in identifying women facing domestic violence.
4. Create a training cell in the hospital, which would train the other staff of the hospital.
5. Network with other organizations working on women's issues for mutual support and sharing.

Services

1. Counseling: Trained counselors help women to build their strength so that they can rebuild their lives.
2. Legal aid: Through our collaboration with Majlis and Lawyers Collective, we provide legal aid to women. Lawyers are available twice a week at the centre.
3. Temporary shelter: There is provision for temporary shelter for a short period at two shelters in the city. The hospital also provides 24 hour shelter under medical observation.

Activities

1. Training: is one of the ongoing activities of the centre. The hospital staff is being sensitized to gender issues so that they are able to screen women survivors of domestic violence and refer them to the centre. A group of hospital staff has been trained as key trainers. A core group of 12 has emerged as the training cell of the hospital. They are now conducting training for the rest of the hospital staff. The core group also has intensive discussions/debates and mock sessions to review their role and develop further as trainers.
2. Research: A few short studies were conducted in the initial phase to understand the hospital systems and procedures. Every year we would analyze the counseling process based on the case records of the women registered at Dilaasa.'
3. Documentation: Every activity of the centre and its processes are being documented to enable us to evaluate the work of the centre.
4. Networking: Dilaasa is networking with women's organizations, legal aid agencies, shelters and other groups working with women survivors of domestic violence for mutual support, referral and sharing.

Conclusion

There is a need for an affirmative action to protect girls, young and elderly women from domestic violence and establish human rights for women. It must address the following areas of intervention.

1. **Improve Women's Economic Capacities**: Improve women's access to and control of income and assets, recognize her shared right to the family home, and incorporate the principle of division of community property in divorce laws. Productive assets and property are critical to strengthening the economic and social status of women, providing income opportunities and improved respect for women outside marriage and family.

2. **Strengthen and expand Training and sensitization Programs**: Programme designed to train, sensitize and inter-link those working at critical entry points to identify and treat abused women should be a priority, with one aim being increased accountability across institutions. Such programmes should be tailored for medical personnel, the judiciary, counseling and other support service providers.
3. **Dilaasa** model of one stop crisis centre housed in the public hospital to facilitate collective intervention of medical staff, police and NGO must be replicated through out the country.
4. **Effective use of the Media to build Public Awareness**: Mobilization of communities around campaigns such as that for "Zero Tolerance of Violence" requires improved skills and capacity among NGOs to enter new forms of dialogue with journalists and media personnel to heighten awareness of human rights and their significance for addressing domestic violence.
5. **Programmes designed for the batterers**: must be introduced in both the state and voluntary sectors. In order to promote a holistic approach to prevention as well as intervention, the deficiency in programmes designed for men needs to be addressed.
6. **Addressing Domestic Violence through Education**: Prevention of domestic violence ultimately depends upon changing the norms of society regarding violence as means of conflict resolution and traditional attitudes about gender. To achieve this, there must be introduction of gender and human rights in the curricula of schools, universities, professional colleges, and other training colleges. Along with this, there must be recognition and commitment to the principle of free compulsory primary and secondary education for girls.

REFERENCES

Agnes, Flavia, 1988, "Our Fight Against Wife beating" in Rehana Ghadially *Women in Indian Society-A Reader*, Sage Publications, Delhi.

CWDS Crimes Against Women: Bondage and Beyond, Centre for Women's Development Studies, 2002, New Delhi.

Deoshali, Padma, Purnima Maghnani and Dr. Seema Malik, 2005, *Establishing Dilaasa-Documenting the Challenges*, Cehat.

Ghaswala, Bakula, 1998, " 'Astitva' Battles Domestic violence" in Shirin Kudchedkar and Sabiha al-Issa, *Violence Against Women and Women Against Vilolence*, Pencraft International, Delhi.

ICRW Domestic Violence in India: A Summary Report of a Multi-site Household Survey, New Delhi, 2004.

Jagori, "Didn't We Ban It 40 Years Ago?" (2003), New Delhi www.jagori.org

Lohia, Shaila, " Domestic Violence in rural Areas", in Shirin Kudchedkar and Sabiha al-Issa *Violence Against Women and Women Against Vilolence*, Pencraft International, Delhi, 1998.

Mathur, Kanchan, (2004), *Countering Gender Violence: Initiatives Towards Collective Action in Rajasthan* Thousand Oaks (California), Sage Publications, London.

Dabir, Neela, (2000), *Women in Distress*, Rawat Publications, Jaipur.

Jaising, Indira (ed.), (2001), *Law of Domestic Violence: A User's Manual for Women*, The Lawyers Collective, Delhi.

Patel, Vibhuti, (2002), *Women's Challenges of the New Millennium*, Gyan Publications, Delhi.

Patel, Tulsi (ed.), (2006), *Sex-Selective Abortion in India*, Gender, Society and New Reproductive Technologies, Sage Publications.

10.

DEVELOPMENT OF WOMEN'S EDUCATION IN BANGLADESH

SAMINA SULTANA, KHANDOKER MAHMUDUR RAHMAN AND RUBA RUMMANA

Introduction

Challenges to a developing country are manifold. While suffering from lack of capacity to utilize natural resources, shortages of human expertise, and numerous economic challenges, a developing country also bears the burden of numerous social challenges. As a result, the problem of priority setting becomes a dilemma for policy makers. Social and economic disparities between genders take questionable priority as families strive hard to have two square meals a day. Amid this challenging socio-economic backdrop, we are going to examine how a developing country like Bangladesh has faced the challenge of development in education sector, particularly education of women.[7]

The importance of education encompasses almost all sectors of a developing country. The ultimate result of education can be observed in terms of productivity enhancement via development of social capital. Therefore, the productivity gap between genders would exist if there is disparity in education between genders. Since independence in 1971, Bangladesh Government experimented with different approaches towards development of women education. We can broadly divide these efforts into two eras, pre-'90 and post-'90 eras.

Challenges

Right after independence, like any other new nation, the government had to fight against piled up problems of the past in various sectors. Enormous industrial and agricultural challenges, coupled with unprecedented famine threw the government into gigantic challenges. The social problem like gender disparity in education could hardly be imagined to have priority when government was fighting famine and facing teething problems of politically stabilizing a country at its onset. Budget allocations for various sectors were mostly gender-blind, therefore, significant and specific allocation particularly contributing to women education cannot be traced.[9] Even though it was evident from numerous social researches that gender discrimination exists in education, particularly parents were more interested to spend for boys' rather than for girls' when it comes to education[10], probably the insurmountable political and economics challenges outweighed the government's priority in adopting policy measures to reduce gender discrimination in education.

Therefore, pre-90 era, if anything can be seen as development of women education, could only be termed as "moral persuasions" to encourage families to send their daughters to school. No specific budget or other policy tools applications could be traced. Even though a number of educational institutions were established, e.g., girls' schools and colleges, etc.; however, no trace of long run policy measures could be seen.

In 1990, delegates from 155 countries including Bangladesh, as well as representatives from some 150 organizations agreed at the 'World Conference on Education for All' in Jomtien, Thailand, held by UNESCO, to universalize primary education and massively reduce illiteracy before the end of the decade. 'The World Declaration on Education for All: Meeting Basic Learning Needs', and 'Framework for Action: Meeting Basic Learning Needs' were signed. These agreements, most likely, did have significant impact on subsequent government policy measures regarding universal primary education, with specific policy measures to improve women education. It is evident that the post-'90 era is marked by active government policy towards universalizing primary education, and special emphasis was given on girls' education through various supportive tools. These agreements were synergized by agreements reached at the UN Millennium Summit in September 2000, where Millennium Development Goal (MDG) was born as a common framework of universal development goals. The MDGs reflect the actions and targets contained in the Millennium Declaration that was adopted by 189 nations.

The key challenges to women's education, therefore, were of two primary dimensions. First, to increase the rate of enrolment of girls at educational institutions, second, to hold them on track, i.e., to reduce drop-out rate in order to maintain a consistent rate of enrolment all through the subsequent stages.[1]

It is worth mentioning that, the government correctly identified that gender discrimination in education was partly due to economic reasons, and partly due to social reasons – emanating, again, from economic reasons. In a traditional Bengali family set-up, man is seen as the leader, decision-maker, and bread-earner of the family (this assumption probably holds good for other countries as well in the Indian sub-continent). Thus, if the bread-earner has anything left after spending for his family to be spared for his children's education, he will most likely choose to educate his boy(s), and not his daughter(s). Alternatively, if daughter(s) is(are) ever sent to educational institutions, she will not progress farther than the boy(s) as family supports educational advancement more of boys than girls. It is not because he is discriminating based on his personal liking or disliking of boys vs. girls, rather it is more because of his perception based on the rationale that the boy has to get along with the rest of the society and make himself able to earn, for that the boy(s) needs more education than girls! However, recent data show that this trend is gradually diminishing and the difference between expenditure for boys and expenditure for girls are reducing (see Table 10.5).[2]

Development in a Planned Way

Out of eight goals in MDG, the second and third goals are relevant to our analysis in order to understand the development of women's education in Bangladesh. The second goal of MDG is aimed at attaining universal primary education for all by 2015. The third goal is aimed at promoting equality between men and women, and to empower women. The third goal is, actually, partially relevant because consideration of gender-equality in education will only be applicable to our analysis.[3]

Meeting the second goal of MDG is indicated by three major dimensions: (a) Net Enrollment Rate in Primary Education (this rate is defined as the number of children aged 6-10 years currently enrolled in primary schools), (b) Drop-out and completion Rate (drop-out rate is the rate of students enrolled in school but not completing the grade); (c) Adult literacy rate (ages 15+ years). The youth literacy rate reflects the effectiveness of primary education programs over time. Because of insufficient data for this indicator, the adult literacy rate for people over the age of 15 is used to measure progress. According to the MDG Mid-term Progress Report published in 2007, the adult literacy rate has increased from 37 per cent in 1990 to 54 per cent in 2006. Bangladesh must intensify its efforts urgently if it is to achieve its target of 100 per cent adult literacy by 2015.[3]

To achieve the MDG target, Bangladesh has to increase the primary school enrolment rate from about 73.3 per cent (in 1992) to 100 per cent by 2015, and raise the primary school completion rate from 62 per cent (in 1994) to 100 per cent by 2015. Bangladesh has also to reduce the drop-out rates from 38 per cent in (1994) to zero per cent by 2015. In addition to MDG goals for education, Bangladesh has to reduce the gender gap in enrollment as well. The goal for Government of Bangladesh is to attain a ratio of female to male at 50:50 by 2015.

To achieve these ends, government has taken a number of policy measures in line with MDG targets. The Compulsory Primary Education Act, 1990, has made primary education (Class I to V) in Bangladesh free and compulsory for all children. In the context of constitutional provisions and the Primary Education (compulsory) Act 1990, the national strategy for achieving the goal of universal primary education is anchored on the following principles:

(*i*) "That no child be deprived of education for lack of teachers, learning materials and adequate space;

(*ii*) That no child be subject to disparity of access to primary education arising from gender, income, family, culture or ethnic differences and geographic remoteness;

(*iii*) (To ensure) the quality and relevance of primary education by intensifying efforts to improve learning contents and materials and carry out reforms in the primary education system."

As a result, the education sector has been receiving the highest budgetary allocation in recent years - the proportion has been roughly around 14 per cent of total budget allocation during 2002-2003 to 2006-2007.[4] Table 10.1 reveals this fact.

***Table 10.1*: Allocation to Education Sector in National Budget (2002-03 to 2006-07)**

National Budget for Financial Year	*Total Allocation to Education as % of Budget Allocation to All Sectors*
2002-2003	15.17
2003-2004	13.69
2004-2005	12.80
2005-2006	14.91
2006-2007	15.62

Source: Ministry of Finance, Finance Division - Annual Financial Statement (2004-2005), Budget Summary, 2005-2006 and National Budget Summary, 2006.

Bangladesh, so far, has recorded success in increasing primary school enrolment. This includes creating gender balance, which is due largely to the introduction of stipend programs, free supply of textbooks, tuition fee waiver and cash incentives provided by the government. At the primary education level, the net enrolment ratio increased to 87.2 per cent in 2005 against the target of 79.2 per cent (according to Mid-term MDG Progress Report, 2007, UNDP). This is up from 60.5 per cent in 1990. If that trend continues, Bangladesh will meet its target of 100 per cent net enrolment in primary education by 2012, three years ahead of 2015. Another survey, by Bangladesh Bureau of Statistics shows that the primary enrollment rate in 2005 was actually 80.4. Apart from variations in publicly available data, we may conclude that no matter how much success has been achieved in primary enrollment, the low rate of completion rate may act against this success and pull the adult literacy rate down, as will be explained soon in the following sections.

Table 10.2 summarizes the trend in net enrolment ratio at primary and secondary levels.

***Table 10.2*: Percentage of Children Enrolled in Schools, 2005**

Gender	*Children, 6-10 years (primary)*		*Children, 11-15 years (secondary)*	
	2000	2005	2000	2005
Both sexes	75.1	80.4	65.3	69.9
Boys	74	79.50	59.4	66
Girls	76.4	81.3	71.5	73.9

Source: Household Income and Expenditure Survey, Bangladesh Bureau of Statistics

It is evident that, enrollment rate is rising for both sexes and more girls are enrolling than boys. As the rate is defined as the number of children aged 6-10 who are currently enrolled in primary schools, the faster increase in population of that age group may pull down the rate by the slower increase in students' enrollment.

Table 10.3 that summarizes the trend of enrollment ratio by gender.

***Table 10.3*: Enrollment Ratio by Gender**

Indicators	*Base year (1992)*	*Current Status (2005)*	*Target (2015)*
Ratio of girls to boys in *primary* education	45:55	53:47	50:50
Ratio of girls to boys in *secondary* education	34:66	50:50	50:50
Ratio of girls to boys in *tertiary* education	25:75	36:64	50:50
Ratio of literate women to men, 20-24 years old	42:58	46:54 (2002 data)	50:50

Source: MDG Mid-term Progress Report, 2007, Government of Bangladesh

It is evident from the table that for primary enrollment, boys have fallen behind girls (the ratio of girls to boys stands at 53:47). The enrollment target has been met at secondary level, achieving a ratio of 50:50. However, in tertiary education, girls are way behind boys, even though the ration improved from 25:75 in the base year (1992) to 36:64 in 2005. This trend, coupled with high drop-out rates, has resulted in slow improvement in adult literacy rate.[11]

The enrollment scenario would be clear from the drop-out/completion rate. The following table summarizes the gender-wise drop-out/completion rate, based on latest available data from Bangladesh Bureau of Educational Information and Statistics:

***Table 10.4*: Dropout and Completion Rate (2001)**

Grade/cycle	*Dropout Rate (%)*		*Completion Rate (%)*	
	Total	*Female*	*Total*	*Female*
Primary (Grade 1-5)	33	NA	67	NA
Junior Secondary (Grade 6-8)	19.8	72.2	81.2	22.8
Secondary (Grade 9-10)	52.9	54.8	47.1	45.2
High Secondary (Grade 11-12)	42.7	41.5	57.3	58.5

Source: Bangladesh Bureau of Educational Information and Statistics, Nov. 2002

It is evident from the Table 10.4 that as one moves from lower to higher grades drop out problem goes upward. In 2001, the dropout rate is substantial for girls in the junior secondary section. This is a critical area in which Bangladesh's performance is poor and marked by a lack of credible and representative information. A 2005 baseline survey on primary education by the Ministry of Primary and Mass Education, Government of Bangladesh, shows that about 53 per cent of school entrants of primary school age continue to Grade 5.

Getting back to the issue of female drop-outs, there could be a question why girls are dropping out as they move forward. The answer could be found in socio-economic status of women and priority of families in the past to educate their boys and not advancing girls for further studies.[6,8] However, the recent data suggest that the trend is changing for better (see Table 10.3). The monetary cost for education, in the form of books, tuition and transportation explain this divergence between genders. Another reason could be, that only primary education was free at some point of time in the past, so families could not afford to send their daughters to school.

This gap in gender enrollment, partially, was addressed by various NGOs (Non-Government Organizations).[12] The most prominent NGO contributing to this sector is Bangladesh Rural Advancement Committee (BRAC). They operate schools that function under a non-formal primary education model. These schools, operating under two different models, admit students of 8-10 years. Eligible children were those who had never enrolled in any school or who had dropped out of the formal school system. These children attend 4 years of primary school and cover the entire 5-year curriculum (Grades 1-5) with all the competencies set by the National Curriculum Textbook Board (NCTB) of Bangladesh. Even though NGOs were found active in providing free education in line with government initiatives, however, their effort in secondary education is still lacking. In 2002, government initiated the "Secondary Student Stipend Program" to uplift girls from this situation.

The objective of the program can be categorized under short term and long term. Its short term objectives are increasing female enrolment in grade VI-X, assisting them to pass the board exams, growing their interest in studies and preventing them from early marriages. Under long term objectives of empowerment of women, reducing gender disparity, and increasing the social status of females and finally recognizing the girl-child as an economic asset are laid down. Even when the girls continue their secondary education, their incompetence prevents them from continuing further studies resulting in drop-out. However, there are signs that this attitude of discrimination is waning. The following table (Table 10.5), showing gender-wise expenditure for education, exhibits minor difference in private expenditures between genders.

It is evident from the Table 5 that, average private expenditure per primary student varies widely between types of institutions. Overall, the average annual per student expenditure is the highest in case of government primary schools (Tk.2,554) and the lowest (Tk.1,682) in case of community schools. Except in the case of community schools, guardians living in urban areas spend on primary education significantly larger amounts per student per annum compared to guardians living in the rural areas. Per student annual expenditure in non-government schools and madrashas (schools of religious stream) located in urban areas is significantly larger compared to non-government institutions in rural areas.

An important observation from Table 10.5 is that, per primary student average private annual expenditure does not vary much between boys and girls (in both rural and urban areas), regardless of the type of institution. Per girl student expenditure is somewhat higher compared to boys, particularly in urban areas for most types of institutions. The findings reveal that guardians no longer discriminate against girls.[2]

***Table 10.5*: Primary Education: Average Annual Private Expenditure per Student by Location (Rural and Urban) and Type of Institutions, 2005, in Taka**

Types of Institution	*Rural*			*Urban*			*Total*		
	Boys	*Girls*	*Both*	*Boys*	*Girls*	*Both*	*Boys*	*Girls*	*Both*
Government schools	2,551	2,463	2,507	2,755	2,690	2,724	2,596	2,511	2,554
Non-govt.(regd.) schools	2,145	1,974	2,060	3,728	3,470	3,603	2,545	2,327	2,438
Non-govt. (non-regd.) schools	1.785	1,775	1,781	2,568	2,746	2,663	1,938	1,939	1,939
Community schools	1,729	1,670	1,700	1,675	1,541	1,609	1,719	1,643	1,682
Non-govt.(regd.) madrasha	1,740	1,723	1,733	3,654	4,070	3,855	2,230	2,423	2,324
Non-govt.(non-regd.) madrasha	1,798	1,714	1,756	2,733	3,067	2,893	2,015	2,012	2,014

Source: Education Watch Report, 2006

Apart from the problems as stated above, inadequate infrastructure in school manifests in the form of insufficient teachers, lack of informative books, unskilled teachers, adverse teacher student ratio, poor communication system, and lower salary structure of teachers, inferior quality of mid-day meal, unsafe drinking water, unhygienic sanitation facilities, unpleasant learning environment, and absence of co-curricular activities, political influence and inefficient governing body. All these factors, in some way or the other, result in drop-out problem, irrespective of gender.

Another reason for higher rate of drop-outs as students progress to subsequent levels, is the sharp rise of private cost of education. Here is a word of caution on what we mean by "free primary education". It is free in the sense that, tuition waiver and free books are given by the education provider (both government and non-government institutions alike). However, in addition to these costs, families have to bear the expenses of other educational items for students. These include, but are not limited to, private tuition, scripts, stationery, school bags and umbrellas, school dress, transport, lunch/tiffin, entertainment, medical treatment, energy (kerosene, electricity), and other costs. In a recent survey conducted by Education Watch (published in December, 2007), it is estimated that the private cost of parents of a student at grade V is 5.9 times higher than the private cost of parents of a student enrolled at class I (this comparison is done for students enrolled at government primary schools). This progressive rise of cost of private expenditure might have significant impact on growing drop-out rates as students progress through subsequent stages.

Tertiary Level Situation

The success of female enrolment in primary and secondary level becomes inconsequential when we come across the female to male ratio in tertiary level as 36:64 (UN 2005) in 2002. Education in this level is not adequately linked to the job market. According to the Labor Force Survey, under-employment rate for female is 52.8 per cent compared to 7.4 per cent for males. Social factors like early marriages, high fertility rate, and feeble health conditions for women constrain the female participation in higher education. So the aim of attaining equal share between male and female in tertiary education by 2015 will not be realized unless policy intervention is made at this stage.

Current Trend

The recent data shows that, whereas the MDG required Bangladesh to maintain a female to male students' ratio in primary enrollment as 48:52 in 2005, Bangladesh actually achieved (mid-term report, 2007) 53:47. That means girls now excel boys in terms of primary enrollment. For secondary education, the targeted ratio (50/50) has already been achieved.

Therefore, government has been able to remove gender disparity at the primary and secondary levels of education. None of the countries in South Asia except Sri Lanka has achieved this milestone. The Government has prepared a National Work Plan for universal primary education. Special initiatives have been taken to ensure distribution of books and stationeries free of cost to the extremely poor and in remote regions of the country. In FY 2007-08, about 15 thousand primary teachers will be recruited of which 60 per cent will be females. This will bring the current student-teacher ratio of 55:1 down to 46:1. 55 lakh primary students will be given monthly stipend at the rate of Taka 100. Actions are underway to bring back drop-outs in 11 thousand teaching centres. In the next fiscal year, 10 thousand teachers will be trained. As many as 18186 classrooms will be built. 6.5 lakh persons from among those who have attained literacy through mass education program will be provided with income generating training through continuous education within the next fiscal year. Mosque and temple-based child and mass education will be strengthened.

Alongside the secondary female stipend program, the Government is also introducing stipend program for the poor male students. 63 per cent of the non-government budget allocation of the Ministry of Education is spent for salary subventions of the teachers and staff of non-government educational institutions. In the revised budget of the current fiscal year there is an allocation of Taka 3 thousand 13 crore for this purpose. In order to make this huge spending cost effective, the allocation against each institution will be linked with performance. An Independent Inspection Body will undertake performance evaluation. Steps are being taken to provide special training for the teachers. Emphasis has been laid on English language and vocational education. Information and statistics on education are being enriched.

Postscript

It can be noted that, Bangladesh has shown significant progress towards primary and secondary enrollment.[5] However, achievements have been overshadowed by poor performance in areas of female education, drop-out problem at secondary and tertiary levels, as well as poor infrastructure in schools. Higher education is a crucial input from the point of view of human development. This education will ultimately lay out the economic and social well being of an individual, and society at large. Both the Government and private bodies need to be more active in this regard. There is a considerable number of graduates in Bangladesh without employment, suggesting that education has not been diffused in the right direction with the right motive. Female education, a strong indicator of human development, should be addressed immediately by government policy interventions.

REFERENCES

Millennium Development Goals, (2005), *Progress Report*, Bangladesh, by UNDP.

Financing Primary and Secondary Education in Bangladesh, (2006), *Education Watch Report*, by Campaign for Popular Education, Bangladesh .

Millennium Development Goals, (2007), *Mid-term Progress Report*, Bangladesh, by UNDP and Government of Bangladesh.

National Budget of the Peoples' Republic of Bangladesh, 2006-2007.

Bangladesh Education Sector Overview, Japan Bank for International Cooperation, Final Report, March 2002.

Ain O Salish Kendro (ASK), (2004), Bangladesh Mohila Parishad, and Steps Towards Development, Summary of CEDAW Report to Supplement the Fifth Periodic Report of the Government of Bangladesh to the UN Committee on the Elimination of Discrimination Against Women, Dhaka.

CPD Occasional Paper Series, (2003), Bangladesh's Population Policy: Emerging Issues and Future Agenda, March.

Akter, Shaheen, (2005), *Occupational Segregation, Wage Discrimination, and*

Impact on Poverty in Rural Bangladesh, Journal of Developing Areas v 39, no. 1.

Amin, Sajeda, (2006), Selective Inclusion or Active Discrimination? Women and the Labour Market in Bangladesh.

Conditional Cash Transfers and Educational Gender Gaps: Insights from Bangladeshi Households, Background Paper for the Bangladesh Gender Assessment, Washington DC: The World Bank, April 2006.

Annual Report, (2007), Asian Development Bank.

Report on Primary Education in Bangladesh, (2005), Challenges and Successes, jointly published by Bangladesh Bureau of Education Information and Statistics, and Bangladesh Ministry of Women and Children Affairs.

11.

ATTITUDE TOWARDS SCHOOL INFRASTRUCTURE AMONG GIRLS OF PRIMARY SCHOOLS

A Survey in West Bengal

DEBDULAL DUTTA ROY AND AMRITA PANDA

Infrastructure is recognized by all to be the major bottleneck to development (Rao, 2005). Dr. Manmohon Singh, the Prime Minister of India, recently gave major thrust on infrastructure facilities in education. He asserted *"While growth generates wealth, we also need to invest in equitable social and physical infrastructure, catering to the needs of marginalized sections of our society which still need to catch-up with the more advanced regions"* (PM Reviews Mid term appraisal, 2005). Large number of marginalized sections of our society lives in the villages. With a view to harness the socio-economic growth of the villages, paramount importance is to equip our village schools with suitable infrastructures and to assess the attitudes of students towards infrastructures. Latter is useful in understanding their comfort and difficulties in using the infrastructures. Current study examined attitude of rural girls towards school infrastructures. As the study was conducted in the rural schools of West Bengal, it is important to pay special attention to the school infrastructures in the state.

School Infrastructures in West Bengal

Eradication of illiteracy happened to be one of the major programs of the Govt. of West Bengal. Following the census, 2001, literacy rate of West Bengal (69.22 per cent) was above 65.4 per cent. Female literacy (60.22 per cent) was lower than male literacy (77.58 per cent). Statistical information about school infrastructures is mainly based on DISE data. In 2005-2006, DISE studied 59223 schools covering 49559 of all the districts (n=20) of West Bengal. State elementary education report card by DISE most of the government managed primary schools (N=42706, 87 per cent) are located in the rural areas and most of the rural students (N=6211720,

86 per cent) are enrolled there. There are very few private schools in the rural areas (N=88). The primary schools are made of pucca structure (63 per cent) and partially pucca structure (16 per cent). Schools have various facilities, namely; common toilet (66.9 per cent), girls' toilet only (21.8 per cent), drinking water facility (81.5 per cent). Teachers are trained (70.9 per cent). Irrespective of rural and urban differences, pupil-teacher ratio is less (1:48) than 2004-2005 (1:50). Similarly, student-classroom ratio decreased to 52 from 57 in 2004-2005. Both boys (50 per cent) and girls (50 per cent) are getting relatively more textbooks. Very few students get school uniform (8 per cent). And uniforms are mainly for girls (97 per cent). There were very few studies about availability of school infrastructures in West Bengal.

Mukherjee and Mandal (2005) conducted systematic studies in Coochbehar and Bardhaman Districts to understand school infrastructures. They did not find completely pucca structure of building. For most schools, side walls of the structure might have been pucca but the roof was either of tin or partially asbestos or of totally asbestos. Drinking water sources were tube-well constructed by Gram Panchayet. Schools were lacking adequate facility of urinal and electricity connection. Number of classrooms available for the purpose instruction was in an average 3. Partition wall in between classrooms for most school was made-up of bamboo sheet, thus criss-crossed between/among classes. Particularly when one class is not held because of teacher's absence, the neighbouring classes could not be taken or if taken with lot of trouble. Overall teacher student ratio was 1:53. During teachers' absence or other pre-occupations, students of all classes are accommodated by removing the partition walls in between classes and instruction was delivered by a single teacher. Students used to sat either on the floors whether earthen or pucca or they made their own arrangement. They brought own mattresses, gunny bags/ plastic sheets for the purpose of sitting.

Primary School Infrastructures in Rural Areas of West Bengal

Following the statistical report of the Elementary Education in Rural India, 2005-06, there were 42793 primary schools (87 per cent of 49894 schools of all classes) in West Bengal.

Most of the schools (95.53 per cent) were established before 1994. 62 per cent (less than 9.18 per cent of national average) school buildings were made-up of pucca structure. 41.55 per cent classrooms (63.79 per cent) were in good condition. Average number of classrooms was 2.7 (higher than national average 2.7). Number of single classrooms (18.87 per cent) was higher than national average (14.13 per cent). Student-classroom ratio

(54.36) was higher than national average. Approximately, there were 6 teachers. 92.50 per cent schools received school development grant in contrast with the national average of 72.58 per cent. Out of them, 8.23 per cent schools failed to utilize the sanctioned grant. Quite small number of schools (23.73 per cent) had boundary wall. 83.03 per cent of schools had drinking water facility. Schools had common toilets (68.04 per cent). Toilets only for girls were available in 21.66 per cent of schools, in contrast to the national average of 27.09 per cent. Most of the schools were not electrified (95.6 per cent, national average = 84.48 per cent) had no electricity. Almost all schools had blackboard (99.7 per cent, national average = 7.46 per cent). 33.15 per cent (National average = 45.45 per cent) of schools had play ground. 85.25 per cent (national average = 67.02 per cent) schools got TLM grant. 57.77 per cent schools (National average = 43.65 per cent) had book banks. 21.80 per cent (National average = 51.13 per cent) schools had medical checkup. Above studies focused only availability of different infrastructures in schools but not the attitude towards them.

Attitude

Throughout the history of psychology, the notion of attitude has played an essential role in the explanation of behaviour. For example, a search of Psych INFO with the keyword 'Attitude' revealed more than 12000 articles published from 1992 to 2002. Gordon Allport (1954), an early pioneer in attitude research, characterized the concept of attitude as distinctive and indispensable to social psychology. Allport (1954) defined attitude as a mental and neural state of readiness, organized through experience, exerting a directive or dynamic influence upon the individual's response to all objects and situations with which it is related.

Assessing attitude is complex as it is unobservable hypothetical construct. It must be inferred from measurable responses indicating positive or negative evaluations of the attitudinal object. It may be inferred from three basic components. (Breckler, 1984). All three are related, and more they are consistent with each other the more stable is the attitude.

The *cognitive component* consists of the person's thought process, perceptions and beliefs and evaluations about the attitude object. For example, students may think that school provides adequate space to sit in the classroom.

The *affective component* gives an emotional or feeling aspect to the attitude which, results in an object being liked or disliked. In the example of adequate space in above, student may feel warmth or liking for the school.

The *behavioural component* refers to the tendency to act towards the object in a consistent and characteristic way. Again, following the above example, student may want to attend the class regularly.

There are five basic characteristics of attitude. These are:

Valence: It is the degree of positive or negative feeling about an attitude toward an object that predicts what attitude scales normally measure.

Centrality: It is the extent to which an attitude is a part of a person's self-concept and reflects the individual's identity.

Interrelatedness: It is the extent to which an attitude is related to a person's other attitudes.

Stability: It is simply an attitude's resistance to change.

Salience: It is a person's conscious awareness of the attitude.

Attitude Towards School Infrastructures

Each infrastructure has set of qualities. By experiencing these qualities, students form different attitudes towards infrastructure. For example, students assume that school is safe through experience of school building's capability to protect students from internal and external environmental threats. Student's attitude towards infrastructures can be inferred from 3 kinds of responses as cognitive, affective and conative. Cognitive response is based on student's perception. For example, school toilet is used by all students. Affective response is very much psychological in nature. It includes student's emotional tones. For example, School toilet is adequate for privacy. Conative includes motor functions or actual behaviour. For example, I go to school toilet if need.

Attitude towards infrastructures is assumed to be multidimensional in nature. Again their multidimensionality is assumed to vary with respect to various types of infrastructures. The multidimensional attitude towards infrastructure has been studied in the industrial (Dutta Roy, 1989, 1991, 1992), hospital (Dutta Roy, 1997) and bank settings (Mukhopadhyay, 2005) but no such studies were made in the school settings. Therefore, current study will examine relationship among the multi facets of the attitudes towards school infrastructures by developing a questionnaire to assess them.

Current study focused on nine attitudes towards infrastructure as cleanliness, safety, comfort, adequacy, exploring, reliable, easiness, equal opportunity and willingness to participate in school activities. The assumptions behind each attitudinal variable are given below:

Cleanliness: Cleanliness is the absence of dirt, including dust, stains, bad smells and clutter. Purpose of cleanliness includes is to make school free from offensive odor, dirt and contamination of germs and of diseases. Classroom becomes dirty due to unused papers, wastage materials of tiffin-box, dusts coming through windows and doors, etc. Good cleaning habit among students is important for classroom cleanliness. Brooming and washing are common means to make classroom clean. Clean classroom and toilet are healthy for the students. It protects students from diseases and germs. Students before starting class usually clean the classrooms with brooms. In some schools, sweepers are available for cleaning the classroom and toilets. Clean classroom, toilet, mid day meal, medical check up is assumed to affect student's motivation to attend school.

Like classroom, fresh and clean water is important in school. Clean water means absence of toxic substance. Presence of toxicity can be understood through foul smell, turbidity, unwanted color, etc. The main source of water is rainfall. In West Bengal, the state is endowed with large ground water sources. It is tapped by means of heavy and medium duty tube wells. Schools are allocated with such tube wells. Following Human Development Report of West Bengal, 2004, 83.2 per cent of habitations are under rural water management.

Safety: Safety is the state of being "safe" (from French *sauf*), the condition of being protected against any failure, damage, accident, errors or harms. Some of the safety systems in school are pucca building, covered electrical wares, safe drinking water, not slippery in the toilet, wall-fixed blackboard, clean food and careful health check up. School maintains several safety systems to protect students like keeping emergency phone numbers, first aid kit, fire extinguishing cylinders.

Comfort: Comfort refers to feeling of pleasurable ease, a state of being relaxed and feeling of no pain. Feeling of comfort in learning at classroom and in uses of different infrastructures makes students at ease and relaxed.

Easiness: Like comfort, easiness plays important role in forming attitude towards school infrastructures. Easiness refers to posing no difficulty. Answering or asking questions to teachers with fear, difficulty to learn lessons, to take teacher's note or to follow teaching learning materials cause feeling of uneasiness in students.

Adequacy: Adequacy refers to feeling of sufficiency to satisfy a requirement or to meet a need. Adequate sitting position, illumination in classroom, drinking water, privacy in toilet use make students motivated towards school.

Exploring: It refers to systematic searching, examining or investigating. Students through learning process in classroom tend to explore the surroundings. Teachers, books, teaching learning materials play critical role in development of exploring attitude.

Reliability: It refers to dependability or consistency. Reliabile teachers, friends and textbooks develop interpersonal trust and good teacher-student interaction. It motivates students to attend the school regularly.

Equal opportunity: School infrastructure should be easily accessible to all the students. There should not be any prejudice or discrimination based on race, colour, age, gender, national origin, religion, mental or physical disability in participation of school sports, cultural program, accessing books and in getting mid-day meal.

Willingness to participate in school activities: If there would be equal opportunity for access of infrastructures, students will be interested to participate in sports, cultural programs, mid-day meal and health check up program. They will be willing to attend the school regularly.

Objective of the study was to examine attitude of girls in primary education towards different qualities of school infrastructure across different demographic groups.

Methods

Sample: 3-tier sampling (districts, blocks and schools) were followed in sampling the schools.

Districts selection

Data were collected from schools located in the rural blocks (wherein 75 per cent are engaged in agricultural activities) of 6 districts (Table 11.1). In all the districts, female literacy level is lower than male literacy. This gap is high in South 24 Paraganas and Bankura.

***Table 11.1*: Distribution of Literacy Rate Across Six Districts Based on 2001 Census**

Districts	*Total Literacy*			*Rural Literacy*		
	Male	*Female*	*D*	*Male*	*Female*	*D*
Howrah	83.2	70.1	13.1	80.7	64.5	16.2
North 24 Pgn(s)	83.9	71.7	12.2	76.7	61	15.7
South 24 Pgn(s)	79.2	59	20.2	77.9	56.1	21.8
Hooghly	82.6	67.2	15.4	79.7	62.1	17.6
Bankura	76.8	49.4	27.4	75.8	47.6	28.2
Maldaha	58.8	41.3	17.5	56.6	38.4	18.2
Average	77.42	59.78	17.63	74.57	54.95	19.62

Note: D = Male-female gap in literacy level

Of all the above districts, rural population is high in Maldaha (92.7 per cent), Bankura (92.6 per cent) and in South 24 pgs (84.3 per cent). Relatively, urban population is high in North 24pgs (54.3 per cent), Howrah (50.4 per cent) and Hooghly (33.5 per cent). Likewise, more no. of rural primary schools managed by the Govt. are in Bankura (96 per cent), Maldah (95 per cent) and in South 24 Pgs. (93 per cent). And there are 86 per cent, 73 per cent and 63 per cent rural primary schools in Hooghly, Howrah and

N.24 Pgs. respectively. Student enrolment varies across districts. In Bankura (1:90), Hooghly(1:75) and Howrah (1:65), schools to cater more students in rural areas. In Maldah (1:43), South 24pgs.(1:55) and in N.24 Pgs.(1:59), schools cater to relatively less no. of students. Following DISE report of 2005-06, Development grant is higher in South 24pgs. (95.2 per cent), Bankura (93.8 per cent), Maldah (93.2 per cent) and in Hooghly (89.9 per cent) than North 24 Pgs. (69.5 per cent), Howrah (82.5 per cent). But TLM grant is higher in South 24pgs. (93.8 per cent), Bankura (92.5 per cent), Maldah (92.3 per cent), Hooghly (83.5 per cent) than Howrah (79.9 per cent) and North 24 pgs. (67 per cent).

Selection of Rural blocks

Like selection of districts, 12 rural blocks were selected from the above six districts based on following criteria:

a. Literacy rate of the rural blocks. From each district the highest and the lowest literate block is selected;

b. At least 75 per cent of the population is involved in agriculture;

c. Availability of local transport facilities;

d. Availability of administrative support in emergency.

Selection of Schools

20 primary government schools were selected from 12 rural blocks in 6 districts of West Bengal. In school selection, attention was paid to availability of students with mixed community and easy accessibility of schools for collection of data.

School Infrastructures

During collection of data, besides observation and interview with teachers, a school report card was administered to the Head of the Institution to understand infrastructure facilities of school.

Area

50 per cent of the schools under study were established before independence of India. Usually, local educated and uneducated people donated the land to develop culture of education in the neighbouring areas. Average, school occupied 23.68 katha land with a SD of 20.29. Market (Mean=2.68 km, SD=4.27 km) and block office (Mean=3.74 km, SD=3.80 km) are more than 2 kms. away from the school on an average but the main road with local transport service (rickshaw, Jeep , small car etc.) is near (Mean=1.10 km, SD= 1.91 km). Out of the total area, few schools (39 per cent) had their own playgrounds. Flower and vegetable garden were not found resulting difficulty in garden based teaching system.

Water source

Tube well rather tap water is the main source of drinking water. Some schools (16 per cent) had no tube wells. Tube wells of some schools required major repairing. In most of the schools, local people used tube wells. Only 5 per cent of the schools used tap water.

Toilets

Except one school, all schools had toilets. Many schools had no toilet for girls (76 per cent). Students and teachers used both open (27 per cent) and shaded toilets (50 per cent). Toilets were not clean as most of the schools had no sweepers. The average no. of toilets in each school was 4.

Windows and Doors

Classrooms of many schools had 3 windows and 1 door on average. Windows were wide as a result some schools did not require artificial illumination, but for some schools windows were blocked by the houses of local people. Students in these schools found difficulty to write on.

Electricity

Some schools arranged own meter for electricity. Only 56 per cent of the schools had electricity. Some schools arranged only one bulb of 40 watts per classroom.

Enrolled Students

Few students out of the total students of schools studied in class IV. Though some schools had over loaded students. In one school 100 students were accommodated in one classroom. Following the obtained data from school report card, the average no. of students in the primary schools were 207, among which mean enrolment of students in class four was 56 with SD=27.87. During visit, on an average 29 students with SD 9.76 were present.

Teacher Qualification

Most of the teachers possessed Higher Secondary degree (51 per cent) and few possessed graduate (25 per cent) and school final (19 per cent) degrees. Teaching in local language is important in primary school education. Therefore presence of para-teachers is important. Very few schools had para teachers (6 per cent). Comparing the overall student teacher distribution, the student teacher ratio was 34:1, and the student classroom ratio was 40:1.

Teaching Learning Materials

Teaching learning materials (TLM) are most useful instruments in concept formation and cognitive skill development. It is advisable to design TLM by the students under the guidance of teachers. Classroom teaching will be based on TLM. Regarding use of TLM, pocket board, map (94 per cent), chart (89 per cent), models (72 per cent) were mostly used. Few schools used flash cards (67 per cent) and work cards (44 per cent). Most of the schools prepared teaching learning materials through school teachers or through professional workers. Some schools bought materials from Kolkata or from nearby cities.

Book Banks

Book banks help students and teachers in acquiring different kinds of knowledge. Most of the schools (77 per cent) had book banks. Usually, the Head or school authority managed it. In some schools, due to security reasons, school authority keeps books in his house.

Mid-day Meal

Mid-day meal system was available in all schools. Some schools provided rice, dal, vegetable curry and boiled eggs. Local women of self-help group under village education committee were engaged in preparing meals in separate room. Most of the schools arranged one storeroom to keep groceries. Some schools used own office room to keep groceries.

Health Check-up

Medical team visit is common practice for primary school. Only 50 per cent of the schools had regular health-check up facilities. Health check up includes testing height, weight, eye and major physical ailments.

Sample Characteristics

Students were asked to participate voluntarily in this study. Some criteria were followed in selection of participants as (a) ability to read and write in Bengali and (b) appeared not as retarded in intelligence to the teachers. 308 girls participated in this study. One 24-item schedule was administered to them for understanding their age, caste, religion, and socio-economic conditions. Their mean age was 9.47 with SD was 1.15. About 2/3 of the girls were Hindus (64 per cent) and approximately 11/3 were Muslims (34 per cent). Socio economic questionnaire includes 9 variables; (i) frequency of taking meals (ii) study guidance at home (iii) occupation of guardians (iv) types of house roofs (v) type of house walls (vi) sources of drinking water at home (vii) types of illumination at home (vii) types of toilets at home and (ix) number of rooms. All the variables were coded and scored. The scores ranged from 9 to 32. The mean score was 21.25 with SD was 4.50.

Instruments

A questionnaire of 68 items with yes and no response category was developed to assess 9 attitudinal dimensions (cleanliness, safety, comfort, adequacy, exploring, reliability, easiness, equal opportunity, willingness to participate in school activities) of attitude towards school infrastructure quality. Considering categorical response patterns, rational equivalence technique was used to assess reliability of the final questionnaire. It is noted that reliability coefficient for the total scale was 0.90, indicating that 90 per cent of the observed score variance is true variance, i.e., due to 'true' individual differences among samples, where by only 10 per cent of the observed-score is attributable to error variance. Content validity in this study was examined in terms of item-total correlation. Point bi-serial correlation coefficient was computed to determine item-total correlations (Table 11.2).

***Table 11.2*: Description of the Questionnaire**

Attitudes	*No. of Items*	*Mean*	*SD*	*rbi*	*rtt*
Cleanliness	5	0.73	0.26	0.60	0.58
Safety	7	0.65	0.26	0.58	0.68
Comfort	5	0.75	0.22	0.55	0.42
Adequacy	12	0.77	0.13	0.43	0.58
Exploring	12	0.76	0.13	0.38	0.50
Reliability	5	0.76	0.21	0.57	0.50
Easiness	7	0.83	0.20	0.56	0.68
Equal Opportunity	5	0.67	0.28	0.62	0.63
Willingness to Participate	10	0.70	0.17	0.43	0.50

Results and Discussion

Districts: Table 11.3 shows significant and positive correlation among 9 attitudes. Therefore Wilks' Lambda was used to determine district wise differences.

***Table 11.3*: Inter correlation among attitude variables (N=308)**

	Mean	*SD*	*1*	*2*	*3*	*4*	*5*	*6*	*7*	*8*	*9*
1. Cleanliness	0.73	0.26	1.00								
2. Safety	0.65	0.26	0.50	1.00							
3. Comfort	0.75	0.22	0.43	0.46	1.00						
4. Adequacy	0.77	0.13	0.36	0.47	0.38	1.00					
5. Exploring	0.76	0.13	0.12	0.11	0.12	0.33	1.00				
6. Reliability	0.76	0.21	0.31	0.37	0.39	0.32	0.26	1.00			
7. Easiness	0.83	0.20	0.34	0.49	0.51	0.43	0.26	0.53	1.00		
8. Equal Opportunity	0.67	0.28	0.20	0.00	0.10	0.27	0.37	0.28	0.16	1.00	
9. Willingness to participate	0.71	0.17	0.40	0.38	0.34	0.39	0.24	0.28	0.33	0.22	1.00

N.B. All variables were significant at 0.01 level

Table 11.4: Attitude Towards School Infrastructure by Districts

Attitude	N-24_pgs (n=38)		Howrah (n=74)		Bankura (n=46)		Maldah (n=56)		S_24_pgs (n=40)		Hooghly (n=54)			
	M	SD	M	SD	M	SD	M	SD	M	SD	M	SD	F	p
Cleanliness	0.68	0.23	0.86	0.18	0.79	0.23	0.54	0.2	0.87	0.2	0.61	0.29	20.26	0.00
Safety	0.47	0.18	0.74	0.24	0.78	0.18	0.5	0.32	0.67	0.25	0.7	0.18	14.66	0.00
Comfort	0.63	0.18	0.89	0.13	0.83	0.16	0.61	0.2	0.74	0.29	0.74	0.18	19.40	0.00
Adequacy	0.75	0.11	0.83	0.14	0.8	0.14	0.71	0.13	0.78	0.09	0.75	0.11	6.73	0.00
Exploring	0.78	0.1	0.79	0.1	0.74	0.12	0.74	0.17	0.81	0.15	0.72	0.14	3.45	0.00
Reliability	0.76	0.17	0.87	0.19	0.8	0.21	0.64	0.19	0.68	0.22	0.77	0.18	10.35	0.00
Easiness	0.83	0.15	0.94	0.13	0.88	0.14	0.63	0.19	0.81	0.21	0.87	0.17	24.46	0.00
Equal Opp.	0.63	0.23	0.79	0.2	0.61	0.3	0.69	0.31	0.71	0.28	0.54	0.28	6.33	0.00
Willingness	0.6	0.17	0.76	0.17	0.78	0.18	0.63	0.12	0.72	0.16	0.72	0.13	10.48	0.00

Attitude towards infrastructure depends upon infrastructure quality. In this study, data were collected from 6 districts. Out of them, Maldah district is far away from state capital and Howrah is close neighbouring district of state capital. Table 11.4 shows students of Maldah district perceived poor quality of school infrastructures and those of Howrah district perceived best quality of infrastructures in a significant manner [Wilks' Lambda = 0.35, Rao's R (45,1318) = 7.61].

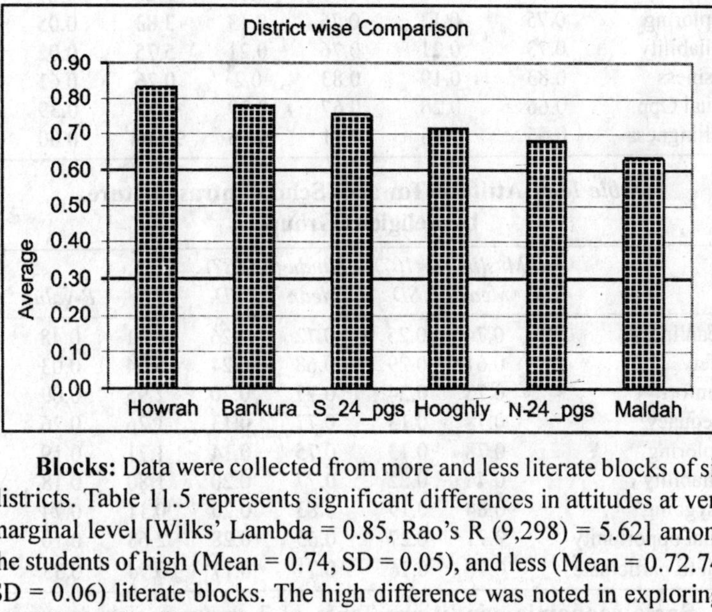

Blocks: Data were collected from more and less literate blocks of six districts. Table 11.5 represents significant differences in attitudes at very marginal level [Wilks' Lambda = 0.85, Rao's R (9,298) = 5.62] among the students of high (Mean = 0.74, SD = 0.05), and less (Mean = 0.72.74, SD = 0.06) literate blocks. The high difference was noted in exploring, reliability, and willingness to participate into cultural and sports programs. This phenomenon is very high among students of high literate blocks. Due to unavailability of adequate sample, interaction effect of districts and blocks could not be accounted.

Religion: Religion has marginal significant effect [Wilks' Lambda = 0.92, Rao's R (9,284) = 2.82] on variation in attitude towards school infrastructure. Table11. 6 shows that except safety, no significant mean difference was noted between the groups. Muslim girls reported less safety than Hindu girls.

***Table 11.5*: Attitude Towards School Infrastructure by literacy in Blocks**

	Less Literate		*High Literate*			
	Mean	*SD*	*Mean*	*SD*	*F*	*P-value*
Cleanliness	0.74	0.25	0.73	0.26	0.83	0.36
Safety	0.64	0.25	0.65	0.26	0.85	0.36
Comfort	0.73	0.23	0.75	0.21	3.10	0.08
Adequacy	0.76	0.09	0.77	0.15	1.20	0.27
Exploring	0.75	0.13	0.76	0.13	3.83	0.05
Reliability	0.73	0.21	0.76	0.21	5.75	0.02
Easiness	0.83	0.19	0.83	0.2	0.26	0.61
Equal Opp.	0.66	0.26	0.67	0.29	0.73	0.39
Willingness	0.65	0.16	0.71	0.16	28.88	0.00

***Table 11.6*: Attitude Towards School Infrastructure by Religious Groups**

	Muslim (n=107)		*Hindu (n=187)*			
	Mean	*SD*	*Mean*	*SD*	*F*	*P-value*
Cleanliness	0.74	0.25	0.72	0.26	0.51	0.48
Safety	0.61	0.29	0.68	0.24	5.04	0.03
Comfort	0.73	0.24	0.77	0.20	2.95	0.09
Adequacy	0.78	0.13	0.77	0.13	1.26	0.26
Exploring	0.78	0.13	0.75	0.14	1.71	0.19
Reliability	0.74	0.22	0.77	0.20	1.80	0.18
Easygoing	0.84	0.19	0.83	0.20	0.11	0.74
Equal opportunity	0.71	0.27	0.65	0.28	2.68	0.10
Will to participate	0.70	0.16	0.71	0.17	0.94	0.33

Socio-economic condition: Table 11.7 shows socio-economic condition had significant effect [Wilks' Lambda = 0.84, Rao's R (9,112) = 2.32] on differences in attitudes especially on feeling of adequacy, exploring and easy going. Students of low SES group possessed significantly high score on easy going, exploring and adequacy.

Discussion

Attitude to school infrastructure quality is important for spreading literacy. It places central role in the use and maintenance of school infrastructure. Current study examined attitude toward nine qualities of school infrastructure of girls of different demographic backgrounds. Results revealed three things (a) multidimensional properties of attitudes; (b) within group variation of attitudes and (c) differential pattern of attitudes across demographic groups.

***Table 11.7*: Attitude by Socio-economic Condition (N=122)**

		Low SES (n=65)	*High SES (n=57)*	*F*	*p-value*
Cleanliness	Means	0.76	0.72	0.75	0.39
	SD	0.27	0.24		
Safety	Means	0.67	0.61	1.47	0.23
	SD	0.22	0.28		
Comfort	Means	0.78	0.73	1.17	0.28
	SD	0.19	0.24		
Adequacy	Means	0.79	0.73	6.50	0.01
	SD	0.11	0.15		
Exploring	Means	0.78	0.71	7.21	0.01
	SD	0.13	0.16		
Reliability	Means	0.76	0.74	0.27	0.60
	SD	0.19	0.23		
Easygoing	Means	0.88	0.76	12.99	0.00
	SD	0.16	0.22		
Equal opportunity	Means	0.68	0.60	2.00	0.16
	SD	0.28	0.31		
Will to participate	Means	0.71	0.66	2.53	0.11
	SD	0.18	0.16		

Socio economic condition did not interact [Wilks' Lambda = 0.89, Rao's R (9,104) = 1.37] with religion and literacy in blocks [Wilks' Lambda = 0.90, Rao's R (9,110) = 1.39].

Multidimensionality

Results show positive and significant inter-correlation among nine attitudes. This suggests perception of one quality of infrastructure leads to influence another quality. For example, perceiving the school as clean helps the girls to perceive the infrastructure as safe, comfortable, adequate, explorable, reliable, easiness to access, equal opportunity and willingness to participate in sports and cultural programs. In other words, a cognitive schema is formed within girls about the school covering all infrastructure qualities.

Within Group variation of Attitudes

Results show 74 per cent girls possessed overall positive attitude towards the school infrastructure. This suggests more attention should be paid to change in attitude toward school infrastructure quality among the girls. Many girls thought that school infrastructures were not safe and were not equally accessible. This is a serious concern for infrastructure management in school. Government should pay much attention in designing and managing school infrastructures.

Attitudes Across Demographic Groups

Planned infrastructure management requires distribution of attitudes across different groups as this provides insight about identification of sufferers. Results noted variation of attitudes by districts, literacy level in blocks, religion and socio-economic condition of students. Students of Maldah districts had poor level of positive attitude and those of Howrah districts had very high level of positive attitudes.

Attitude change takes place with level of literacy. Girls of more literate blocks reported high positive attitude than those of less literate blocks. This difference was high in exploring, reliability and willingness to participate attitudes. High attitude in exploring suggests that girls of more literate blocks assume that available school infrastructures namely, teachers, books, teaching learning materials, help them for systematic searching, and examining or investigating. They like to depend on teachers, friends and text books. They feel high interpersonal trust in teacher-student interaction. Finally, they like to participate in sports, cultural programs, mid-day meal and health check up programs in school.

Results noted religion wise difference in the attitudes. Muslim girls perceived less safety in schools than Hindu girls. Girls living in low socio-economic condition had positive attitude towards school than those of high socio-economic condition. This suggests effect of exposure on attitude change. Poor students got little access to evaluate current school infrastructure due to less exposure. On the other hand, due to more exposure, students of high socio-economic condition reported positive attitudes towards school infrastructure.

Findings are important in managing school infrastructure. Usually, attention is paid to student or teacher infrastructure ratios. This helps in getting insight about accessibility of infrastructure but it fails to generate insight about users' attitude towards school infrastructure quality. Current study noted this issue. Based upon the results, concerned school authority can take appropriate measures in managing school infrastructures. Demographic wise difference helps to identify specific target groups who need better school infrastructures.

To conclude, current study may be considered as platform for future planning of TQM (Total quality management) in school.

REFERENCES

Allport, G.W. (1954). Attitudes in the History of Social Psychology. In G Lindzey & Aranson (Eds), *Handbook of Social Psychology*, Vol. 1, Reading, MA: Addison-Wesley.

Breckler, S.(1984). Empirical validation of affect, behaviour and cognition as distinct components of attitude, *Journal of Personality and Social Psychology*, 47,8, 1191-1205.

Dutta Roy, D. and Ghosh,M. (1997) Assessing the health of a hospital - A process state approach. *Management and Labour studies*, 22,1,6-12.

Dutta Roy, D. (1991) A model of change in Organizational health to improve Quality of life, *Social Science International,* Vol. 16, No.4, pp. 189-191.

Mukherjee, S and Mandal, A. (2005). Primary education in West Bengal-More concerns than complacency, In Mandal,A. (ed.) *Rural Development in West Bengal*. New Delhi., Northern Book Center.

PM Reviews Mid-term Appraisal, *Yojana*, 49, 41-42.

Rao, S.L. (2005). Use of forex reserves. *Yojana*, 49, 5-8.

12.

WOMEN DEVELOPMENT THROUGH TECH-VOC EDUCATION

A Case Study in Overseas Teacher's Perspective

S. RENUKADEVI

Introduction

Education is considered the most important aspect of nation building. Education for national development should include education for self-reliance, personal development, social development, production capacity, social Integration & political understanding. (Pillai, 1995). With equality in reality, men and women should, equally contribute to national development. Pundit Jawaharlal Nehru once said, 'To Awaken the people, it is woman who must be awakened; once she is on the move, the family moves, the village moves and the nation moves'. The UNESCO Conference in 1962 underlined the importance of the access of girls and women to technical and vocational education for economic and social development.

Considering the fact that women play an important role in the nation building process and the fact that many of the women have contributed in the field of science and technology, women education, particularly technical and vocational education should be given a high priority. The development of women education includes many strategies, the most important one being the training of the trainers of women. This article highlights the details of one such training of trainers' programme, which was aimed at imparting knowledge on Women development through technical and vocational Education.

Women Development in the National Policies

In the National Policy on Education (1986), provisions regarding Women Education have been made. Part IV of the policy named 'Education for Equality' includes 'Education for Women equality'. It states "Women Studies will be promoted as part of various courses and educational institutions encouraged taking up active programmes to further women's development. It further states, "Major emphasis will be laid on women's participation in vocational, technical and progressive education at different levels". The Policy of non-discrimination will be pursued vigorously to eliminate sex stereotyping in vocational and professional courses and to promote women's participation in non-traditional occupations, as well as in existing and emerged technologies.

The National policy on Education Review committee (1990) made various recommendations in the context of women's Education, the dimension being:

1. Access to education and quality of learning
2. Content of education and gender bias
3. Vocational Education
4. Training of teachers and other education personnel.
5. Research and development of women's studies
6. Representation of women in the educational hierarchy
7. Empowerment of women
8. Adult Education
9. Resources
10. Management.

The National Perspective Plan for Women Education (1998-2000 A.D) formulated some important specific objectives for women education so that women may also participate in the area of social, cultural, economic, and political and also in education. One of the important objectives to be obtained by 2000 A.D. in regard to women's education is the impetus to enroll in various professional degree courses so as to increase their number in medicine, teaching, engineering and other fields substantially. The recommendation reads:

- A fruitful rapport has to be established between the community at large and the teachers and other education personnel.
- Diversified courses leading to occupational preparation should be of parallel duration to the general secondary courses. At least 30 per cent seats should be reserved for girls in apprenticeship training courses on a non-transferable basis.
- General and vocational training courses should be combined so that prospect of career immediately on completion of schooling may attract girls from weaker sections.
- There is a need to open more colleges and Polytechnics for girls, especially in rural areas.
- Girls should be encouraged to enter in professional courses.
- Vocational and technical education for women, both formal and non-formal, should be a major feature of the programmers of rural universities.

- Women's Universities and Women centres in colleges need to take an active role in women development.

Background of the Study

The National Policies clearly spell out the need for Women development through formal and non-formal programmes. The policies and committees suggest the need for technical and vocational education for women. Moreover, recommendations are offered for having teachers for women development initiative and also establishing centers for women studies. Many University departments are offering courses for the empowerment of Women (Mishra, 2005).

National Institute of Technical Teachers' Training & Research [NITTTR], Chennai has been involved in Women empowerment issues through some of the projects like Canada-India Institutional Cooperation Project (CIICP), Community Polytechnics Scheme (CPS), and Centrally Sponsored Project for Integrating Person with Disabilities in to the main Stream of Technical And Vocational Education (CPWD). The Government of India has been consistently involved in Human Resource Development of other developing/ underdeveloped nations by training the teachers/ administrators from overseas countries.

NITTTR, Chennai has been offering training to overseas teachers and administrators in areas like Curriculum Development, Environment Management, Pedagogy, Educational Media production for the past few years. It was decided to offer 8 weeks programme on "Women Empowerment through technical and Vocational Education" for overseas teachers. The programme was approved by Ministry of External Affairs.

To study the efficacy of women development through technical and vocational Education, an evaluation of the eight-weeks programme conducted at NITTTR, Chennai exclusively for women teachers and administrators, was done to evolve a prescription for women Development through Technical and Vocational Education.

Objectives of the Study

The objectives of the present study are to:

1. Analyse the expectations of the participants
2. Alanlyse the contents/process of the programme
3. Evaluate the usefulness of the programme
4. Analyse the feedback/output of the programme

Sample

As per the approval of Ministry of External Affairs, applications were received from teachers and educational administrators of various countries.

11 participants attended the programme. The trainees represented the Countries like Iraq, Yemen, Nepal, Myanmar, Botswana, Lesotho, Tajikistan and Uzbekistan. Out of 11 participants, 7 are teachers and 4 are administrators.

Procedure

Programme

The programme titled 'Women Empowerment Through Technical and Vocational Education' was conducted from 7th Jan 2008 to 29th Feb 2008. The Programme was conducted at the Department of Education NITTTR, Chennai. Several faculty /resource persons participated and enriched the programme.

Objectives of the Programme

The objectives of the programme were:

1. To understand the basics of Women Empowerment
2. To comprehend the issues related to Women Empowerment through Technical & Vocational Education
3. To understand the relevance of technology for Women
4. To acquire knowledge of use of interpersonal relationships
5. To understand the balancing of Work, Education and Home
6. To understand the process of Guidance and Counselling
7. To apply Leadership Skills in Women Empowerment
8. To use appropriate strategies for Women Empowerment
9. To Develop Innovative practice of Women Empowerment

Contents of the Course

In the planning stages of the programme, a basic draft curriculum was prepared by the course coordinator, which was placed before the expert committee. On incorporating the expert opinions, the following content was accepted under the curriculum of the programme.

The contents of the programme –curricula includes components like Indian culture, Technical Education in India, Ice breaking, Women Empowerment introduction, Principles of Learning, Management and Simulation games, Classroom communication, Instructional Objectives, Adolescence, Success, a winning strategy, Stress Management, Student Motivation, Instructional Planning, Women & Leadership, Women and Vocational Rehabilitation, Role of Women Empowerment, Portrayal of Women in media, Multimedia, Media Production, People skills, Etiquette and Manners, Women Empowerment – An international perspective, Transformational Leadership & Feminist Leadership, Entrepreneurship

Development, Rural women Empowerment, Neuro-Linguistic Programming, Women & Leadership and Personality Development.

Process

Though there are several strategies that are available, after a detailed discussion, the following strategies have been identified and used. The strategies were:

1. Ice Breaking Sessions
2. Lecture-cum-Discussion Sessions by eminent resource persons
3. Guided-Practice session
4. Educational visits
5. Development of Media
6. Development of a Project

Output

The participants are expected to have enhanced competencies in Women Empowerment through Technical and Vocational Education.

Discussion

Participants' Expectations

Their expectations about the programme included

- Knowledge of new innovations, Advanced technologies, Research methods, curriculum development and Environment
- Knowledge about how women should be empowered for economic and social development
- Knowledge about research and importance of technical education to women
- Knowledge to improve the work as a women manager
- Strategies for encouraging women to take training
- Knowledge of women empowerment
- Relevant knowledge to conduct such programmes in their country

Country Report Analysis

An analysis of the country reports of the participants revealed that all the participating countries like Iraq, Yemen, Nepal, Myanmar, Botswana, Lesotho, Tajikistan and Uzbekistan have women development cells. Women have been trained through Formal and non-formal programmes. The Governments have special provision of support services. The countries have been concentrating on a career-oriented curriculum. Entrepreneurship is promoted among women. All the countries are examining some form of reservation for women in parliament. All the participants felt that "Women are the anchors of the nation".

Analysis of Projects Developed by the Participants

Each participant was asked to identify a suitable topic for empowerment in his or her respective countries. The projects completed by the participants include:

1. Women Empowerment in Tajikistan
2. Gender Sensitization and Women Development in Iraq
3. Role of Women in development of Science and Technology in Uzbekistan
4. Setting up guidance and counseling centres for rural women in Botswana & Lesotho
5. Technical Training for rural women in ASEAN Country
6. Women Empowerment through the Basic vocational training
7. Setting up women empowerment Units (Tailoring, Embroidery, Fast food)

Analysis of Feedback

A detailed analysis of the feedback was made and the following observations appear to be tenable.

1. The rating of the training is "good", "Very good" and 'Excellent"
2. The ratings for facilities provided are "very good" and 'Excellent"
3. All the participants felt that they have gained sufficient knowledge of women empowerment
4. And they all appreciate the need for these types of programmes
5. The trainees expressed happiness that they were able to know the strategies of Women Empowerment in other countries including India
6. The trainees expressed the opinion that they will be conducting similar programmes in their country.
7. Many of the participants expressed willingness to know more and work in this area of women development
8. They also observed that the quality of the training was very good.
9. They were highly interested in completing their project work and they also expressed willingness to continue to work in this area.

Analysis of the Efficacy of the Programme

Though the programme objectives and content were framed in general, the training schedules and topics were planned keeping in mind the expectation of the different technical teachers/administrators from different countries, from different ethnic backgrounds, from different religion and culture.

It was observed that in the beginning of the training, the participants were not interacting much. At the end of the ice breaking session, the total group was tuned to interact freely among themselves.

The trainees participated actively in all the discussion sessions. The participants showed interest in training technology and guidance and counseling. Most of the participants wanted guidance in running non-formal programmes for rural and underprivileged women. The content of the programme was found to be very useful for all the participants.

The programme highlights that subsequent conduction of the programmes of the kind will help in evolving a model of training for heterogeneous groups. It also reveals that such training programme for women empowerment will enables us to engage in research and comparative studies and also enable the sharing of expertise of different regions.

Conclusion

The present chapter highlights the empowerment of women through training of trainers programme. The policies with reference to women development have been detailed. The programme conducted for the overseas participants was found to be very effective resulting in sharing of knowledge, scope for further research and it will also be helpful in evolving a model of training for women development.

REFERENCES

Pillai, J.K. (1995). *Women and Empowerment*. New Delhi: Gyan Publishers.

AIU (1991). *Directory of Women's Studies in India*. New Delhi: Association of Indian Universities.

Mishra, R.C. (2005). *Women Education*. New Delhi: APH Publishing House.

Raju, M.L. (2007). *Women Empowerment Challenges and Strategies*. New Delhi: Regal Publications.

Sidhiqui, M.H. (1993). *Women Education: A Research Approach*. New Delhi: Ashish Publishing House.

13.

EDUCATION AND EMPOWERMENT OF WOMEN
An Issue for India

DULAL MUKHOPADHYAYA

Prologue

Jawharlal Nehru once said, *'To awaken the people, it is the woman who must be awakened. Once she is on the move, the family moves, the village moves and the nation moves.'*

Men and women are almost equal in the total global populace. But still women are not given equal status with men and this unequal gender role in socialization process operates in every society. Like men-folk, women must have equal roles to play for the progress of the society.

Today, the human civilization has changed from agricultural society to cybernetic age where knowledge is considered as capital and knowledge industry is considered as the most demanding industry in the world. But strangely enough this societal change has little impact on women-folk of the society. Though fewer number of women, all over the world, have achieved equal and sometimes higher status than men; but these are stray incidents.

In informal process and formal arena of education often the authority tries to reinforce the socialization process of preparing girls to be soft, dedicated, polite, peaceful, tolerant, passive and submissive.

In the majority of societies girls grow up with a notion of temporary membership in her natal home and considered as a reproductive machine in the family of 'in-laws'. Their productive role becomes limited to household chores.

Gender inequality is a global phenomenon; only the manifestations vary in form and degree in different cultures. Some of the developed countries of the world have given the franchise right to their women only a few decades ago. There are fewer women in the higher administrative positions in the U.K. than in India. Though more than 80 per cent of British women are earning members, majority of them are confined to low paid, low skilled part-time jobs or are in secretarial posts. The situation in U. S. A. and Japan is also not very encouraging.

The pre-colonial India was primarily a patriarchal society wherein women were completely under male dominance. The upper class women of this period were predominantly home confined but the women from the peasant and lower income groups of the societies had to work outside their home to supplement their family income. This trend remains almost unchanged in the modern India particularly in rural areas.

The Concept of Women Empowerment was voiced in the International Women's Conference in Nairobi in 1985. In this Conference women's empowerment was considered as 'a distribution of social power and centre of resources in favour of women'. But without improving the educational participation of women in education this is not possible.

This affects improvement of the nation in terms of both economy and growth on one hand and individual on the other. Education helps empowerment of women by developing 'intrinsic capacity, inner transformation of one's consciousness to overcome barriers, access resources and traditional ideologies.'

Ultimately empowered women develop some special qualities in their lives. Some of these are as follows:

They

- are able to transform their lives;
- can organize themselves effectively;
- are able to identify their own problems and can solve these problems;
- can take care of their own learning process;
- are responsible and accountable for and reflexive on their values; beliefs, motivation, rights and duties, and obligations;
- can create physical security (shelter, food and health) and a safe social environment;
- are able set their own goals and can develop their own strategies;
- can organize their own resources;
- can do their own work and evaluate them.

Thus empowered women can resist different problems affecting their own lives and the societies like criminal and terrorist activities, rape and violence against them, improving educational standards, restore cultural heritage, control their own health and reproductive systems, remove alcoholism, etc.

> *"... the daughter carrying years of fear*
> *and betrayal on her haggard nape*
> *stares at her mother's face*

at the dried mouth of an old lioness
and dreams, dreams of killing her once more
because of their great semblance and rancour
because of their great weakness and pain
the embrace of defeat which she wants
the embrace of feminine truth,
will we, Mother, ever reach the depths of delirium
and find one another united with other
strangers we call wretched
on the other side of the Social river?"

(DACIA MARAINI, Demeter found a new)

Introduction

The progress and development of the nation is measured on different yardsticks. Among them education is the most important indicators. Quality, progress and development of education indicate the growth of the country. Different documents conclusively prove that the quality and growth of education in ancient India was quite high and the lives and living standard was also very good. At the same time education of women was considered very important at that time.

Women in the Ancient Age

The status of women in India has gone through many changes over the past few millenniums. It is also very difficult to know exactly the status of women in different period of times but researchers and grammarians, like Katyayana and Patanjali, have thrown some lights on it from the old scriptures and from other sources.

In the early Vedic periods there was no gender discrimination. There is enough evidence that in the society the women had equal rights with men during the 'Rig Vedic' periods (1500 – 1000 BC). In the 'Atharva Veda' we find that the people considered the 'success of woman depended upon her proper training during the Brahmachrya.' [Vijayalaksmi, Pandit, P. 1997]

In the 'Rig Vedic' verses we also find that women married at the mature age (12 to 16 yrs. and could choice their husbands. Both boys and girls had 'initiation (upnayana). Very few girls continued their studies because of hard lives and different austerities had to be taken at different stages of their student- lives. So some of them only contended with such hard lives and in depth study of the Vedic lore and other women preferred cozy home lives. They engaged themselves in cultivating arts and crafts and became good housewives. They were known as 'Sadyovadhus'.

But among the girls who took seriously the study of 'God-realisation', some of them were very good in the prevailing ways of learning. They were known as 'Brahmavadinis'. In the Vedic literature 27 such 'Brahmavadinis' were mentioned, e.g. Gargi, Maitreyi, Visvanara, Lopamudra, Apala, Saswati, etc. 'Once in the presence of King Janaka, he (Yajanavalkya) held a discussion with learned Brahmanas. Among their interlocutors was a lady named Gargi Vachaknavi, who greatly distinguished herself in the discussion.' (Key, F.E., 1964). That position of women in the societies deteriorated from the later Vedic ages (1000 to 300 BC). Altekar (1957) wrote:

> "The discontinuation of Upanayanam, the neglect of education and the lowering of the marriage age produced disastrous consequences upon the position and status of women": [Altekar, A.S. 1957]

In the 'Mahavarata' we find a glimpse of it:

"A wife is half the man, his truest friend;
A loving wife is a perpetual spring
Of virtue, pleasure, wealth; and faithful wife,
A sweetly speaking wife is a companion
In solitude, a father in advice,
A rest in passing through life's wilderness."

(Translated by Monier Wiliums)

The dual standard of the society set up by Manu prevailed in the Indian society until the 'Vakti Cult' movement and later reformist movements initiated by different leaders of the society in different forms.

Women in the Middle Ages

The status of women in the mediaeval society further deteriorated due to various reasons. Child marriage, practices of sati, prohibition of widow marriage were considered in a ritualistic way among the Hindus. The status of women among the Muslims was no good than this. Though we find some literate women among the Muslim community also. Practice of purdah among the women started at this period. Among the Rajput women in Rajasthan the 'Jauhar' was practiced to save the chastity of women. Among the Hindus polygamy was a part of the lives and among the Muslims polygamy was accepted in the name of religion. Among the rich Muslims 'Zenana Mahal' was very popular. In some parts of the country the system of 'Devadashi' or 'Temple Women' was prevailed and both the rich people and the 'Temple Priests' sexually exploited them.This continued for many decades till the rise of the 'Vakti Cult' movement. One of the women leaders of the 'Vakti Cult' movement was "Mirabai'. She was a saint, a poet and a singer. At that time women felt some sigh of relief from the orthodox society. Messages of 'Guru Nanak' were unique in this context. He tried to spread the messages of equality among men and women of the society. This had a very effective impact on the societies in some parts of India.

Women in the Colonial Past

***Table 13.1*: Women in Administrative jobs**

No. of Posts in I.E.S. held by	*1921-22*
Men	
Europeans	200
Indians	120
Vacant	53
Women	
Europeans	31
Indians	02
Vacant	09

Then came the East India Company (EIC) with a mission and vision to engulf the entire country for material gain. After 1857 the grip of the colonial rulers tightened after the 'Sepoy Mutiny', the first organized freedom struggle of India.

In the beginning the EIC brought missionaries for their own purpose and that continued up to the third quarter of the eighteenth century.

In 1813, 'the Chartered Act' entrusted the EIC to educate the people but there was no mention of women's education. The Wood's Dispatch (1854) gave emphasis on girls education and accepted the declaration of the Governor General of Bengal that emphasized on women to improve the moral of the people of India. The Despatch observes:

> 'The importance of female education in India can not be overrated; and we have observed with pleasure the evidence which is now afforded of an increased desire on the part of many of the native s of India to give good education to their daughters.'

In 1882 the Indian Education Commission (Hunter Commission) discussed the education of women with special emphasis. Recommendations of the Education Commission (1882) made it possible the entry of women to the profession of teaching and nursing.

According to the above Commission Report the number of School going children (at 15 per cent of the population) was 16.28 per cent for males and 0.84 per cent for females (1881-82). This shows the status and condition of women at that time.

It is to be mentioned here that after 1917 the position of women in higher Governmental position was improved due to the change of policy of the Government. According to Naik and Nurullah (1974) :

> 'The policy of the Public Service Commission of 1887, which was so vehemently upheld by Curzon and his successors, was thus officially buried (in 20th August 1917) and a new era of rapid Indianisation of the Education Department set in.'

Thus it opened up the entry of both male and female Indians in administrative jobs. The following figures will prove this:

***Table 13.2*: Literacy rates During the British Rule**

Year	*Literacy Rates in %*	
	Female	*Male*
1901	0.60	9.83
1911	1.05	10.56
1921	1.81	12.21
1931	2.93	15.59
1941	7.30	24.90

(*Source*: Census of India)

The Government of India in its resolution (October 1, 1919) accepted the plight of women's education and recommended :

> "The education of girls needs more financial fostering than that of boys, primarily education must mainly be free. Scholarships and studentships must be given lavishly; grant-in aid must be calculated more generously and greater expensiveness of secondary education has to be practically recognised."

In 1925 the National Council of Women was established and in 1928 the first 'All India Women's Conference was held and the conference demanded the same type of education for both men and women. Karve established the SNDT Women's College in Bombay (now Mumbai) in 1916, which was recognised as university in 1938. All of these had influenced positively towards the development of women education in India.

But long before that 'the Vakti Cult' movements and later movements of the leaders like Vidyasagar, Ram Mohan, David Hare, Bethune, Derogeo, Vivekananda, Gandhi, Karve, Ranade, Madam Came, etc. had made much headway towards the development and empowerment of women. 'The Brahmah Dharma' movement had also made visible contribution in this case.

At the end of the British rule in India, the position of literacy rates was as follows:

All through the British rule the total traditional education system was systematically destroyed and in its place a new education system was developed purposefully for the benefit of the rulers. In 1931, Gandhiji made a press statement at Chatham House, London:

"Today India is more illiterate than it was fifty or a hundred years ago, and so is Burma, because the British administrators, when they came to India, instead of taking hold of things as they were, began to root them out. They scratched the soil and left the root exposed and the beautiful tree perished."

India Wins Freedom: Women in Independence India

'Long years ago we made a tryst with destiny, and the time comes when we shall redeem our pledges, not wholly or in full measure, but very substantially. ...A moment comes which rarely comes in history, when we step out from the old to the new, when an age ends, and when the soul of a nation, long suppressed, find utterance.' [A Tryst with Destiny: Nehru, 1947]

Women in Education

The National Policy on Education–1986 observed:

"Education will be used as an agent of basic change in the status of women. In order to neutralize the accumulated distortions of the past, there will be a well-conceived edge in favour of women. The National education System will play a positive interventionist role in the empowerment of women. It will foster the development of new values through redesigned curricula, text books, training and orientation of teachers, decision makers and administrators."

But what is the actual status of women in the education arena? Let us ponder over some hard statistics on educational progress of women after independence:

***Table 13.3*: Educational Progress of Women after Independence**

Year		*% Literate*		*M/F (%)*
	Persons	*Male (M)*	*Female (F)*	*Literacy Gap*
1951	18.33	27.16	8.86	18.30
1961	28.31	40.40	15.34	25.06
1971	34.45	45.95	21.97	23.98
1981	43.67	56.50	29.85	27.65
1991	52.19	64.20	39.19	25.01
2001	65.38	75.75	54.16	21.69

Note:

(1) For 1951, the population male, female and persons refers to effective literacy rates and the break up of Rural, Urban and male- female components are crude literacy rates.

(2) Literacy rates for 1951,1961 and 1971 Censuses relates to population aged five years and above. The rates for the 1981,1991 and 2001 Census relate to population aged seven years and above.
(3) The 1981 Literacy rates exclude Assam where census could not be conducted and the 1991 literacy rates exclude Jammu & Kashmir where Census could not be conducted due to disturbed conditions.
(4) The 2001 Census, literacy rates exclude entire Kachchh district, Morvi, Maliya-Miyana and Wankaner talukas of Rajkot district, Jodiya taluka of Jamnagar district of Gujarat State and entire Kinnaur district of Himachal Pradesh where population enumeration of Census of India,2001, could not be conducted due to natural calamities.

(*Source* : Census of India 2001)

This gender disparity exists still in the enrolment in primary and secondary levels of education. This is shown in the Table 13.4.

***Table 13.4*: Percentage of Enrolment in Primary and Secondary Levels of Education**

Year	*Primary Education*		*Secondary Education*	
	Boys	*Girls*	*Boys*	*Girls*
1997-98	62.3	48.0	23.6	15.9
1998-99	62.7	48.2	24.0	16.3
1999-00	64.1	49.5	25.1	17.1
2001-02	63.6	50.3	26.1	18.7

The Table 13.5 shows the enrolment in Higher Education (HE) in the recent years. After the 1990s the change of the scenario in HE is changing slowly. In 1995 only 36 per cent of women were in HE but in 2005 the rate is 40.50 per cent.

***Table 13.5*: Women's Enrolment in Higher Education**

Year	*Total Enrolment*	*Women Enrolment*	*% of Women*	*M/F Gap (%)*
1995-96	6574005	2363607	36	28.00
1996-97	6842598	2514511	37	26.00
1997-98	7260418	2722062	37	26.00
1998-99	7705520	2932993	38	24.00
1999-2000	8050607	3112090	39	22.00
2000-01	8399443	3306410	39.4	21.20
2001-02	8821095	3514450	39.84	20.32
2005-06	11028020	4466348	40.50	19.00

Source: UGC

Thus gender gap decreased from 28.00 per cent (1995-96) to 19.00 per cent (2005-06) due to various actions taken by the different government sectors, especially after NPE-1986, which states:

'... The policy of nondiscrimination will be persuded vigorously to eliminate sex stereotyping in vocational and professional courses and to promote women's participation, as well as in existing and emergent technologies.' (NPE, Government of India, 1986).

Women's Empowerment

Before going to discuss 'women empowerment', we should have a clear working definition of the term empowerment. The National Empowerment Center, Massachusetts (Chamberlin, J.2006) has identified the following qualities of empowered people:

1. Having decision-making power.
2. Having access to information and resources.
3. Having a range of options from which to make choices (not just yes/no, either/or.)
4. Assertiveness.
5. A feeling that the individual can make a difference (being hopeful).
6. Learning to think critically; learning the conditioning; seeing things differently; e.g.,
   a. Learning to redefine who we are (speaking in their own voice).
   b. Learning to redefine what we can do.
   c. Learning to redefine our relationships to institutionalized power.
7. Learning about and expressing anger.
8. Not feeling alone; feeling part of a group.
9. Understanding that people have rights.
10. Effecting change in one's life and one's community.
11. Learning skills (e.g., communication) that the individual defines as important.
12. Changing others' perceptions of one's competency and capacity to act.
13. Coming out of the closet.
14. Growth and change that is never ending and self-initiated.
15. Increasing one's positive self-image and overcoming stigma.

[Chamberlin,J. 2006]

The above qualities of empowerment show that the term is a complex, multidimensional and related to mental, physical, emotional, social and spiritual aspects of one's life and society. So it also depends on the situational variables and should be considered from the point of view of demands or requirements of the respective populations.

Paulo Freire (1970), a noted educationist and social reformer, had used the term "transformation". According to Freire empowerment entails more than just adequate adjustment. It entails the transformation of those involved and their society. Redistribution of power is central to this emancipation.

Claessen and Van Wesemael(1992) had defined women empowerment as follows :

> "(Empowerment is) a process of women acquiring the experiences, knowledge, tools and techniques to be able to transform their lives and the society. Within this process transformation of the existing power relations is crucial."

This definition covers different aspects of empowerment:

- *The physical*: control over body and sexuality, including protection against sexual violence;
- *The economic*: access to and control over resources and income;
- *The legal*: strengthening of position within the legal system;
- *The organisational/political*: self-organization, self-help and collective action to bring about transformation;
- *The ideological*: self-respect, confidence and equal status vis-a-vis men. An essential part is the right of women to have access to information and know-how". (Claessen, J. & Wesemael,1992)

a) Why Women Empowerment?

Before going to discuss 'Women Empowerment' let us see the position of women in India from the Report of the Working Group on "Empowerment of Women" for the 11th Five Year Plan (2006). The crime clock maintained by the NCRB reveals a shocking figure:

- Crime Committed Against Women every 3 Minutes
- Molestation case every 15 Minutes
- Rape case every 29 Minutes
- Sexual Harassment case every 53 Minutes
- Dowry Death case every 77 Minutes
- Cruelty by Husband and Relatives case every 9 Minutes

–The National Crime Records Bureau (GOI), 2004

Care, development and attention of the children depend mostly on the living condition and social status of women. Again as a mother, woman has a special role in nurturing the children. The population of girl child in every society is almost 50 per cent of the total child-population. Upbringing of these children mostly depends on the mother. So mother's status bears a direct impact on the future life and development of the girl-child.

Since time immemorial, women have played, and continue to play, a key role in conservation of basic life support systems, such as land, water, flora and fauna. So they should have a special role and status in the society.

There is an undisputed relationship among economic status, social equality, social integration and health of women. The effect of social integration and economic inequality bears a negative impact on the health of women. Poverty is the result of social and economic inequality. In a given population the outcome indicators of health (mortality, morbidity and life expectancy) are directly related to the standards of living (Wilkinson, 1992). Inequality in the service sectors is still a matter of concern. The Table 13.6 will show the poor employability among women in different service sectors.

Various international studies have shown a close relationship between income inequalities and excess mortality rate. Kennedy et.al.(1996) showed that income inequality was directly related to the total mortality rate in a given population. In India millions of women perish due to this socio-economic inequality, because malnutrition, high birth rate proportion, female infanticide, and early marriages of girls are rampant especially among rural women. Low literacy rate among rural women of low socio-economic status is one of the main reasons of these problems. In India the economy of the country more or less depends on agriculture.

***Table 13.6*: Women's Employment in the Organized Sector by Major Industry Divisions**

Division & Industry	*Women Employees (in Thousands) as on 31-03-2001*		
	Public Sector	*Private Sector*	*Total*
Agriculture, Hunting, Forestry & Fishing	48.3	464.4	512.8
Mining and Quarrying	55.6	8.4	64.0
Manufacturing	93.0	937.0	1030.0
Electricity, Gas & Water	44.7	1.3	46.0
Construction	63.2	4.0	67.3
Wholesale & Retail Trade & Restaurants and Hotels	17.4	29.4	46.8
Transport, Storage & Communications	174.9	8.1	182.9
Financing, Insurance Real Estate & Business Services	184.8	60.2	245.0
Community, Social & Personal Services	2177.2	577.3	2754.5
Total	2859.2	2090.1	4949.3

Source: India, Ministry of Labour, Directorate General Employment and Training, 2003.

The Government of India has made a Press Statement (November 28, 2007) where several causes of disparities were sated. Some of these are as follows:

- During the past ten years, the labour force participation rate (the share of working-age women who work or are seeking work) stopped growing, with many regions registering decline.
- More women than ever before are actually in work. The female share of total employment stayed almost unchanged at 40 per cent in 2006 (from 39.7 per cent 10 years ago)
- At the same time, more women than ever before are unemployed, with the rate of women's unemployment (6.6 per cent) higher than that of men (6.1 per cent).
- Women are more likely to work in low productivity jobs in agriculture and services. Women's share in industrial employment is much smaller than men's and has decreased over the last ten years.
- The poorer the region, the greater the likelihood that women work as unpaid contributing family members or low-income own-account workers. Female workers contributing to family, in particular, are not likely to be economically independent.
- The share of women in wage and salaried work grew during the past ten years from 42.9 per cent in 1996 to 47.9 per cent in 2006. However, especially in the world's poorest regions, this share is still smaller for women than for men

(GOI, Press Release, November 28, 2007).

More than 65 per cent of the Indian population still lives in rural areas and agriculture is their main source of livelihood. So development of rural India is a major concern for any developmental project undertaken by the authority. Again almost 50 per cent of the rural population are women. In rural India women share the major responsibilities inside and outside the family, so their development in different fields of their lives is essential for development of India because it will ultimately increase the economy, health and other related areas of the country.

For this reason the Government of India has taken up 'various activities and programmes for women participation, such as National Rural Employment Guarantee Act (NREGA), Prime Minister's Rozgar Yojana (PMRY), Swarnjayanti Gram Swarozgar Yojana (SGSY), Swarna Jayanti Shahari Rozgar Yojana (SJSRY) and Sampoorna Grameeen Rozgar Yojana (SGRY)' (GOI, 2007).

Empowered people have the ability to direct and control their own lives. Thus if successful empowerment of women can be done, it will ultimately raise India as a whole and future citizens will be properly developed starting from their mothers' laps, because empowered women may develop some special qualities in their lives. Some of these are as follows:

They

- are able to transform their lives;
- can organize themselves;
- are able to identify their own problems;
- can solve these problems themselves;
- can take care of their own learning process;
- are responsible and accountable for and reflexive on their values, beliefs, motivation, rights and duties, and obligations;
- can creates physical security (shelter, food, health) and a safe social environment;
- are able set their own goal;
- can develop their own strategy;
- can organise their own resources;
- can do their own work; and
- can evaluate their own work.

Thus empowered women can manage different problems of the societies and their own lives like criminal and terrorist activities, rape and violence against them, low educational standards, restoration of cultural heritage, control their own health and reproductive systems, removal alcoholism, etc. and they will do all these things in a caring, responsible and safe way.

b) Education and Women Empowerment

Different committees and commissions have accepted that education is the most important ingredient in the empowerment process. The female population consists of 50 per cent of the total population. So their education is also equally important for the development of a nation. In the International Conference on Population Development (1994) it was recommended to remove any sort of bias, which can cause any type of discrimination and inequalities between men and women. The World Conference at Beijing (1995), the Convention on the Elimination of all Forms of Discrimination against Women (CEDAW, 1979); the Copenhagen Declaration (1995) and the Millennium Goals (2000) had formulated plans to eliminate gender discrimination and women empowerment. Again education is considered as a human right. The Beijing Platform for Action lays down critical areas of concern for women, which are listed in the following box:

Critical areas of concern

1. Women and Poverty
2. Education and training of women
3. Women and health
4. Violence against women
5. Women in armed conflict
6. Women and economy
7. Women in power and decision-making
8. Institutional mechanisms for the advancement of women
9. Human rights and women
10. Women and media
11. Women and environment
12. Girl child.

The EFA Global Monitoring Report (2002) states, "... where right to education is guaranteed, people's access to and enjoyment of other rights is enhanced."

In the International Women's Conference at Nirobi (1985) the concept of Women's Empowerment was introduced where empowerment was considered as 'a distribution of social power and centre of resources in favour of women'.

'Achieving gender equality, however, is a grindingly slow process, since it challenges one of the most deeply entrenched of all human attitudes. Despite the intense efforts of many agencies and organizations, and numerous inspiring successes, the picture is still disheartening, as it takes far more than changes in law or stated policy to change practices in the home, community and in the decision-making environment. In many parts of the world rape is not considered a crime, goes unpunished and continues to be used as a tool of war. Even in highly developed countries, violence against women of all kinds is routine and often condoned' (World Economic Forum, 2005).

In the light of heightened international awareness of gender issues, it is a disturbing reality that no country has yet managed to eliminate the gender gap. According to the report of the World Economic Forum (2005) the most successful countries that have narrowed the gap are the developed countries. Among them are the Nordic countries, with Sweden standing out as the most advanced in the world. These are followed by New Zealand (6), Canada (7), United Kingdom (8), Germany (9) and Australia (10), countries that have made considerable progress in recent decades in removing obstacles to the full participation of women in their respective societies. France (13) ranked ahead of the United States (17) among the

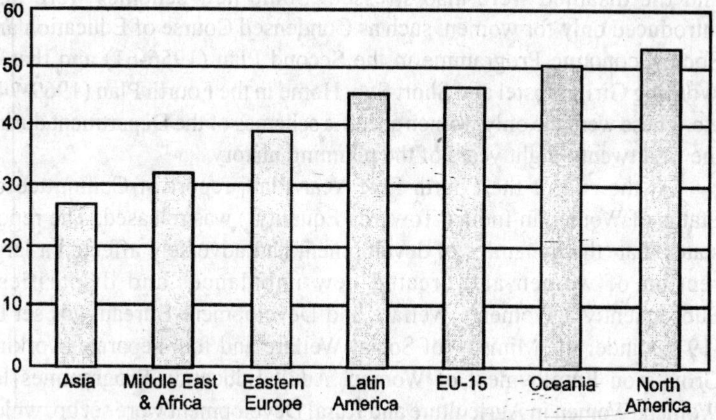

Figure 13.1.*Educational attainment of Women in some selected countries (WEF, 2005)*

58 nations. Seven East European nations hold places among the top 25, with Latvia (11), Lithuania (12) and Estonia (15) the highest ranking in that group. Switzerland (34), Italy (45) and Greece (50) perform poorly, lower in rank than many of the East European group, and below Latin American nations such as Costa Rica (18), Colombia (30) and Uruguay (32). Brazil (51), Mexico (52), India (53), Korea (54), Jordan (55), Pakistan (56), Turkey (57) and Egypt (58) occupy the lowest ranks. This is shown below in a graphical form.

c) Five-year plans and the Empowerment of Women

After independence the status of Indian women was low in almost every sphere of women's lives and the condition of women in the rural sectors was even worse.

So from the First Five Year Plan the planning strategies on women and children in the country have changed from 'welfare' to 'development' to 'empowerment'. The approach in the First Five Year Plan (1951-56) was to 'promote the welfare of women' so that they can play their 'legitimate role in the family and the community'. In the plan paper the commission stated, 'the position and functions of women differ to a great extent in different communities, and therefore, community welfare agencies will have to work out their programmes and activities according to the specific requirements in which they work'.

In the subsequent plan periods (the Second, Third, Fourth and Fifth Plans, including the four years of Plan holiday) the emphasis was mainly on 'welfare', though other categories of welfare such as the old and the disabled were also stressed. Some new schemes were also introduced only for women, such as Condensed Course of Education and Socio-Economic Programme in the Second Plan (1956-61) and that of Working Girl's Hostel and Short Stay Home in the Fourth Plan (1969-74), etc. These were the only women specific schemes of the Department during the first twenty-eight years of the planning history.

At the end of the Fourth Five Year Plan, report of Committee on Status of Women in India ('Towards Equality') was released. The report states that 'the dynamics of development had adversely affected a large section of women and created new imbalances and disparities.' Subsequently a Women's Welfare and Development Bureau was set up (1976) under the Ministry of Social Welfare and four separate Working Groups on Employment of Women, Adult Education Programmes for Women, Women in Agriculture and Rural Development were set up, which was a positive shift from 'welfare' to `development' in the Sixth Plan (1980-85). The thrust areas were *health, education and employment.* Stress was given on rural women in different sectors of agriculture, dairying, poultry, small animal husbandry, handlooms, handicrafts, small-scale industries, etc.

In the Seventh Plan (1985-90) stress was on employment generation of women (both skilled and unskilled) through proper education and vocational training. The Department of Women and Child Development was set up in 1985. In the same plan period attention was also given on girl child along with woman. The aim was to give girl-child centred space for physical and mental development before marriage.

The Eighth Five Year Plan (1990-95) tried to ensure that 'benefits of development from different sectors do not bypass women and special programmes are implemented to complement the general development programmes.' The Government declared her policy to develop 'every child'. National Plan of Actions (1992) was declared, one for the children and the other for the girl-child.

The Ninth Plan (1997-2002) made two significant changes: 'Empowerment of Women' and 'Women's Component Plan'. The policy of 'Empowerment of Women' was adopted to create an environment so that women can freely exercise their rights both within and outside home, as equal partners along with men. For this purpose a 'National Policy for Empowerment of Women' was approved (2001). Secondly, 'Women's Component Plan' attempted to convergence existing services, resources, infrastructure and manpower available in both women-specific and women-related sectors.

The main thrust of the Tenth Five Year Plan (2002-07) was three pronged strategy of social empowerment, economic empowerment and providing gender justice to create an enabling environment of positive economic and social policies for women and eliminating all forms of discrimination against them and thus advance gender equality goals.

Social Empowerment - Create an enabling environment through adopting various policies and programmes for development of women, besides providing them easy and equal access to all the basic minimum services so as to enable them to realize their full potential.

Economic Empowerment – Ensure provision of training, employment and income generation activities with both forward and backward linkages with the ultimate objective of making all women economically independent and self reliant.

Gender Justice – Eliminate all forms of gender discrimination and thus enable women to enjoy not only de jure but also de facto rights and fundamental freedom on par with men in all spheres, viz, political, economic, social, civil, cultural etc.

The Eleventh Five Year Plan (2007- 12) gives stress on Gender Issues. The vision or philosophy of empowerment for the XI Plan is *Inclusive and integrated economic, social and political empowerment with gender justice*. The extent of empowerment of women in the national hierarchy is determined largely by the three factors – her economic, social and political identity and their weightage. The proposed plan has given stress on these three issues.

In the Eleventh plan the above crucial areas of concern, to a large extent, are considered as the thrust areas that are required to be kept in view in the Eleventh plan, while priority will continue to be laid on health, nutrition, education, income generating activities, relief and rehabilitation for women in distress.

Where is the way?

In defining empowerment, especially for women, we have mentioned some determinants:

- *The physical*
- *The economic*
- *The legal*
- *The organizational / political and*
- *The ideological*

The above stated determinants can be divided into two categories: the first three determinants are the actions to be considered for empowerment programmes which will improve the living conditions of women and the last two refer to the necessary conditions for taking action. The term "ideological" here implies that the participants must be taught a certain ideology like self-confidence, self-esteem, self-expression, self-respect, etc. that are important for empowerment process. These issues are not ideologically bound. They are linked to an individual process of development and to the development of self-awareness (Claessen, J.1992).

The National Policy for the Empowerment of Women (2001) was announced on the basis of some objectives to strengthen and enhance the process of empowerment: The policy was:

(*i*) Creating an environment through positive economic and social policies for full development of women to enable them to realize their full potential.

(*ii*) The de-jure and de-facto enjoyment of all human rights and fundamental freedom by women on equal basis with men in all spheres – political, economic, social, cultural and civil.

(*iii*) Equal access to participation and decision making of women in social, political and economic life of the nation.

(*iv*) Equal access to women to health care, quality education at all levels, career and vocational guidance, employment, equal remuneration, occupational health and safety, social security and public office, etc.

(*v*) Strengthening legal systems aimed at elimination of all forms of discrimination against women.

(*vi*) Changing societal attitudes and community practices by active participation and involvement of both men and women.

(*vii*) Mainstreaming a gender perspective in the development process.

(*viii*) Elimination of discrimination and all forms of violence against women and the girl child; and

(*ix*) Building and strengthening partnerships with civil society, particularly women's organizations.

(The National Policy for the Empowerment of Women, GOI, 2001)

To make these goal a practical reality the following components of empowerment of women are to be given special priorities with immediate effect :

a) Economic and social component
b) Education component and
c) Health component

For economic and social empowerment of women the following actions are to be taken :

(*i*) To develop knowledge and skills in modern technologies.

(*ii*) Agri-based and allied professions should be created to ensure self employment for rural women.
(*iii*) Rightful place of women to free them from their gender imposed roles.
(*iv*) Technologies which are labour saving, drudgery reducing, income generating and productivity increasing should be given wide publicity and their use should be encouraged through pragmatic extension.
(*v*) Women should be given opportunities to have control over production and resources.
(*vi*) More access to financial resources of the family should be developed, etc.

Education is said to be the most important and key element to sustainable development and empowerment of women because this factor alone is related to many other factors of the society; but till now literacy level of women is alarmingly low, especially in rural India. A majority of the poor women live in a situation, which makes them unable to have access to education. Some of the reasons are as follows:

(*i*) Daily struggle for wage, fuel and fodder,
(*ii*) Rigidly defined social norms and roles which prevent them to interact with others and lack of opportunities to come together and use collective strength.
(*iii*) Low image and lack of confidence due to lack of education.
(*iv*) Lack of adequate and gender sensitive education infrastructure, etc.

Health component is again related to education and economic condition of the people. 'Health standards of a country reflect the social, economic, political and moral well being of its ordinary citizen. Economic and social growth of a society and country is directly dependant on the health of its constituents. These access difficulties can be due to:

1. Geographical distance
2. Socio-economic distance
3. Gender distance' (Deogaonkar, M. 2005)

Healthy living conditions and access to good quality health care for all citizens are not only basic human rights, but also essential prerequisites for social and economic development. The most sensitive indicators of health of the society are infant and maternal mortality rates. Women suffer a lot due to poor healthcare facilities. It affects much on the total reproductive systems on women and thus ultimately affects on the health of the children. So active and practical programmes are to be taken for the women from the grass roots levels.

Conclusion

Our Respected President of India, Smt Pratibha Devisingh Patil reminded us:

> "It is also a matter of concern that the male-female gap in literacy rates continues to be unacceptably high. This divide is sharper in rural areas. Women's literacy and education has to be made a priority. If we make women literate, they will be self-reliant and the beneficial impact on society will be manifold. It has been observed that where the women are literate, the rate of infant mortality comes down and the quality of life improves. Also, when women are taught how to read and write they in turn begin to send their girl child to school, breaking the pattern of social gender discrimination, which is a strong barrier to girls' education. It is important that in schools, girls must get equal opportunity to study and acquire necessary skills and knowledge. Specific education programmes, with targets, should be launched for education of girls."
>
> [Speech by the Respected President of India, Smt Pratibha Devisingh Patil, on the occasion of the International Literacy Day- 2007]

The discrimination against women was found to be maximum among families of low socio-economic conditions than in middle and high socio-economic status families. The discrimination of women is also present even in higher status families in hidden, subtle and disguised form. Consistent discrimination develops insecurity and this insecurity breeds anxiety. Ultimately it also affects on the their health, child rearing practices, thinking abilities, etc. All these traits, being negatively related to the development of their abilities and intellectual capacities, affect their adjustment in different fields of the society. Thus a major portion of the manpower in the society remains unused and underused. And the country's preparations for her plans for the empowerment of women remains unattended and unfulfilled over the years. Now we are in the morning of a new millennium and vowed to enter into a learning society. Will it be possible to leave behind a large number of the populace, the women of our country?

It requires education, because it liberates mind, thought process and other material and non-material gains for the present and for the future. We are visioning a society where every men and woman will have equal rights, equal status and equal position in the family and society. Tagore visioned such a society:

Where the mind is without fear
and the head is held high;
Where knowledge is free;
Where the world has not been

broken up into fragments by narrow
domestic walls;
Where words come out from
the depth of truth;
Where tireless striving stretches its
arms towards perfection;
Where the clear stream of reason
has not lost its way into the dreary
desert sand of dead habit;
Where the mind is led forward by
thee into ever-widening thought and
action...
Into that heaven of freedom, my
Father, let my country awake.

— Rabindranath Tagore

REFERENCES

National Perspective Plan for Women 1988-2000, (1988), Department of Women and Child Development, GOI, Ministry of HRD.

Country Report: Fourth World Conference on Women, (1988), Beijing 1995. Department of Women and Child Development, GOI, Ministry of HRD.

Chamberlin, J. (2006), A Working Definition of Empowerment. The National Empowerment Center,Lawrence, Massachusetts.

Freire, P. (1970), *Pedagogy of the Oppressed*. New York: Seabury Press.

Claessen, J., & Wesemael, L. Van (Eds.). (1992). Reading the word and the world: Literacy and Education from a Gender Perspective. Oegstgeest: VO.

Govt. of India. Country Report: Fourth Conference on Women, Beijing, 1995.

Department of WCD, Ministry of HRD, New Delhi.

Census of India 2001 (2001): Provisional Population Totals. Registrar General and Census Commissioner, GOI.

Planning Commission, Government of India. Tenth Five Year Plan 2002-2007. Volume II.

United Nations. World Population Monitoring 2001: Population, Environment and Development (ESA/P/WP.164). Draft. New York: Population Division, Department of Economic and Social Affairs, United Nations, 2001.

Caldwell, J. "Education as a factor in mortality decline: An examination of Nigerian data," Population Studies, 1979,Vol 33, 3, 396-413.

Wilkinson R.G. (1992), Income distribution and life expectancy. BMJ.

Kennedy B.P., Kawachi I, Prothrow-Stith D (1996), Income distribution and mortality: Crosssectional ecological study of Robin Hood Index in the United States. BMJ.

Report of the Working Group on 'Empowerment of Women for the XI Plan (2006),

Ministry of Women and Child Development, Government of India, New Delhi.

Speech by the respected President of India Smt Pratibha Devisingh Patil, on the occasion of the International Literacy Day, New Delhi, 8th September, 2007.

Women In India, Central Statistical Organisation, Ministry of Statistics and Programme Implementation, Government of India, New Delhi: 2002.

Programmes for Women : Annual Report of UGC 2005-06, New Delhi.

Women's Empowerment: Measuring the Global Gender Gap (2005), World Economic Forum, Geneva.

CONTRIBUTORS

ARYA, VIJAY VRAT, Ph.D., is Associate Fellow in the Department of Higher & Professional Education (DHPE), National University of Educational Planning and Administration, New Delhi. He has sizable contribution to his credit in various journals and also for assisting in various research projects in the area of higher education.

DATTA, KARUBAKI, Ph.D., is presently Reader in the Centre for Himalayan Studies, North Bengal University. She has published many scholarly articles in journals and has edited three books related to the Himalayan region.

DUTTA HAZARIKA, SUJATA, Ph.D., is Assistant Professor in Department of Humanities and Social Sciences in Indian Institute of Technology, Guwahati. Her area of interest includes Sociological aspects related to Gender and Displaced Communities, Technology and Society, Alternative Science, Complimentary and Alternative Medicine.

DUTTA ROY, DEBDULAL, Ph.D., is member of faculty of the Psychology Research Unit of the Indian Statistical Institute, Kolkata. He was the recipient of awards from Indian Science Congress Association, Indian Congress on Quality, Environment, Energy and Safety Management Systems, Madras Psychology Society and Pondicherry Psychology Association.

ILIŠKO, DZINTRA, Ph.D., is the Chair of Institute of Sustainable Education, Latvia and a senior researcher and the docent at Daugavpils University. Her fields of interest are multicultural education, Religious Education and issues related to sustainability.

INDERSEN, JAYA, Ph. D., was professor of higher education at the National Institute of Educational Planning and Administration. She has been a visiting professor at the University of Manitoba, Canada and a visiting scholar at the University of Michigan, USA. Currently she is a freelance consultant and conducts training workshops for capacity building. She has several research publications to her credit.

LEÃO, CELINA PINTO, Ph.D., is presently at University of Minho, Portugal as an Auxiliary Professor and as a researcher with the Algoritmi Center. Her main interests are in modelling and simulation of processes, and in the application of new methodologies in the learning process of numerical methods and statistics in engineering.

MUKHYOPADHYAYA, DULAL, Ph.D., is Professor of Education of Faculty of Education in University of Kalyani, India. He has to his credit many papers in different journals of national and international repute, apart from four books on Instructional Technology and Educational Management. He is also acting as a member of editorial committee in different professional journals on Education.

Nelasco, Shobana, Ph.D., is presently Reader in Fatima College, teaching Economics for last two decades. She has completed MA., M. Phil(with distinction) and Ph.D in Economics and M.B.A, in Finance. She has, to her credit good number of publications.

Paira, Anjana, MA, M.Ed., is a Research Scholar in the Department of Education in Faculty of Education *(Vinaya Bhavana)*, Visva-Bharati, Santiniketan. Her area of research is zoomed over Tribal women education with special reference to attainment juxtaposition of tribe groups.

Panda, Amrita, M.Sc., received her Masters in Experimental Psychology from University of Calcutta, India. Presently she is at Psychology Research Unit of Indian Statistical Institute, Kolkata, India, as a Project Assistant.

Patel, Vibhuti, Ph.D., is Professor of the University Department of Economics, and Director, Department of Post Graduate Studies and Research of SNDT Women's University, Mumbai, India. She was a visiting faculty at the Development Studies Institute of The London School of Economics and Political Science.

Pimentel, Carina, M.E., at present preparing her Ph.D. thesis in Production Engineering, at the Algoritmi Research Center. Her main research interests are related with mixed integer programming, lot sizing and scheduling, optimization problems and with engineering gender studies.

Rahman, Khandoker Mahmudur is currently Assistant Professor, School of Business, United International University, Dhaka, Bangladesh. His research interests include competitive brand management, quality management in service enterprises, and gender issues in business.

Rodrigues, Cristina S., Ph.D., is currently lecture in the Engineering School at the University of Minho and a research member of the Algoritmi at the University of Minho, Portugal.

Roy, Rajarshi, Ph.D., is associated with a national research-cum-training institute located in Kolkata, under Ministry of Human Resource Development, Government of India and dealing with restricted sphere of Education.

Rummana, Ruba is working as an Assistant Professor in the Department of Arts and Sciences, Ahsanullah University of Science and Technology, Dhaka, Bangladesh. Her principal areas of interest include Gender, Development Economics, Women Entrepreneurship and related issues.

S. Renuka Devi, Ph.D., is at National Institute of Technical Teachers' Training & Research, Chennai as Assistant Professor of Department of Education. She has published papers in National and International journals and has conducted number of programmes for Engineering and polytechnic College teachers, including Women Empowerment Programmes for overseas teachers and administrators.

SULTANA, SAMINA, Ph.D., joined the teaching profession in 1971 and retired as Professor and Chairman of the Department of History, Jagannath University. At present she is council member Asiatic Society, Bangladesh.

WIZARAT, KAUSAR, Ph.D., is Assistant Professor in the Department of Higher & Professional Education, National University of Educational Planning and Administration, New Delhi. Her area of working is Higher Education with specialization in planning and management. She has presented papers on gender issues in national level conferences and contributed several research papers in reputed journals.

INDEX